ANCESTOR OF THE WEST

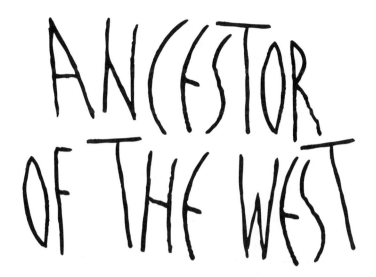

ANCESTOR OF THE WEST

WRITING, REASONING, AND RELIGION IN
MESOPOTAMIA, ELAM, AND GREECE

Jean Bottéro, Clarisse Herrenschmidt,
and Jean-Pierre Vernant
With a Foreword by François Zabbal
Translated by Teresa Lavender Fagan

THE UNIVERSITY OF CHICAGO PRESS
CHICAGO AND LONDON

JEAN BOTTÉRO is emeritus director of L'École pratique des hautes études, Paris. He is the author of *Mesopotamia: Writing, Reasoning, and the Gods* (University of Chicago Press, 1992).
CLARISSE HERRENSCHMIDT is a researcher at CNRS.
JEAN-PIERRE VERNANT is former chair of studies in comparative religions at the Collège de France. He is editor of *The Greeks* (University of Chicago Press, 1995).

Originally published as *L'Orient ancien et nous: L'écriture, la raison, les dieux*
© 1996 Éditions Albin Michel S.A.

The University of Chicago Press, Chicago 60637
The University of Chicago Press, Ltd., London
© 2000 by The University of Chicago
All rights reserved. Published 2000
Printed in the United States of America

09 08 07 06 05 04 03 02 01 00   1 2 3 4 5
ISBN: 0–226-06715-7 (cloth)

Library of Congress Cataloging-in-Publication Data
Bottéro, Jean.
    [Orient ancien et nous. English]
    Ancestor of the West : writing, reasoning, and religion in Mesopotamia, Elam, and Greece / Jean Bottéro, Clarisse Herrenschmidt, Jean-Pierre Vernant ; translated by Teresa Lavender Fagan.
        p.   cm.
    Translation of: L'Orient ancien et nous.
    Includes bibliographical references and index.
    ISBN 0–226-06715-7 (cloth : alk. paper).
    1. Middle East—Civilization—To 622. 2. Writing—Middle East—History. 3. Middle East—Religion. I. Herrenschmidt, Clarisse. II. Vernant, Jean-Pierre. III. Title.
DS57.B6813   2000
939.'4—dc21   99–23113

Contents

995.86

Foreword

FRANÇOIS ZABBAL

This work examines the Mesopotamian legacy; more specifically, it looks at three of the major inventions produced by the society that in the fourth millennium B.C. grew out of the encounter between the Sumerians and the Akkadians on the land that is today known as Iraq: writing, reasoning, and religion. The development of writing is examined through its relation to the thought and religiosity that it engendered as soon as it appeared, and as it was adopted by other peoples—the Semites of Syria, who improved it, and the Greeks, who perfected it. At the culmination of a long evolution, it was reasoning—or "reasonings," as Jean-Pierre Vernant says—and universal religions that proved to be the tributaries of writing, capable of establishing generalizable and decontextualized norms.[1]

A search for origins would imply processes of transmission, but here the authors look at the specific historical configurations of these three inventions in some of the cultures that accepted, adopted, or transformed them. Each of these cultures, in its own way, and depending on its individual material, social, and cultural circumstances, therefore made use of a common legacy. In the present work we will not witness the stages of an evolution that was crowned by Greek reasoning or Hebrew monotheism. While the Mesopotamian paternity of civilization has been steadily substantiated, in the western part of the Old World at least, the numerous and enduring tributaries of that paternal source did not all flow into a single current. On the contrary, those tributaries never ceased to change, grow, or fuse. Thus, just like material goods and technologies, Mesopotamian ideas simultaneously flowed into the East, into Persian territories, and into the West, toward Syria and farther, into Greece. Adopted and modified by Achaemenid, Aramaean, Hebrew, and Greek cultures, these ideas sometimes underwent more or less radical changes, and sometimes they remained unchanged, reappearing here and there in currents of thoughts, myths, or beliefs.

The fact that the two entities artificially named the East and the West inherited those ideas in no way signifies that only two large branches grew out of the civilization that was born close to six thousand years ago in Mesopotamia. As usual in history, the question of origins holds surprises for whoever is prepared to reject an ideological view of cultural identity. And so behind the notion of the "West" one discovers many Islamic influences. As for Islam, which we often attempt to reduce to the "East," it also conceals many of the tensions that exist between its East and its West, and it has had to confront the venerable Orients beyond its boundaries—India and China. Do we seek to understand civilizations and to date the great bifurcations of their history by focusing on peoples, cultures, and empires? Or do we seek, on the contrary, to isolate the constituent elements of the "West" beginning in most distant antiquity and reconstruct the paths along which they were transmitted up to the dawn of modern time?

The direct descendants of Mesopotamia, throughout its multimillennial history, have been numerous and diverse. And insofar as the incomplete documentation can reveal, there appear to have been constant exchanges and commerce between different cultures. Although the presence of Semitic peoples within the entire Fertile Crescent did not fade, Indo-European populations, or those of unknown origin, continued to flow into the region or to appear at its frontiers. Some groups disappeared without leaving any noticeable trace; others, variously documented, were absorbed in other groups, not without having first benefited from Mesopotamian influence: for example, the Elamites—whom Clarisse Herrenschmidt examines in part 2—Mesopotamia's neighbors to the southeast, who were gradually conquered at the end of the second millennium by the Indo-European Iranians and by the Hittites from Asia Minor, who were also Indo-European. But all these peoples participated in some capacity in the same civilization, through commercial exchanges, peaceful or violent invasions, and conquests. The diffusion of cuneiform writing, invented in Mesopotamia, bears witness to this, as do the fragments of the rich mythology that inspired the authors of the Bible and that were also known by the Greeks.

As the Mesopotamian era drew to a close in the first millennium B.C., the principal actors in the region, who were to remain in place up to the advent of Islam, included the Iranians (represented by the

Achaemenid Empire, which fell under Alexander the Great, and later by the Sassanians); the Greeks (for whom the Hellenistic and then the Greco-Roman kingdoms assured a lasting presence and a primary influence throughout the Middle East); and finally, the Aramaeans, the Semitic peoples who in the second millennium founded kingdoms in Syria, including Damascus, best known from its treatment in the Bible.

Thus on the eve of Islam three great millennial cultures—one Semitic and the others Indo-European—enriched the entire region. And yet their unique personalities continued to stand out above the blending that occurred. This is seen in the renaissance of the Iranian culture under Islam, beginning in the tenth century A.D., as well as in the continued presence, up to the ninth century, of the Aramaean influence, expressed in the Aramaic Syriac language adopted by the Nestorians and the Jacobites, through which a large part of the Greek philosophical and scientific legacy passed into Arabic. Meanwhile, the centuries of the Hellenization of the Middle East had assured the legacy of the Greeks such that one need look no further than in the schools of philosophy and theology that continued to teach Greek thought following the Muslim conquest.

It would be useful, then, to note here that the Aramaeans, and more generally the western Semites, followed a different path from that of the eastern Semites, which Jean Bottéro presents in chapter 2. For from the Mesopotamian vantage point, they were the ones who formed the closest link between the Semites from the Arab peninsula and the Arab-Muslim culture, which in the eighth century became a great imperial culture before falling before the Persian and Turkish Empires. In fact, the Arabic language appears to be the heir of the Aramaic millennium, since it flows into the same mold and even absorbs entire sections of the Aramaic lexicon. The Aramaean culture had experienced its greatest development after the annexation of the kingdoms of Syria by the Assyrians, the Babylonians, and the Achaemenid Persians. After adopting the alphabetic system from the Phoenicians, Aramaic became the international language of the Middle East; and that status was reinforced during the reign of the Achaemenid Persians. It replaced all the Semitic tongues in the Fertile Crescent and eliminated the eastern Semitic languages, Assyrian and Babylonian. Aramaic writing is at the origin of so-called square-letter Hebrew script and, through the intermediary of Nabataean, of the Arabic writing system.

It is thus through writing that Arabic can be connected to Aramaic and, further, to Mesopotamia. There is more certainty to this connection than to one involving myths and religion, which has been scantily documented with respect to the Arabic peninsula before Islam. The inquiry that the present work undertakes into the relations between writing, reasoning, and religion can therefore have no equivalent for the pre-Islamic Arabic world. It is fully justifiable for the Islamic period, however. To be convinced of this one need only mention the central place occupied by writing in the Muslim dogma. Nowhere else has a theology of the "Religions of the Book" been similarly developed around ideas of increate text and of the falsification of earlier revelations.

In truth, of the two branches of Mesopotamian civilization, the western branch is today in a better position to reclaim its past. Close to two centuries of archeological discoveries, of deciphering and analyses, have enabled the West to conquer ever more vast expanses of its own history, and in the meantime to restore the East's past, as well. Well before biblical archeology, the exploration of the Middle East by European travelers reconstituted what the nineteenth century named "sacred geography." Research into biblical sites, following that of Greco-Roman civilization, was gradually accompanied by inquiries among Arab nomads, who were believed to be a reflection of the Hebrews before Israel.

The unexpected result of archeological excavation was to push the past back several millennia, upsetting the myth of the two ultimate origins of the West: Greece and the Bible. Jean Bottéro has shown elsewhere the important consequences of the discoveries of Assyriology on the vision of the past, and Jean-Pierre Vernant has shown how the positive reasoning of the Greeks was formed not ex nihilo but out of cosmogonic myths borrowed from Mesopotamia.[2]

This idea of an "Eastern" origin of the West, though it still encounters much resistance, continues to make headway. It is not certain, however, that it will triumph as long as the ideology of origins remains impervious to the facts that have been established by historical knowledge. And we must perhaps wonder whether the West's endless conquest of its own past and of that of other civilizations should not be accompanied by similar research undertaken by those civilizations into their own origins.

This is a long way off, insofar as the East is concerned, in spite of the undeniable vestiges in the very soil of the Middle East and of the growing controlling presence of archeological digs by Eastern states. In truth, the distant past, highlighted by prestigious monuments, is often placed in the service of nationalistic ideologies, in an age when the advent of Islam continues to be considered the unprecedented founding moment of the Arabs. Yet it is not certain that religious dogma alone is responsible for this reductive vision of history. Such dogma—which considers the Koranic Revelation as the "seal," or closure, of earlier revelations—has never prevented the investigation of other cultures and civilizations. Scholars in ancient times, moreover, eagerly welcomed the Greek and Persian cultural patrimonies and explored the history and scientific accomplishments of other peoples. As for Mesopotamia, it seems that as great a thinker as Ibn Khaldun was well aware of his rich heritage: "Where is the science of the Persians . . . ?" he asked. "Where is the science of the Chaldeans, of the Assyrians, the Babylonians? Where are their works and the results they gathered?"[3]

Translator's Note

In the three very stimulating essays that follow, the authors frequently cite original texts, of which they provide French translations. Wherever possible, I have used the standard English-language translations of those texts and have cited the appropriate references. When a published translation could not be obtained, I have translated directly from the French version.

I wish to take the opportunity here to acknowledge the invaluable assistance of Matthew Stolper of the Oriental Institute at the University of Chicago. Professor Stolper painstakingly read and critiqued the first draft of the translation, for which I am truly grateful.

ONE

Religion and Reasoning in Mesopotamia

JEAN BOTTÉRO

CHAPTER ONE

The Birth of Civilization

In my youth—so many years ago!—I spent a lot of time with old Aristotle, who had a profound effect on me through his way of viewing the world, of asking and answering universal and essential questions, questions that today are of very little interest to anyone anymore but on which, in a sense, everything depends. Aristotle taught me, among other maxims, that in order to really understand things, one has to witness their birth and watch them grow. If I want to learn everything there is to know about an insect, for example, I must do more than simply dissect it, for then I am only looking at a cadaver, a mechanism that has been fixed and has become anything but the true insect: in order to observe it not just as an admirable though inert machine, but as an unpredictable creature directing its own movements and subject to laws even more complicated than those of mechanics, I must observe it alive, watch it live—that is, see its birth, its development, and its actions. Aristotle was right.

The goal and purpose of the present essay is precisely to explain the birth and the growth of the culture—the way of thinking and living—in which we have been immersed for generations in order better to know, appreciate, and understand it, and then perhaps to be able better to live it. This is the culture that defines us, the one in us, that which distinguishes us from the many other peoples who solve the problems of existence faced by all mankind in a different way—the Chinese and the Japanese, for example, not to mention those whom we readily call "primitive." This civilization, which we call ours, is freely called "Western," but in fact it reaches far into the Middle East. For if we discuss our civilization not as partisans but as anthropologists, and especially as historians, we see it gather and encompass not only the Greco-Latins, the heirs of

Christianity, but also the Muslim world; in other words, almost the entire Arab world. A multitude of peoples, here and there, share too many concepts, values, principles, rational and emotional reactions, too many identical cultural parameters, for us not to group them all, beyond their otherwise secondary divergences, under the heading of a single and same civilization, that is, our own: theirs as well as ours! Slowly but surely, and above all through its technological innovations—but everything comes out of that!—our civilization is well on the way to conquering the world. This does of course raise serious issues, not only for others but for ourselves, as well, especially in relation to others. Thus we have an additional reason to look at our civilization very closely once again and to attempt to form a just notion of it by witnessing its birth and the way in which it developed.

Many still believe, as has for a long time been claimed, that in going back through the centuries in search of the sources of our common civilization, the search ended on one hand with Greece and Hellenism—with its enlightenment, its promotion of Man, its discipline of the mind and its intelligence—and on the other with the Bible, the world of ancient Israel with its religiosity, its absolute monotheism, and its moralism. For whether one likes it or not, it is a fact that these two rivers, at the beginning of our time, eventually combined their waters into Christianity, around which a coherent and conquering cultural system was established. And a few centuries later, when an equally expansive Islam was established, it was also erected on a group of primarily religious and ultimately biblical convictions, ideas, and choices. These biblical influences were, moreover, at least in time and among the educated, who always govern culture, equally though sporadically imbued with a general perspective focused on traditional Greek ideology. Thus it was with good reason that our common civilization has been traced to that double origin, biblical and Hellenic; it was considered born of those parents, whose lives and maturation had occupied a bit more than the first millennium B.C.

Today we must go back even further in time because in the last century, after years of work by many talented scholars, treasures were taken out of the land—and out of oblivion—in the eastern part of the Mediterranean. In Egypt, Asia Minor, Syria, Mesopotamia, Iran, as far as southern Arabia, we have uncovered a prodigious wealth of monuments and documents bearing witness to civilizations much older than those of the Greeks or the people of the Bible and which an almost complete oblivion had left buried in a 2,000-

year-old darkness. What is more, we have gradually come to realize that it is impossible that these civilizations did not count for something, that they did not play a part in the education of our ancestors from Greece and Palestine; we've come to realize that neither Hellenism nor the Bible could constitute absolute beginnings and that we have to return to that essential rule of history: There is always something that came before. Now, after a hundred and fifty years of not only uninterrupted archeological discoveries, which uncovered remains that continue to be examined, but above all of the deciphering of hundreds of thousands of texts that have been read, analyzed, compared, and joined together—in short, dealt with like gigantic archives that are systematically stripped to the bone—when we question the genealogy of our own civilization, we now see things more clearly. Its parents have already been identified; we can now hope to meet our oldest identifiable relatives in a direct ascending line. Where might they be found?

The Hittites of Asia Minor, whose impact did not extend beyond the limits of the second millennium, left something of themselves in the Aegean world, and from there in Greece. But they primarily served as a relay and a rest stop on the journey, transmitting what they themselves had received from an even older source—the southeast. Egypt, in its originality and its magnificence, until shortly before the Christian era remained essentially self-contained: a window of Africa onto the Mediterranean. Egypt's neighbors to the east were an entire bloc of Semitic peoples—about whom I will speak later in more detail—who appear not even to have known Egypt very well before the first half of the second millennium and who, undoubtedly for a long time, were already culturally organized and not very receptive to whatever might come to them from that foreign and exotic Nile River basin. These same Semites, in Palestine and above all in Syria, from at least the middle of the third millennium, formed a certain number of small states that sometimes more or less rapidly disappeared. Although they were politically divided, they nevertheless possessed a common culture to which each group made its own contribution but whose structure most probably owed at least its development to the influence of the highly perfected culture of fourth-millennium Mesopotamia. A striking example of Mesopotamia's seminal influence on this region is the following: around 2500, right in the heart of Syria, the land of Ebla had already received from Mesopotamia not only a writing system, an essential cultural element, but at minimum a written culture and a good number of rituals and customs.

In order to take into account honestly all that has been revealed by the vast work of unearthing the past, pursued throughout all the regions of the eastern Mediterranean, until we have evidence to the contrary we must turn to Mesopotamia if we wish to see the great spring, now more than six thousand years old, that has fertilized lands and centuries. It is a wellspring to which, directly or indirectly, the Greeks and the authors of the Bible all went to find the source of their own civilizations, before giving birth, through them, to our own. If I wish to reveal the most distant origins of our civilization that are known today, it is to Mesopotamia that I will now take us.

I say "the most distant origins known today"; not, contrary to what I perhaps seemed to promise in speaking of "birth," the absolute origins. This is for two reasons: first, human affairs are too complicated, too interdependent, too linked, visibly or invisibly, for us to imagine them appearing in a short span of time, like an individual who comes into the world. Let us remember that in history, there is always something that came before, and let us not forget that the most ancient ancestors and predecessors of our race wandered the earth for hundreds of thousands of years before us.

The other reason is that, as an Arab proverb says: "The past is dead," disappeared, erased, and thus unknowable as it truly was. In order to rediscover it indirectly, we need "testimony" that comes straight from those who lived in a given time and that can provide us with some authentic notion of it. These can be what we call "monuments": tools, containers, dwellings, works of art, and so on, which, like all artifacts, retain something of their creators that can be elicited by questioning the objects methodically and intelligently, as archeologists do. There remain vast quantities of such objects, which people have scattered about ever since the most ancient times and which excavators discover every day. But those objects say very little, their answers are often ambiguous and uncertain; and especially, owing to their very material nature, they prove absolutely unsuitable for ever responding to the great essential questions that deal with the mind and the heart of mankind, much less the vicissitudes of people's behavior and lives: we can at best just glimpse some turning points in them, some vague stages in history. The only data that come from the past and that can respond directly to all our questions are documents—texts. They are exact, detailed, precise, and most often unquestionable. For they are written, and writing is materialized language, fixed and transportable far away in time and space—language, the most perfect instrument of human communication, since it can express almost all the thoughts, visions, memory, even the feelings of the one who is speaking. Documents therefore comprise the surest, the most complete, the most indispensable sources for our rediscovery of the past. And even if they do not necessarily clarify everything, when they are joined to each other and, if possible, to what is revealed by other monuments, they enable not only the statements, the direct awareness, but—in order to fill in the inevitable gaps—the connections, reflections, deductions, and prudent conjectures of which historians know how to make use and thanks to which we can succeed in "knowing more about it."

Before Mesopotamia we have only a huge mass of monuments—which leaves us in the hazy darkness of "prehistory." But in Mesopotamia we have discovered amazing quantities not only of monuments from all ages, the oldest of which go back to the age "of cavemen," around 70,000 B.C., but more important we have found objects that are a thousand times more precious. They teach us things distinctly and frankly and respond in plain language to our inquiries concerning the stages in the life, the thought, and the civilization of those times. These discoveries are the close to a half million documents—an enormous collection!—that we now possess, even if we bear in mind that they encompass the three millennia in which the local civilization lived and that certain periods are better documented than others—and some not at all. Moreover, as they are by definition written, obviously the documents only appeared along with writing, which was invented and launched, in this land in particular—in the form of a mnemonic device for accountants—around the end of the fourth millennium. I will speak later about this invention and the stages and consequences of it.

Thus not only is our information concerning the origins of Mesopotamian civilization limited to four or five thousand documents that are almost incomprehensible because of their mnemotechnic nature (which indeed do instruct us, sparingly and in the haze, in the harsh and laconic manner of ancient monuments), but they go back only to the time of the invention of writing—so that the most distant discernible origins of the civilization of the land which I have brought into the spotlight can go no further back than to around the end of the fourth millennium. If one thinks about it, this isn't too bad, but it can, after all, be deceptive! In fact, as I have suggested, and as we shall soon see, we have the means to go even further back and to catch a glimpse, at least from a wide perspective, of what one might call the most ancient "history" of the land out of which our own civilization, in its oldest perceptible state, was born.

What was the theater of this venerable succession of events? Everyone has a more or less vague image of it ever since the recent wars that were waged there: ancient Mesopotamia covered approximately the area of present-day Iraq. About two-thirds of the way along its length there is a chain of modest hills that divide the region into its northern territory, Assyria, and its southern section, Babylonia. It was in Babylonia that the scenes that governed the drama played out: the Prologue and Act I. In the third millennium this southern territory was divided into a southern half bordering the Persian Gulf, which was called Sumer, and a northern half, Akkad.

The entire land, at first covered by the waters of a single enormous river, gradually dried out and was exposed, retaining from its earlier waters only the Tigris to the east and the Euphrates to the west, beginning in the seventh or sixth millennium, while the end of the last glacial period in Europe was strongly reducing precipitation and was drying out regions that had until then been lush with vegetation. It was during that time that the neighboring Arabian peninsula (like the more distant Sahara) changed from an inhabitable savanna to the uninhabitable desert we know today. Thus in the fifth or even in the beginning of the fourth millennium at the latest, Mesopotamia assumed the appearance of what the land is today: an "interfluvial" territory (as its name indicates), a large, flat valley of very fertile alluvial soils, successively occupied by populations that came down from the surrounding hills—Kurdistan to the north and the slopes of the Iranian plateau to the east. We know little of these populations since we no longer have anything but their monuments, practically mute archeological vestiges through which we can at least catch a glimpse of the people, settled in small villages, in the beginning isolated and for a long time having a rudimentary culture. These occupants later left their mark, more or less profoundly, on the land and the civilization: for example, the classic technique of making beer in that chiefly grain-growing region, where beer has throughout time remained the principal beverage, was, if we consider the vocabulary relating to it, most likely borrowed from one of those cultures. But I must repeat: for lack of documents, we know almost nothing about them. The two ethnic branches that have been abundantly documented and were visibly dominant—the most noteworthy, the most active, the most directly responsible for the establishment of the local civilization—were the Sumerians and a group we call the Akkadians.

We know very little about the Sumerians and absolutely nothing about their origins. That they existed, both as an ethnic group and as a culture, is irrefutably proved by their language. But because that language is unique and completely separate from all the ancient tongues of the Middle East and its neighboring regions, it is impossible for us to connect the Sumerians, even using some sensible hypothesis, to any linguistic or ethnic family. If one believes as I do an old local myth called "The Seven Wise Men," the Sumerians must have arrived in southern Mesopotamia (we don't know exactly when, but it was probably at the beginning of the fourth millennium at the latest) from the southeast—from "the sea," stresses the myth—perhaps by following the Iranian coast of the Persian Gulf. This is why they frequented and first inhabited the part of the land closest to the Gulf, thus perhaps explaining its name, "the land of Sumer."

On the other hand, we know the Akkadians much better. That name, in part conventional, is given to the most ancient Semites who settled in the region, upstream from Sumer—as long ago as the Sumerians, and possibly earlier. In fact, given their very remote antiquity, they were certainly the most ancient of all Semites. Their first proper nouns appear in our most ancient documents, dating from close to 4,800 years ago. I feel I must emphasize somewhat strongly the essential role of this branch of the Semitic family, both a linguistic and a cultural branch—it is not mentioned enough, in my opinion—in the development of our culture and in our history, and which is still thriving, thank God, not only in the Middle East, but throughout the world. Although we know nothing of the Akkadians' origins, we are in a position to make some legitimate conjectures on the subject. Their language, as it has been sufficiently restored by linguists to its most archaic form, is related on one hand to ancient Egyptian and on the other to Berber, and further, to dialects that preceded Ethiopic in Abyssinia. Thus it is a rather sure bet that at least a very long time ago they frequented a territory that was close to peoples who spoke those various languages. And it is surely reasonable to limit our study to the area of the Arabian peninsula onto the edges of which they would have been pushed during the period of desertification, that is, around the sixth millennium, as it was the only livable place to settle. Thus throughout several millennia a large group of Akkadians occupied the northern edge of what was to become the Great Syro-Arabian Desert, or Syria. They lived there as semi-nomads, devoting themselves primarily to raising sheep and goats. In order to arrive in lush and fertile Mesopotamia, which must have tempted them, they had only to follow the flow of the Euphrates. Some groups among them must have made this move very early on, a move that led them, in the fifth millennium, perhaps, to the edge of the land of Sumer, into the land of Akkad. This is what we know of the most ancient history of both the Akkadians and the Semites.

History as a whole, and at the same time the history of the civilization of the land, began with the encounter and the intermixing of the two populations, the Sumerians and the Akkadians, in the southern section of the territory around the middle of the fourth millennium at the latest. We know absolutely nothing of the circumstances of their meeting, of when, how, or where it occurred. We are only certain that it did take place—like the meeting of a father and a mother when a child is born. For it was from the meeting of those two populations, and from the long symbiosis that meeting stimulated, that Mesopotamian civilization, the ancestor of our own, was born on the ruins of earlier populations.

We can also assert with some certainty that that civilization seems to have been above all the work of the Sumerians: intelligent, active, ingenious, resourceful, all evidence supports the notion that they were primarily the soul, the leaders, and the champions of the nascent civilization. Everything we have learned through many detailed documents about the later history, starting in the middle of the third millennium, indicates not only the presence of the Sumerians but also their superiority. Many Sumerian terms (printed here in roman type) relating to thought, to institutions, and to technology were brought into everyday Akkadian vocabulary (printed here in italics)—and in such cases, as we well know, the word was always borrowed along with the object it denoted. For example, in Akkadian (the language of general use in the land starting at the end of the third millennium), the word *tuppu* was used for the common small clay tablet that was employed the way we use paper as a medium for writing because the use of such a tablet was learned from the Sumerians, who called it dub. Similarly, it was because the Akkadians had received the art and the technique of gardening, of growing fruits and vegetables, from the Sumerians that they also took their word for "gardener": nu.kiri became Akkadianized into *nukaribbu*.

It would be easy to draw a long list of such borrowings: they would uncover the astonishing mass of cultural items of all kinds that the Sumerians poured into the local civilization. Looking briefly at another area, Mesopotamian religion, in its earliest days—for as long as the Sumerian dominance lasted—the supernatural figures of the divinities that were worshipped in their land, the members of their pantheon, as we call it, were not only very many in number—there were hundreds of deities—but judging from their names, the overwhelming majority of the gods were of Sumerian origin: An for the patron god of the sky; Inanna ("Celestial Lady") for one of the most noteworthy goddesses, who, significantly, was the patroness of love; and Nin.urta ("Lord of the Arable Land") for a god responsible for agriculture, to name a few.

Of course, in the face of this Sumerian cultural torrent, the Akkadians did not remain simply the beneficiaries of it: they assimilated and propagated what the Sumerians had taught them, but they contributed to it, as well. In the realm of religion, for example, we see divinities with Semitic names and personalities gradually slipping into the pantheon: Shamash, god of the sun; Adad, god of rain and wind; Ištar, goddess of war; and so on. Also, a new religious spirit became dominant: the gods, whom the Sumerians had a tendency to humanize, sometimes excessively, with the defects, the "down-to-earth" qualities, even the foibles of human beings, gradually came to be viewed in a completely different light and were presented only as very lofty and majestic lords, forever cut off from humans by their very loftiness. And this seems to me, inasmuch as we can judge, to be one of the essential cultural traits unique to Semites in general: a very intense religiosity as well as a sense of the extreme superiority and "transcendence" of the gods.

Religion is not the only segment of the civilization to which the Akkadians made a contribution and with which they shared their unique cultural elements, elements unknown to their Sumerian counterparts. The Sumerians in turn took from the Akkadians the name along with the object: na.gada, which in Sumerian means "herdsman, shepherd," comes from the Akkadian nāqidu; dam.hara, "combat," from tamḫaru; and even sum, the Sumerian name for garlic, from the Akkadian shūmu.

The Mesopotamian civilization, the oldest form of what we know of our own, was thus born in the southern part of Mesopotamia during the fourth millennium, out of the encounter of the Sumerians, who came from the southeast, and the Semites, called the Akkadians, who arrived from the northwest, out of their gradual coming together, their intersecting and cross-breeding, out of their long symbiosis and their reciprocal acculturation, inspired and directed first by the Sumerians, who were already more cultivated and refined on their own, but who were also, by all appearances, more open, more active, more intelligent and clever, and more creative.

These qualities did, however, have their counterparts, and the subsequent history of the region and its civilization suffered the consequences of them. When they arrived in the region, the Sumerians indeed appear to have burned all bridges to their earlier dwelling place and to their kind, if they left anyone behind. To our knowledge they never received the slightest infusion of fresh blood into their population. Thus on an ethnic level they found themselves in a condition of inferiority and weakness in the presence of the Akkadians, for the Akkadians—as we know through the history that follows—always received reinforcements, other Semites, immigrants as they had once been, who came from the same Syrian territories that they had. At the end of the third millennium, for example, a new branch among them emerged, in independent groups or in masses, peacefully or with the intention to conquer, who spoke a Semitic language akin to Akkadian but one that had been sufficiently distinguished from it in the meantime. In Sumerian they were called mar.tu; in Akkadian, *Amurrū* (we say "Amorites"), which means "Westerners," a designation that indicates their point of departure. They quickly allowed themselves to be seduced by the material and cultural wealth of the land and were soon assimilated with the inhabitants, infusing them with new blood and providing vigorous stimulation to their life and to the progress of their culture.

The Sumerians were unable to resist this Semitic flood: so during the third millennium and most certainly in the final third of that period, they disappeared, absorbed by the Akkadian population. And the entire land, its civilization and its destiny, found itself in the hands of the Semites alone, who continued to multiply and strengthen there. And yet two essential elements recalled the ancient Sumerian dominance in at least the realms of culture and, shall we say, the mind, enduring until the end of that civilization's history.

First, although their language, Sumerian, which indeed appears to have been at first the only written language in the land, died off at the same time as those who spoke it from birth, and although Semitic Akkadian replaced it in everyday, then in official, and later in literary usage, Sumerian continued to be used—at first in an official capacity, then as the written language of culture—in religious and scholarly literature, and even in secular literature. It triumphed early on over Akkadian, which had just recently started to be employed in these areas, and later gradually gave way to it, but without ever truly disappearing. And this literary use of Sumerian—even if it necessarily became an impure Sumerian—persisted in the region until the end of its history, around the beginning of the Christian era: not only were Sumerian works still copied in order to be read and studied as sources of inspiration, but scholars used Sumerian while "talking shop," somewhat as academics of our own culture wrote and spoke in Latin until the Renaissance. Can there be any stronger proof than that lengthy endurance of Latin among us to convince anyone of all that we owe culturally to Rome? Similarly, there is no better demonstration of the weighty liminal and fundamental contribution of the Sumerians to the birth and development of the civilization of the ancient Mesopotamians than the Mesopotamians' attachment till the very end to a language that was foreign to their mental habits, even if such a constancy concerned only the educated members of their society.

This is not, however, the only legacy that suggests the Sumerians' essential superiority or the depth of their activities. There is something else that jumps less readily to our eyes but that carries just as much weight. While acculturating and "educating" the Semites in the land, it seems to me, the Sumerians profoundly changed their perspective, their focus of interest, their attitudes toward and the Semites' reactions to the world around them—in short, their mentality, the very orientation of their minds. Wherever we encounter Semites, beyond Mesopotamia, throughout their ancient history—which is only truly revealed to us beginning in the second millennium—we see them through their written works, most often inspired by great passion, reacting with vigor in the face of things and events, endowed with a very lively imagination capable of creating new and striking images; in short, capable of an extraordinary lyricism that makes us easily admire the most powerful of poets among them: I am thinking of many passages in the Bible, from the prophets to the Book of Job, on one hand, and of the oldest Arab poets, of the *mu'allaqāt* and the Meccan surahs of the Koran, on the other.

Yet one looks in vain for such powerful words, such verbal inventiveness, such richness and fantasy of imagery, such vehemence of speech, and such impetuosity of feeling within the entire mass of Akkadian literature, including the poetry. With few exceptions, Akkadian authors, regardless of genre, appear rather stiff, without much warmth, formal; they use powerful and unexpected metaphors sparingly and are great lovers of repetition; in short, to choose a qualifier that expresses well what it means: they are prosaic. On the other hand, what is striking about those Akkadians in just about every realm, beginning in the earliest times, is a sort of curiosity about things, as if they had a need to discern them clearly, analyze them, compare them, understand them, put them in order, and classify them. In short, they placed the mind, intelligence, clarity above all else in their contact with the world, rather than heart, passion, or spirit. Personally, it is difficult for me not to attribute such a difference—I won't say a deformation, but a transformation—to an early education by the Sumerians, who, indeed, as we can easily see only by reading a small portion of their literature and in particular their poetry, seem to have lacked any vigorous involvement in things, any true need for strong or new images or for impetuous discourse, an overflowing imagination flowing into an energetically warm style. Under the influence of the Sumerians the Mesopotamian Semites, at least the educated among them— the only ones with whom we have direct contact through their writings (we will later discuss this aspect of things)—were therefore first transformed in their mental habits, and it was thus that they entered into the civilization of the land, contributed to its inception, and maintained and developed it.

Thus, from the time—certainly at the turn of the third millennium, and perhaps earlier—that the constituent part of the population that was of Sumerian stock and communicated in Sumerian found itself completely swallowed up by the ascendant Semitic element who spoke Akkadian, the social, political, economic, intellectual, and spiritual life of the land—in a word, the civilization— found itself as it would be for two thousand more years: in the hands of the local Semites, the descendants of the ancient Akkadians, who had been acculturated by their Sumerian educators, and the newly arrived Amorites, who were immediately assimilated into the local way of life.

This is why—and I cannot stress this enough, since in my opinion it is of primary importance—even once we admit that Mesopotamian civilization would never have existed, in any case would never have been what we have discovered it to be, without the very rich influence of the Sumerians, it is a fact that when they died out, Mesopotamian civilization was taken over, pursued, preserved, developed, enriched, and finally brought to a close by the Semites alone, shaped by their Sumerian teachers and even having remained faithful to their dialect, but Semitic in their language and thus in their temperament, heart, and spirit.

Powerfully and once and for all marked by "Sumerism," this was certainly a Semitic civilization, a close relative of those that were in turn erected by the other, better-known ancient Semites—the Hebrews, the Aramaeans, and the Arabs—and their civilization was, as such, the precursor of those other civilizations, as well as of our own.

For, beginning at the dawn of history at the end of the fourth millennium, Mesopotamia, a land of alluvia, of rich and fertile soil, owing to its location, its resources, and its industrious and culturally advanced population, found itself destined on one hand for wealth from the fruits of its labor (above all large-scale grain growing and the intensive raising of sheep and goats) and, on the other, to have to look to its neighbors for the materials it lacked: wood for construction and cabinetmaking, stone, and metal. Thus Mesopotamia on the whole produced its own considerable wealth, became powerful, was internally organized with a high standard of living, and was respected and feared by all, to the very reaches of distant lands. But it was at the same time very open, through its trade—either free or carried out through less peaceful means—with all its neighbors, both close and far away: to the west, Asia Minor and Syria on the eastern shores of the Mediterranean, and as far as Egypt (especially after the middle of the second millennium); to the east, Iran, the Arabian shores of the Persian Gulf, and even farther away, the western shores of the Indian peninsula. There is abundant documentation for all this trade activity from as early as the third millennium! These contacts undoubtedly provided the Mesopotamians with the material goods they sought; and their businessmen and soldiers most probably also brought back images, ideas, discoveries that were surely exotic but always quite welcome, even in a highly developed civilization such as theirs.

Mesopotamia exported its surpluses: grain, dates, wool, and the products of an organized "industrial" technology involving the working of leather and fabrics, reeds, wood, stone, and metal. But above all, along with such material goods, the Mesopotamians disseminated their cultural, intellectual, and technical accomplishments in all directions among populations that had not yet achieved—and were far from achieving—a standard of living as high as their own. In the Indus River basin, archeologists have found not only material proof of the passage of the Mesopotamians (their cylinder seals made of carved stone) dating from the third millennium, but in local documents dating from much later they have found clear traces of their highly learned and original astrological system, which the scholars of Babylon had put into place during the second millennium. In the middle of the third millennium at the latest, the Mesopotamians taught the Elamites, who had settled nearby in southwestern Iran, and the people of Ebla, in Syrian territory directly to the northwest, an essential cultural element of incalculable importance—their own writing system and at the same time their languages and the contents of many of their texts. Throughout the Middle East we have found traces of myths dating especially from the second millennium that were clearly developed in Mesopotamia and that, like the myth of the Flood, could scarcely have been imagined anywhere else, along with other literary works written in Sumerian or Akkadian. To cite a striking example, in the middle of the same millennium, undeniably as a response to a pressing request, Hittite scholars in the middle of Asia Minor not only translated the *Epic of Gilgamesh* into their Indo-European language, but they also prepared an abridged edition of it!

This selection of conjunctures seems sufficient to show just how widely, from its beginnings at the end of the fourth millennium and for a thousand years afterward, Mesopotamia generously distributed into the entire Middle East—and even farther—perhaps not the entire system of its civilization but certainly much of its wealth, both material and intellectual.

During the final millennium of its existence, although Mesopotamia at first continued to cause the world to tremble while at the same time attracting its admiration and inspiring a need to imitate, its, shall we say, "civilizing" activities appear to have slowed down. This was not only because, settled in its very high standard of living, it felt little need to raise it further, to innovate, to invent new advantages in ever greater numbers, but also because for centuries, in part owing to Mesopotamia's influence, more or less advanced and brilliant civilizations were developing pretty much everywhere around it, civilizations that no longer had as great a need to seek elsewhere for what they required to improve themselves. And it was above all because in the middle of the first millennium, Mesopotamia, as a political and a cultural power, began to descend to its demise.

At the end of the preceding millennium, a new wave of Semites—who came from the same direction as the Amorites had, who also spoke a language, Aramaic, that had further evolved in the meantime, and whose customs were quite different from those of the supple Amorites who had preceded them a thousand years earlier—had begun to undermine the security, the prestige, and the very existence of the land. Having chosen to remain nomads and live apart from others, they constantly menaced the inhabitants, their fields and towns, and sometimes managed to slip among them to dominate and displace them more effectively. And they were all the more dangerous on a cultural level since they brought a prodigious invention with them, already centuries old, one capable of suppressing and replacing the venerable but always very complicated local writing system: the alphabet. This was certainly enough to disturb and weaken the old, traditional civilization!

When that old civilization lost its strongest support, political independence—Mesopotamia fell into the hands of the Persians in 539 B.C., then into those of the Seleucid Greeks after 330, then two centuries later into those of the Parthians—it approached its demise at an increasingly rapid pace. The old Akkadian language, like ancient Sumerian before it, died, replaced in common usage by Aramaic. Akkadian, with its extravagant script, existed no longer except as it was known and used by the educated, who were themselves increasingly out of touch, scattered into scholarly circles beyond the reach of the average person, circles in which they were content to reread and endlessly comment on the obsolete literary, religious, and scientific treasures of their land. The last trace we have recovered of these final representatives of the traditional culture is a cuneiform tablet dating from A.D. 74 to 75: a stodgy astronomical almanac! It is the last word, the last breath we have of this admirable, 4,000-year-old civilization that changed our world. It was able to disappear because it had over many years gradually transferred its accomplishments, its treasures, to its heirs, our forefathers.

Today, we have seen its birth and its growth; we have seen that civilization fecundate a younger Asia, where, to our historians' eyes, the civilized world, bursting with potential, was concentrated. And we've seen it die, once its work and its time were complete, while its descendants were commencing their own adventure.

There remain a few important points to make. First, we will examine how the Mesopotamians invented what was to revolutionize the world—writing—the use they made of it and how this discovery deeply altered their perspective on and attitude toward the world around them. Next, we will look at how they responded to the essential questions that all people ask themselves concerning the universe and its functioning. Finally, we will try to discover their attitude toward the supernatural world: their religiosity and their religion.

Perhaps through this process of "displaying" we will have the opportunity to perceive beliefs, maxims, proof, ways of seeing and feeling that are still basically our own. If this is the case, then I will not have been wrong to introduce the venerable Mesopotamians as "our oldest identifiable relatives in a direct ascending line."

CHAPTER TWO

The First Writing

The first and without a doubt the most precious of the treasures invented by the ancient Mesopotamians—one that they passed on to us and that has profoundly revolutionized our lives, shaped and considerably developed our minds—is writing. For today we know this with certainty: writing was invented in Mesopotamia around 3200 B.C.

It might be somewhat difficult to admit that writing had to be invented, and therefore that there would have been a time when it was unknown, so integral a part of our everyday lives does it seem to us now. And yet (not even to mention the centuries during which in our own civilization reading and writing were a sort of privilege) when we think about it, it becomes obvious that, after all, writing is not something inherent in our nature, like seeing or eating, but, like art or cooking, it is a cultural phenomenon, just like everything humans have gradually superimposed on their basic animal nature in order to improve their existence. First there is organized speech: one's language—simultaneously the expression and the prolonging of thought, the most perfect instrument of communication, of exchanges with others. It is without a doubt the most basic, the most solid of social ties that draws us from our natural solitude and assures us a close, almost whole contact with others, to whom we thus express—while receiving as much from them— what we feel, what we desire, what we see, what we imagine, what we understand—in short, almost everything that we do and who we are. But this communication through spoken language is limited to those who are standing right next to us. Oral discourse implies the simultaneous presence in space and time of the mouth that speaks and the ears that hear. It lasts no longer than that brief encounter: afterward we can "retain" it, but very imperfectly, through a vague impression of the whole communication or perhaps of a few naturally isolated characteristics, but never exactly as it was originally uttered. Writing enables speech to transcend space and time: once speech in all its details has been fixed and materialized as it was originally intended by its author, through writing it can be distributed completely in all directions. Writing enables us to communicate at long distances and through the centuries. It considerably enlarges the range of language. Moreover, if oral discourse is flowing, continuous, as impossible to retain as running water or as time (one never bathes twice in the same river, as Heraclitus once said), written discourse is consistent and autonomous. In it speech becomes a material object that one can not only examine from every angle but also analyze and dissect into all its parts: its ideas, its themes, its expressions, its images, its words, as far as the particles of its words, on each one of which we can focus our attention, our reflection, not only in order to transpose and use them elsewhere, just as they are or in other ways, but to widen their significance, develop their importance, change it, contradict it, if need be—in short, to go further, or in other directions. In sum, written speech alone can establish an entire tradition, not only in the realm of pure knowledge or understanding, of belief, but indeed also in the realms of taste and the pleasure of communicating—shall we say, in the realm of literature. This is why I have said that the invention of writing revolutionized human thought, and I have suggested that it was, as a gift from our archaic ancestors from Mesopotamia, beyond a doubt their most important, their truly essential contribution to our civilization, indeed to civilization itself.

We would be naive to imagine that the discovery of writing was made all at once, in an instant, the way one finds a pearl. Not only was there "something before," but great cultural innovations, as a general rule, represent developments that are too complicated to have been brought to light and perfected all at once, in one attempt, right away: they always involve a more or less lengthy "history."

The history (the *pre*history—what came before) of writing in Mesopotamia begins with a millennial artistic tradition: paintings on the sides of clay vases and engravings on the stone seals in common use throughout the region. Artists were not only accustomed to projecting and concretely fixing images, to composing small tableaux intended, I won't say to explain, but at least to suggest something in the realm of feelings rather than that of clear vision; but they acquired mastery over drawing, learning to plan out and sketch things in a few strokes: the big-bellied profile of a vase was enough to suggest that vessel, a stem with four shoots to portray the head of a grain plant. Writing was born the day when someone (who? when? under what circumstances?—we'll never have the answers to these questions) understood that by systematically using a given number of such sketches in a design that was uniform enough to be recognizable everywhere, one could, like artists, not only give birth to an emotion, evoke a state of mind, but also transmit a message in plain language. The most ancient documents employing this writing, small clay tablets covered with these pictograms and dating, according to archeologists, from around 3200, indeed offer us a thousand different such sketches, all clearly traced, easy to distinguish from each other, and easy to recognize. This was no longer the fantasy and freedom of artists: it was by all evidence a fixed system.

Why was it developed, and—this much is obvious—in a deliberate fashion? It was not by sheer chance! If we examine these archaic documents closely, we immediately understand what their purpose was. Not only do all of them appear to be covered with these various pictograms, but next to and between the drawings there are specific designs (primarily round in shape, or half-moons, with a specific outline), which quickly appear to be numbers in that their specific designs are often added up at the end—which enables us easily to understand their meaning and the system to which they belong. These were countable documents; therefore it appears highly likely that it was accounting that presided over the birth of this graphic system, which modern archeologists began to discover in 1929. The land and in particular the town (Uruk, present-day Warka, halfway between Baghdad and the Persian Gulf) where all these documents were discovered were already wealthy and prosperous around 3200, due to the methodical exploitation of the richness of the land: there was large-scale farming of grain and dates and intensive raising of sheep and goats, with their derivative industries. It was necessary to distribute these goods, not only throughout the region but abroad, as well, in order to obtain the materials that were completely lacking in that land of mud and reeds. Hence it was essential through rigorous accounting practices to master that vast and complicated movement of goods, or risk waste and financial ruin. The accountants began to understand that if they wanted to keep track of traded goods more exactly than simply by calling upon their fragile memories, all they needed to do was make drawings side by side that would indicate by their very shapes the various objects being accounted for: goods and their usages accompanied by numbers indicating their quantities. In this way they could keep the most complicated accounts exactly up to date, without exposing their business to the weakness and error of their memories. The first known writing system was thus not developed, as we might easily imagine, with the aim of materializing and fixing thoughts for their own sake—this would occur later—but quite modestly, quite dully, as a simple mnemotechnical device, an aid to accounting.

In their original form, each drawing—we say, each sign, each character—thus re-presented (took the place of) the reality whose shape it was reproducing: the vase, the ear of grain. Even if we limit ourselves to looking only at the objects that were to be accounted for and their immediate future uses, it is not difficult to see that there were too many of them for their drawings alone to be used as the basis for a writing system: bull, cow, newborn calf, year-old calf, and so on. It was necessary, therefore, in order to reduce the number of signs to a reasonable and easily manageable quantity (around a thousand in the early days of writing), to resort to a method of simplification: thus one sign could refer to several objects, either because they were closely connected in nature (the pubic triangle could represent the woman; a foot could indicate all the situations in which it played a principal role—standing, being present, walking, carrying and transporting; the ear of grain, all areas involving grain and even the cultivation of grains) or because a convention was being followed (in that land bounded to the north and east by mountains, the sign for mountain could also indicate "what exists beyond," or distant lands). And, as in art, there was the possibility of composing small tableaux by juxtaposing signs, whose joining evoked more, or something other than the mere combination of their respective meanings: the plow + wood = that agricultural tool; + man = its user, the farmer. Thus roughly a thousand signs in all, most of which, it is true, had multiple uses, were enough to create a system that enabled its users to put down in writing at the very least that which was in the realm of accounting.

It was, and this must be strongly emphasized, what might be called a writing system of things: its signs referred immediately—directly or indirectly—to material objects themselves, without going inevitably through the words that expressed them, just as our index finger extended to indicate the direction to follow is immediately understood by everyone concerned regardless of their native language. Such signs are what we call *pictograms* or *ideograms*. A writing system of things denotes only things: concrete things by themselves, stripped of anything that is not part of them, beginning with the more or less subtle relations between things that are marked by the grammar of each language in ways specific to each language.

Since it places only concrete, material realities side by side, such writing is necessarily ambiguous. What is the exact meaning of a series of juxtaposed "things" such as foot + river + fish + woman? Only the person who inscribed those signs to recall an episode in his life would have been able, by calling upon his memory, to reintroduce the notions and correlations that governed the true meaning of the whole: I went to the river; I caught a fish there, which I gave to my woman/wife. Thus composed only of signs for things, writing could recall only to those who produced it the complete and exact meaning of the activity or events in which they had been involved and of which, as good accountants, they wanted to keep an accurate record. In this elemental form, writing was and could only be a mnemonic device, able to recall the known but incapable of teaching the new. This is why the most ancient documents, their complete truth and exactitude, are indecipherable and incomprehensible to us, since we were not witnesses to the dealings that were so laconically recorded in them.

The Mesopotamian writing system made decisive progress toward complete intelligibility (over approximately one or two centuries, we believe, following those early testimonies to its beginnings) when it went from being a writing system of things to becoming a writing system of words. When? How? Thanks to whom? We still do not know. But when we come upon an archaic document in which the sign of the arrow obviously does not refer to that projectile but to a completely different reality, as dictated by the context, that of life, we say to ourselves that here, behind that sign, we have a considerable change in the system. It so happens, in fact, that in Sumerian (and only in that language, which, not surprisingly, given what we know of the Sumerians, suggests that writing was probably also developed by that ingenious people) the word that means "arrow" and the one that means "life" are homonyms (we say "homophones"): they are both pronounced *ti*. Someone who spoke that language understood one fine day that the written sign did not only refer to the object it reproduced or represented, but also to its spoken word in the language, and that that word, a phonetic and pronounceable whole, could therefore also just as easily be evoked directly and immediately by the same sign. And since, still speaking of Sumerian, a large number of words were more or less monosyllabic (an, "the sky"; she, "grain"; sar, "greenery"), signs, at first purely picto- and ideographic, then became pronounceable and phonetic, each one referring to a word that came to be the smallest articulable unit: a syllable. This is how the great transformation of Mesopotamian writing occurred—must have occurred!—when it went from a simple writing of things to the writing of words and sounds. It was no longer directly connected only to concrete things, but to words, to the spoken language, and in that way it became able to reproduce that language—in other words, to cease being purely an evocative mnemonic device—and became a system just as clearly and distinctly meaningful as the language itself: writing was able to fix and materialize language in all its extraordinary capabilities.

Granted, given its very formation, writing remained complicated, because each sign, having first referred to several different objects, thus also referred—in addition—to several different syllables: foot, for instance, referred to du ("to walk"), to gub ("to stand"), and to tum ("to carry"). But it then would have been sufficient to choose from among the mass of signs, keeping only those hundred or fewer (or their phonetic equivalencies) that together would have represented all the syllables of the rather simple phonetic system of the language, in order to create a universal and considerably simplified writing system, a syllabary (like contemporary Japanese, for example, with its seventy-four signs: *a, ka, sa, ta,* and so on).

In fact, events unfolded quite differently. Most probably (this is my own opinion) through an attachment to the primary function of writing, its original capacity to indicate things, writing retained that fundamental prerogative, and signs continued to represent above all real things themselves, to play the role of ideograms. So the Sumerian language, an "agglutinative" language whose words never changed appearance regardless of how they were used in a sentence, was more naturally able to represent each word, always and in all cases, using the same sign for a given word. We have obviously taken into account the Sumerians' ability, newly acquired and duly recognized, to use signs to refer to syllabic values, but that function (which, after all, only came later) must be considered merely as a possible recourse, a pure auxiliary of ideography; for example, it was used to render foreign words, beginning with those borrowed from the Akkadians: thus, "battle" (*tamḫara*) had to be written as dam ("husband/spouse") + ha ("fish"?) + ra ("to strike"). This demonstrates, moreover, the importance Akkadian assumed, especially beginning in the second half of the third millennium, as

JEAN BOTTÉRO

it extended and essentially made universal the phonetic use of signs. For in Akkadian, an inflected language whose words changed appearance depending on their grammatical function, if one wanted to write clearly, it was difficult to express by a single and same character, as in Sumerian, the word sag, "head," which as a subject would have been pronounced *rēshu;* as the object of a verb, *rēsha;* and in the possessive case, *rēshi.*

Throughout the third millennium, writing, the use of which had gone beyond its original function as a simple accounting and "bookkeeping" aid—being employed much more widely and gradually and extending to a growing number of literary genres involving poetry and prose—at the same time became capable of recording everything that could be expressed by the language; writing had come a long way from its initial function of recording basic mnemonics. And writing was organized into a system that to us appears extraordinarily complicated. The number of signs in the writing system was reduced to roughly five hundred—which was not too bad! But those signs had in the meantime become perfectly abstract: not only did they change direction, since scribes acquired a different way of holding the clay tablet that was used as a base (we would say as "paper"), but instead of drawing signs on clay with a pointed tool, which caused smudging, the scribes began imprinting signs with a beveled stylus, which gave their constituent parts a slightly splayed form resembling wedges (cuneiform) or nails (in German, *Keilschrift*). Such a procedure, by eliminating all curves from the signs, turned them into something quite different and increasingly far from the primitive "realist" sketches: they became characters that were completely abstract and thus more difficult to remember. Moreover, each sign retained the common possibility of functioning, as in the beginning, as an ideogram and of referring to things as such while at the same time being able to be used to evoke monosyllabic sounds that made up the words in the language. And since each sign was able as an ideogram to refer easily to several different objects (the foot to "walking," to "standing up," to "transportation"), each sign could concurrently, as a phonogram, refer to several corresponding syllables (du, gub, tum). The context informed the reader not only about which language was being written (Sumerian or Akkadian), just as we can see at first glance whether a text is written in French or in English, but it also revealed, through a collection of ingenious devices that would be unnecessary and too lengthy to list here, the choice of a syllabic reading, so that the hesitations of the readers and the ambiguities of the scribes were rendered if not impossible, then at least reduced to a minimum. In this way writing was quickly formed into a logical, coherent, perfectly manageable system designed to materialize and set down in every detail everything that could be expressed through the spoken language. So true was this that the system was even used, since before the middle of the third millennium, to write a dozen other languages that were all quite different from Sumerian and Akkadian, as well as from each other. And in the middle of the second millennium the same system was used, concurrently with the Akkadian language it was transcribing, as the instrument of communication for international diplomacy throughout the Middle East, including Egypt.

Yet this must be repeated: it was a very complicated system, difficult to acquire and to use, to read and to write. This difficulty was felt in the earliest days: among the four or five thousand ancient tablets that are the oldest examples of the system, the few dozen that obviously have nothing to do with accounting are in fact simple lists and catalogs of signs, organized most often by their shapes and their general meanings (fish, birds, vases, professions and duties). They had no other apparent purpose than to be used by scribes as references, in order to learn their characters and become familiar with them—as in the past our beginning schoolchildren had their primers.

The thorny nature of writing, linked to its extreme complexity, is most likely the main reason that in that land reading and writing were in point of fact never an opportunity offered to everyone, as they are for us (today!), but were only a specialization, a true profession. Naturally, it is not out of the question that a few individuals who were not immersed in manual labor might have (as in China) learned a handful of signs and acquired the ability to decipher and stumble through them. But even among rulers and notables this was highly unusual, and the only people who wrote and read cuneiform were the scribes, the lettered, the copyists, and the secretaries, who began their training at a very young age and continued it for many long years with masters at school (it was called "the house of tablets"). We possess quite a large number of revealing documents that deal with this training. They represent not only scholarly exercises—a sign marked by the firm hand of the master reproduced more or less clumsily by the pupil on a single tablet; more or less awkward and error-filled copies of a few lines of various known, primarily literary works—but also reference works: catalogs of grouped signs, sometimes in two columns, one with the Sumerian sign and

JEAN BOTTÉRO

the other with its Akkadian equivalent; lists of synonyms, antonyms, related words; specialized expressions, for example, legal or business terminology; grammatical treatises in the form of various formulas in Sumerian alongside their Akkadian counterparts, and so on. We have also discovered a few small works that the educated had composed to the glory of their guild, their type of life, and of its advantages, sometimes, moreover, in a slightly ironic tone. Here is a passage from one of these compositions (it dates from the first half of the second millennium) that will shed light on the training, the "profession," and the life of the Mesopotamian writing specialists. It is a dialogue in the course of which a third person questions a pupil, as we might say, or perhaps, given his obviously advanced status, an older student:

"Young man! Are you a student?"
"Yes, I am!"
"If you are, do you also know Sumerian?"
"Yes, I can (even) speak Sumerian."
"As young as you are, how is it that you express yourself so well?"
"Because I have listened to my master's explanations for a long time. Thus I am able to answer all of your questions."
"That is fine, but what can you write?"
"I have already recited (by heart), then written down all the words in [here he cites a certain number of schoolbooks]. I can analyze and construe writing of all the signs. . . . The total number of days I have had to work at school is as follows: I had three days of vacation each month: and since each month has three holidays when one doesn't work, I therefore spent twenty-four days in school each month. And it didn't seem like a very long time to me! From now on I will be able to devote myself to recopying and composing tablets, undertaking all useful mathematical operations. Indeed, I have a thorough knowledge of the art of writing: how to put the lines in place and to write. My master has only to show me a sign and I can immediately, from memory, connect a large number of other signs to it. Since I have attended school the requisite amount of time I am abreast of Sumerian, of spelling, of the content of all tablets.

"I can compose all sorts of texts: documents dealing with measurements of capacity, from 300 to 180,000 liters of barley; of weight, from 8 grams to 10 kilograms; any contract that might be requested of me: marriage, partnership, sales of real-estate and slaves; of guarantees for obligations in silver; of the hiring out of fields; of the cultivation of palm groves . . . including adoption contracts: I can draw up all of these. . . ."[1]

From its listing of tasks at the end, this document shows where their lengthy apprenticeship led most of these "writing professionals": they became what we used to call (I still knew some, sixty years ago) public scribes. In that capacity they found themselves closely connected to people, but above all to the economic, judicial, and political life of the land, the official business of which they were the only ones capable of recording in due form. Through the countless relics we have discovered, and that we continue to discover, the scribes' many-faceted "writings" make the voices of their contemporaries echo all the way to us: thus we are able to hear those voices, originating from just about everywhere in time and space, which enable us to look those ancients in the face, to get to know them—in a word, to reconstruct their history, since this is the benefit of that extraordinary invention, writing.

In the realm of economics, of fundamental importance in a region so rich and so well organized, the secretaries of the many offices, methodically employed to control all activities, have left tens of thousands of pieces of evidence, beginning with the oldest, still indecipherable tablets and from all subsequent periods of the functioning of such an enormously intricate and complicated machine: it was not by chance that "bureaucracy" was taken so seriously in such a perfectly structured land. In the first place, those bureaucrats left an infinite number of lists of the personnel employed at various public or private jobs with their division into groups, the salaries they were paid, and the number of absentees, the "blind," and the dead. Second, through the location of entire archives, we have found lists for the distribution or the packaging and stocking of all sorts of goods and materials, sometimes in daily notes summed up at the end of the month on larger tablets, where the balance is drawn following the monthly removal of what remained in stock. Not to dwell on an endless subject but to cite just one example, dating from around 1780 B.C., that is typical of these ancient practices: we have located in the palace of Mari the details of the foods and ingredients that the royal cook had removed from the storeroom to prepare the king's meals, day after day, month after month, over a period of several years. I'm not sure that we know as much about Francis I or Henry IV.

Inspired by a lofty notion of judicial constraints, even if they had not yet had the idea of formulating them into laws classified into true codes, the ancient Mesopotamians, beginning late in the third millennium, continuously relied on writing to recall and thus to solemnize and perpetuate all sorts of business they constantly engaged in, and their notaries and scriveners have left thousands upon thousands of accounts of that activity: deeds for the purchase and sale of land and slaves; partnership agreements; contracts for the renting of land or livestock, for tenant farming, for interest-bearing loans, for marriage (the wife was obtained following the payment of an agreed-on sum to her family by that of her future spouse), and for adoptions (people had frequent recourse to adoption, for various purposes, including circumvention of certain restrictions: thus one adopted a foreigner so that once he had entered into the family he could be freely given a familial parcel of land that was in itself untransferable); contracts with wet nurses or for apprenticeships—in short, all sorts of business documents, drawn up in due form by bureaucrats and by public scribes, who might have affixed their names and even their seals to the written document alongside those of the parties involved and of the witnesses. It is easy to imagine what a conscientious historian whom writing has enabled to travel back in time can derive from examining such a massive 5,000-year-old archive. I should add that what was true of individuals is all the more so of the political life of that time: the royal notaries and scribes have transmitted royal ordinances, edicts, official acts proclaimed by the ruler, his charitable gifts, his intervention in all matters of daily life in the realm, and even international treaties that he might have negotiated between powerful leaders.

In the domains of administration and justice, the king, the chief judge, was expected to delegate a part of his power to local magistrates. Thanks to the minutes kept by their clerks, we see those magistrates solve legal disputes; rein in excesses, infractions, and crimes; hand down sentences; and pronounce the punishment, either monetary or corporal. Some monarchs were even careful to have these legal decisions gathered and classified, once they were stripped of the specific facts of a given case, thus making them sorts of models both of judgments and of administrative wisdom, gathered into what we erroneously call codes, which nevertheless are very enlightening for us, as they reveal the solutions that were applied to the infinite problems of public life, the meaning of justice, and the "law" that reigned in that land.

If there is a realm where writing, created to eliminate distances, plays its indispensable role to perfection, it is certainly that of letter-writing between distant correspondents. The ancient Mesopotamians, beginning at least in the second half of the third millennium and to the very end, made great use of writing for this purpose, and we have indeed found, from all periods in time, between thirty and forty thousand letters, primarily of an official nature but also some private correspondence. Owing to the highly specialized nature of writing, when correspondents who were not necessarily able to write wished to use it, each missive required the intervention of two professionals: one at the beginning, to write it, and the other at its arrival, to read it. Letters therefore regularly began with a formula of this type: "To So and So (the addressee), say this (you who will read this letter): 'Thus speaks (to you) So and So (the sender, for whom I myself, the secretary, am transcribing the message here).'" Private missives most often concerned business of all kinds rather than sentimental affairs: I have never come across any love letters, and we must assume that the services of the public scribes were too costly for people to have employed them for emotional outpourings. Official letters, found in great numbers from all periods, especially from the first half of the second millennium and from the first millennium, are an inexhaustible source of information dealing with the history of the sovereign, his palace, capital, subjects, and entire land, as well as his relations with the rulers of neighboring lands.

What we find very rarely in letters—information about the chronological, the day-to-day history (since letters were only occasionally dated)—is provided in the documents created by other professional writers in the royal service. By order of the king, they drew up lists of dynasties and of reigns, and within each reign, successive years. For in the absence of a universal era of reference such as ours, which numbers the years before or after the birth of Christ, the Babylonians dated materials by mentioning a defining event from the preceding year: a war, a victory, a political decision, the building of a temple, a palace, or a monument. Thus, for the twenty-second year of Hammurabi's reign: "the year of King Hammurabi [just after the one] when he had a statue of himself erected representing him as the 'Just King.'" Other royal notaries, in more or less protracted and openly biased chronicles, undertook to reconstruct the history of a sovereign, an entire series of rulers, or an entire period. And the annalists, whom the Assyrian rulers brought with them during their annual military campaigns, were similarly assigned to record, in order, episode after episode, and year after year, the unfolding of those attempts at conquest, the submission of the weaker to pay tribute, the annual raids and pillaging for whose successful conclusion these kings were honored—it being of course understood by the writers that those attempts resulted only in victories.

I will not continue listing the huge amount of material that the potential and practice of writing have provided us, material re-

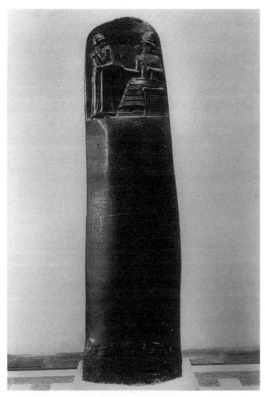

Figure 1. The stela of Hammurabi, discovered at Susa in the winter of 1901–1902, is inscribed with a prologue, 282 laws, and an epilogue. Courtesy of Musée du Louvre. Département des Antiquités orientales. Reproduction interdite sans autorisation. Copyright © Pierre et Maurice Chuseville.

cording a past that would have otherwise disappeared and been long forgotten. It is thanks to the writing professionals and to their hard work that we possess such notable segments of that long road traveled close to three thousand years ago by the ancient Mesopotamians, whose history, life, progress, and downfalls, good fortune and bad we are thus in a position to reconstruct, sometimes with the most significant, the most unexpected, or the most trivial of details.

Not all those who had gone through school in Mesopotamia and had thus made writing their profession—to our advantage—ended up as public scribes, official secretaries, and writers of public acts, or, as we would say, obscure clerks and "pen-pushers"—or more precisely, "stylus-pushers" (dub.sar). The most talented, the most brilliant, the most ambitious, or the luckiest among them could become truly literate men of letters, devoted to literature and living from it, able no longer simply to put down in writing the ideas, feelings, and desires of others, but wishing to transcribe their own thoughts, to create personal written works, and suddenly to rise to the status of true writers: poets, thinkers, or scholars, in all areas of knowledge and taste.

As I have explained, writing—through local distribution and "chronicles," and the sharing of ideas that it made possible—alone offered the means to form solid traditions through the accumulation of exact information, through the pondering of the literal meaning of discourse, through the revision of facts, with everything constantly made available in time and in space to all. In the realm of what I call "occasional literature," that written on a daily basis to respond to specific needs, by secretaries, notaries, copyists, and public scribes—a brief description of which I have provided above—habits, constraints, and formalities of vocabulary, style, presentation, and order were thus developed throughout the centuries. These elements changed depending on the needs, the places, and the times, and were maintained exactly in the various types of documents they characterized: economic and administrative texts of all genres, as well as contractual, judicial, epistolary, and "historical" texts. It is as if, left to the freedom and imagination of individuals, these pieces did not have any value. It is interesting to note that we are still in the same situation: notaries and law clerks know something about this.

Other traditions of form and substance were similarly created and carried on by high-level scholars, writers, men of letters who devoted themselves to the composition of literary works in the strict sense, created not for timely and specific occasions or needs but apparently for the pleasure of it, on request, and intended from the start for everyone, in time and in space—what I call pure literature.

The first collection of literature we have discovered—and it is highly unlikely that an older one will be discovered, given the ancientness and the still-rudimentary use of the writing in it—dates from around 2600! It is difficult and sometimes impossible to understand, decipher, and translate it in its entirety, because one has the clear impression that it is the simple notation of an oral tradition and that writing, still in large part a mnemonic aid, had been used primarily to remind the readers (as educated as the authors!) of discourse that was passed on by word of mouth. Certain literary genres are already apparent in the collection: prayers, religious songs, myths, "advice from a father to his son," and each one is defined by a group of conventions that were subsequently respected to such a degree that many of the works revealed in this venerable "literature" were rewritten in almost exactly the same way at a later date, so that, thanks to these more recent versions, we can more or less deeply probe the texts written so rudimentarily and obscurely around the twenty-seventh century B.C.

I will not dwell here either on these "belles lettres" or on the uniquely literary traditional constants that characterize the various "genres," constants that have been edified and imposed throughout time, thanks to the increasingly expanded use of writing. The main reason for this is that most "literary" works from that land reflect not only preoccupations with taste and aesthetics—the art of writing well to make readers appreciate what is written—but, quite often, other sectors of the culture: "science" or religion, which I will later discuss in greater detail. Elements of style, images, vocabulary, poetic devices (some taken directly from oral discourse, which in Mesopotamia preceded and always accompanied, but over a much wider range, written discourse), and even themes, often repeated exactly from one text to another, or more or less profoundly modified—in short, all that we casually call literature's "tricks of the trade," strictly literary work—repeatedly jump out at us when we simply glance over it, and even more so when we carefully study the countless works of poetry or prose that have been written on cuneiform tablets. I must say that Assyriologists have up to now shown very little interest in examining these works closely, and I am unaware of any serious in-depth study devoted from this perspective to the "belles lettres" of Mesopotamia.

But these literary traditions, which developed out of the use of writing by high-level professionals, are less important than those revealed by works dealing primarily with "scientific" and religious matters—to which I will return, at least indirectly.

CHAPTER THREE

The Intelligence of the World

As we have seen, Mesopotamian civilization invented and perfected the act of writing, and it also gave birth to a specific writing system. This civilization provided itself with the means to set down, to commemorate, to indefinitely distribute, and therefore to deepen and continually perfect what the minds of its thinkers had discovered and developed and what was expressed by its two languages, Sumerian and Akkadian. Through this process Mesopotamian civilization greatly extended its intellectual possibilities, and, it should be said for the record, our own, even if a long time ago we went on, far from the ancient and bizarre cuneiform signs, to that prodigious simplification of writing known as the alphabet, whose history began around the fifteenth century B.C., not far from Mesopotamia, but not in Mesopotamia itself.

I emphasized above how the bearers of that old civilization, the Semites, as well as their Sumerian teachers, seem to us to have been endowed, if not with passion and imaginative and verbal power, then with a great curiosity about things, like a need to discern them clearly, analyze them, compare them, understand them, put them in order and classify them, with true intelligence and clarity.

Equipped with such an intellectual temperament and armed with the incomparable tool of writing, we might have expected those people from the earliest days onward never to have ceased doing their utmost with the means at their disposal to study and attempt to understand the world (their world), to obtain a coherent and balanced idea of it, to respond intelligently to the questions that its existence and meaning—our existence and meaning—endlessly put to us. Such a large vision of the world, translated into countless written texts, is impossible, in these few pages, to describe both completely and in sufficient detail for it to be understood. I will therefore do my best to limit myself to a brief description of two critical realities regarding that vision, realities that, as such, are no longer our own but—and this is also true for writing—that still fundamentally belong to us, and without which our own reality would not have become what it is today. First we will look at the ancient Mesopotamians' general conception of the universe, of its origins and the reasons for its existence, and then at the order they introduced into their intellectual operations in their search for truth, the methodology they developed to advance in their knowledge of things, a method that did not involve physical displacement, a manual and visual form of exploration, but simply an internal use of intelligence—or, to express myself differently, the way they introduced what was to become our "logic," the collection of rules of mental behavior used in the search for knowledge.

Before going any further I must put my cards on the table. A few years ago a unique book was published, one that was powerful and relentless in presenting what its author, Marcel Gauchet, calls (and this is the title of the book) "the disenchantment of the world." Gauchet shows how human beings, at first deeply involved in the supernatural and the divine, whose existence and intervention, humans believed, explained everything around them, gradually became detached from those beliefs, henceforth seeking only in the here and now the answers to the questions raised by the here and now, thus "disenchanting" their way of viewing things, cutting it off from the heavens, and, as we might say today, laicizing it. The ancient Mesopotamians, however lofty their civilization and lively their intelligence, had not yet disenchanted their world—far from it—they had not yet excluded from their intellectual constructs the constant intervention of those gods whose existence they felt forced to postulate, since without the gods humans lacked the ability to answer the infinite questions raised by the world and by occurrences around them. In other words, their religion was still intricately connected to their complete worldview (like filters applied to a lens): all of their views about themselves and the world around them were colored and conditioned by their religion (I will describe that religion as a complete system later in this essay). But it should not be surprising to see religion intervening here more than once, since for the Mesopotamians it was still connected to everything, and because for the ancient Sumerians and Babylonians, as, moreover, for everyone around them, the visible universe was still "full of gods."

This is why what for us are now science and philosophy—fields that at that time did not yet exist—were then what we would call *mythology,* and it was according to the rules of mythology that the ancient Mesopotamians applied their reasoning. Mythology is a primitive form of explanation, and myths, which are its specific expression, might more exactly be defined as "controlled, calculated imaginings." In a world that did not have the means to seek out an always unique truth, people were content to seek out a many-sided likelihood. Faced with an intriguing situation that one wished to explain, without the possibility of proceeding in a purely rational, rigorous, and rectilinear fashion, one imagined how and why that situation had likely come to occur: its cause was invented in the form of a series of events that led precisely to that situation. The series of events, the tale of them, were imaginary, but always calculated in order to end up as closely as possible in the situation one was trying to explain. If I were asked why a storm suddenly arose, I would answer by invoking the laws relating to the humidity of the air, to the formation of clouds, to the phenomenon of the rapid rise of some of them, to their electrical charge. An Indian from Peru would answer the same question by explaining that there is a giant man in the sky with very long legs who is jumping up and down, thus creating the physical shaking of thunder from the sound of his jumping from side to side and lightning by the quick flashing of his eyes. Here, then, is a mythological "reasoning," here is a myth! As for myself, I answered the question with the only explanation that has a chance of being correct and true, taken from the actual nature of the phenomenon, by following the only path that leads from the cause to the effect; but the Indian resorted to his imagination, a calculated imagination adapted to his goal, a mythical explanation that is simply "likely and plausible," for, if it is internally sufficient to account for the problematical phenomenon, not only is it not demonstrated and certain, but it is not the only one that can assume the same role: it is easy to imagine, and there have in fact been imagined in various folklores, many other tales in the same vein that just as plausibly account for a storm, its unexpected arrival, its movement in the sky, its noise and flashing.

The ancient Mesopotamians—whose lengthy tradition of experiences, observations, and reflections, accumulated thanks to their writing, had enabled them to discover the precise cause of a large number of unique phenomena—had recourse only to mythology to confront the great and infinite questions raised by the world around them, its contents and its functioning. They made a "rational" use of that mythology, and in that way created an intelligent and balanced image of the universe, an image that was at least likely, since they did not have the means to discover the true image—nor, most probably, do we, at least at the present time, and in spite of all our knowledge.

Thus the Mesopotamians described the universe around them as a huge hollow spheroid whose top, luminous and brilliant, they saw, and that they called "Above" or "Sky" (Sumerian: an), and whose lower hemisphere, like its inseparable complement, they deduced, and called "Below" or "Underworld" (ki), necessarily dark and lugubrious, like all that is subterranean. The sheer plan of this enormous sphere was in their view occupied by the sea, salt water, a specific and irreducible substance that, according to them, was not at all a mixture of water and salt. In the middle of the sea, like an island, there emerged what we call the earth—obviously flat— whose simultaneously central and superior part was, it went without saying, Mesopotamia, the center of the world. The earth rested on a huge underground table of fresh water, the same that was found in drilling a well and that burst from the ground through springs. Above them, in the expanse of the sky, a number of luminous bodies circulated tirelessly: stars and planets, an age-old observation of which, under the ever-limpid eastern sky, had inspired the Mesopotamians to note the infallible regularity of the stars' movements and their eternal passing by. The largest and brightest of these bodies each presided over half of time: the day and the night. How could those people not have observed many other earthly phenomena with as much curiosity, some occurring with perfect regularity (such as the spring swelling of the two rivers), others occurring completely arbitrarily (such as floods, rains, the changes in the direction of the wind, the swift arrival of a storm)? How could one explain all the mysteries, the obscurities, the ambiguities of such a gigantic panorama, the least detail of which visibly surpassed any human forces by far? And how could one account for the secrets of the germination of grain and other plants within the soil and the growth of animals and humans in the darkness of the maternal womb? How to explain the extraordinary properties of fire, both destructive and purifying, able to change solids into liquids and to cook what was raw? Why were there those strange and irrepressible impulses of physical love? The world, in truth, was full of mysteries.

In order to shed light on these mysteries while appeasing their irrepressible curiosity and a primordial desire to know (that quality unique to the very nature of humankind, as my old friend Aristotle once said), throughout an endless development of the thinking process, about which we know nothing and never will know anything, the ancient Mesopotamians, like so many other peoples, called on the means they had at hand: on mythology, on calculated, controlled imagination. Behind or within each of those problematical phenomena they thus imagined types of drivers, stimulators, or directors: the sky and the underworld, the sea and the earth, the sun, moon, and stars all had within them or behind them (this situation does not appear ever to have been clarified, nor was their exact natural position ever defined—which was not, moreover, simple!) their own master, conductor, leader; likewise fire, the growth of plants, the descendants of animals and of men, the passions of love—and other phenomena, such as that which suddenly throws men against each other: war.

Thus in the image they had created of the world around them, that world seemed to be doubled with an entire group of beings, invisible, of course, but whose existence was no less certain since, without them, nothing could be explained—everything would have been absurd. These beings, clearly superior to humans, were given the name of "gods." The ancient Mesopotamians had filled their world with gods, a world that without the divinities would have been filled with enigmas. Thus there were many gods, by definition, since each one had to direct and operate his or her own domain, his or her own parcel of the universe. The Mesopotamians were polytheists. And in order to have an idea of those same invisible gods who ultimately existed only at the bottom of their "controlled imagination," they found nothing better than our own image: the Mesopotamians were anthropomorphists. Their gods had to be similar to us but still, by definition, infinitely superior to us in intelligence, power, and longevity: it was inconceivable that, given their role, those gods were, like us, subject to death and to the short interval of time that death allows us here on the earth.

Another series of questions remained, inquiries that were just as pressing and at first unsolvable, and that related not to the condition and functioning of things but to their origin: Where did the world come from? And perhaps above all, since mankind is always most interested in itself, why were humans put on the earth? What was the meaning of their existence, the significance of their presence here?

Once again, the only means of "knowing" (of responding plausibly to the question) was the mythological imagination. It has been relied on so often throughout the centuries that more than one response has been given to those questions: as I have stressed, only the truth is unique; probability can be protected in many ways. In Mesopotamia, however, a single, fundamental certainty never varied, since it was in strict logical agreement with the existence of the supernatural world: it could only have been through the gods that the universe and mankind had been created. Each likely hypothesis, each myth giving some detail of that creation—and the myths were often contradictory—presented things in its own way, but they all attributed the origin of the universe and of humans to the sole will and intervention of the gods. It was only in how events unfolded, in the means and stages of cosmogony—the birth of the universe—that explanations differed; each explanation was as "likely" as the next, but varied depending on the point of view adopted by the author, who was conditioned by his time, his vision of things, and thousands of other peculiarities in his thought and his life. We must not lose sight of the fact that the documents, the cuneiform texts in which we glean the details of the myths, are from various periods in the long span of the local civilization and its contemplation, and each is from a different place and by a different author; thus we can justify their inconsistencies, which in no way detract from the role they played.

To look at only one example, some myths advanced the proposition that the world was born the way humans and animals were born, through natural procreation, following the coupling of divine parents: the god from Above, from the sky (An), impregnating the goddess from Below, the earth (Ki), to give birth to the framework of our existence. Sometimes it was a series of generations: the sky giving birth to the earth, which had given birth to the rivers, and so on; or there might have been a string of successive creations of all that keeps us alive by a single and same god, depending on specific needs. Some also imagined a sort of enormous initial chaos, settled by the struggle between two gods, one of which carried off the Above with him, and the other, the Below, thus making the first framework of an orderly world appear. The birth of the world has also been presented in an, shall I say, "industrial" mode, as the result of technical operations analogous to those that were being used to invent and produce manufactured products: in this scenario what was stressed was the careful preparation of the plans, which necessitated a gathering of experts and decision makers, that is, the greatest of all gods, who perfected, in every detail, the plan for the great work, which was then carried out according to that plan.

The reader will have noted that the precise actions the gods took in creating the world, regardless of the myth chosen, are never clearly defined, nor is the specific creation process described: not being able to imagine everything in detail, people remained somewhat in the dark, using verbs with vague meanings, such as *to make, to prepare, to construct, to give birth.* This is because on one hand the ancient Mesopotamians never really managed to imagine things very precisely, but also and above all because the primary effort of thought was put into connecting what they believed to be the true, supernatural causes with their effects, in order to demonstrate how greatly the universe and all that it contained, its existence as well as its functioning, depended solely on the gods, whatever their methods of intervention might have been. There was, however, one more thing: it was not possible to represent the gods as pulling the world out of nothingness, which was unimaginable. In order to create the world, the gods always began with a preexisting matter: the enormous chaotic mass, or clay to shape, or yet an already created part of the world. The ancient Mesopotamians never asked themselves the insoluble question of the absolute origin of things. Perhaps we must see in this the effect of their perspicacity and their intelligence: What was the use of losing oneself in the meanderings of complicated myths and of multiplying the most confused imaginations in the single goal of providing specifics, judged to be futile and supererogatory, especially given the difficulty of imagining everything?

There is every chance that the very urgent question of the origins of mankind was not only debated on the mythological level, but could have given rise, like the question of the beginnings of the universe, to divergent speculations. To our knowledge, however, one of them appears to have won out over the others and to have eliminated them, inasmuch as through what we have discovered in this area we have found only the one. That speculation even became the subject, around 1750 B.C., of a masterpiece of local literature, a great mythological poem in twelve hundred verses, two-thirds of which we have been able to recover, quite enough to be able to understand its importance and what came afterward. We call it the *Supersage,* a translation of the Akkadian Atraḫasīs, the name of the poem's hero. I will summarize it here since it provides a clear view of the beautiful, logical, coherent, and intelligent image that the ancient Mesopotamians had developed of mankind's reason for existing, of the fundamental and irreplaceable role that had been assigned to humans, and of the place they held in the enormous and complicated mechanism of the universe.

The poem begins well before the appearance of mankind: thus there were still only gods, and consequently they were forced—at least some of them, those who were considered inferior to the others—to work in order to obtain what they needed: to eat and to drink, to be clothed, to decorate their bodies, to have shelter. These "worker" gods labored under the orders of the greater gods whose only task was to govern. One day the divine workers, fed up both with wearing themselves out working and with being treated differently from their "bosses," essentially went on strike. It was then that the most intelligent of the gods, the great Enki (Akkadian: Ea) intervened. He proposed the creation of a replacement for the striking gods, one capable of carrying out the same work with as much assiduousness and efficiency but who would never be able to demand a change in status, as the divine strikers had successfully done. That replacement would be the human being: he would be assured intelligence and productivity through the presence in his body's raw matter of the blood of a second-level god who was sacrificed for this purpose; and it would be impossible for him ever even to dream of being raised to the status of a god, since he was made of the same raw material—clay—that would one day reclaim him (a common expression in Akkadian for dying was "to return to clay"). Thus a prototype of a human was put together, approved by the delighted gods, and then put into production, if I may put it that way (the passage has many gaps and part of it is missing), through seven initial couples.

The humans immediately got to work, and since (although they were indeed irrevocably destined by their own nature to die) their lives were still very, very long (this is a well-known trait of local imaginations)—because they never fell ill, experienced no infant mortality, and benefited largely from the fruit of their labor, even if they only ate what was left after they had abundantly served the gods—they increased quickly and extraordinarily, as did the din that arose from their large numbers. They were so noisy that the king of the gods, Enlil, unable to sleep owing to the racket, decided to decimate them (at the risk of annihilating them). First there was an epidemic, but the god Enki saved them; then there was drought and its necessary consequence, famine, but they were again saved by Enki. So Enlil, furious to see his plans thwarted, resolved to annihilate mankind purely and simply, through a scourge without remedy: flood. But the very clever Enki taught his protégé, the king of the land, who was nicknamed Supersage, to build a boat in which he would carry his wife, as well as pairs of all the animals, and this would assure renewal on every level. In the end, since Enlil, the king of the gods, protested (stupidly, one must say) against the fact that a man was saved and that the human race would therefore survive along with the inconveniences to his rest, Enki erased the cause of the dispute: in the future not only would humans live for a much shorter time, but infant mortality as well as the sterilization—either pathological or voluntary—of many women would greatly reduce their numbers. The mythical age, the one when creatures were formed and, if necessary, touched up, was thus concluded; the historical age began, the one of which we have a record and that, without the slightest break since that time, inaugurated and governed our own history.

In order better to understand and penetrate this portrait of the origins of humans and their place in the universe, we must keep in mind that such a mental construct is the result of a mythological reflection; in other words, I will repeat, an exercise of the imagination, controlled by the concern for adapting history thus constructed for one's own goals. Imagination does not create, however; it can only reproduce, combine, and transpose images and situations encountered elsewhere. The authors of the myth of Atraḥasīs clearly transferred into that vision of the world and of humans a state of affairs that at that time was familiar to all inhabitants of Mesopotamia and to others in the surrounding region—that is, the economic and social conditions that governed the relations of property owners, people who were well provided for financially, and the masses, the laborers, who worked the land of the privileged in order to yield a profit, primarily to the advantage of the owners, and, by association, to their own. To these old mythologers, therefore, the world was the landed property of the gods, and of the gods alone, a huge reservoir of raw materials to work in order to transform them into all sorts of useful and sumptuary consumable goods. And humans were put on the earth to carry out that work and thus to play the role of servants to the gods. We must recognize that this was a perfectly intelligent vision, one completely adapted to people's own experience, a noble vision not lacking in grandeur in a still "enchanted" and clearly theocentric world, a vision whose logical and lofty meaning was derived from the double awareness that humans could not cease to work the materials that nature provided them and that not only was the human being not the master of the universe, but that he was a temporary inhabitant destined to die. In the myth of Atraḥasīs, that unchangeable law, against which one senses not the slightest form of rebellion—the ancient Mesopotamians knew how to accept the inevitable and bow to it—is explained by the necessity of separating the gods from humans with an unbroachable chasm. We know this through other sources, thanks to a good number of documents. It was believed that upon death only two things remained of the deceased: his body, fixed in a position of sleep, which was buried and which, more or less quickly, would return to clay, thus obeying the gods, who had made it out of clay; and the insubstantial and ethereal vision that one kept of the deceased in one's thoughts, in dreams, in visions, in a haunting memory; for the ancient Mesopotamians, this was the "ghost" of the dead person, who, introduced into the earth through burial, went to the underworld, that huge, silent, and black cave, the mirror image of the celestial and luminous hemisphere. All the dead without exception went to that place together—this was their destiny. There was no "judgment" to assign a different fate to each individual depending on the morality of his behavior during his lifetime; in the underworld the dead led less a life than a larval and torpid existence (like the "sleeping" cadaver), sad and melancholic, for all time.

We must recognize that such a view of the world and of our human condition, however merely plausible it might have been, was at least rational—it was logically deduced using a great deal of intelligence, if not poetry, and it repeated known statements and convictions: theocentrism and the ultimate superiority of the gods, the only masters of all that existed; the obviously servile and laborious condition of human beings' existence; their inescapable condemnation to death as well as the impossibility of imagining them "returned to nothingness," an abstract and unimaginable notion. I have therefore not been wrong to suggest an intelligent image of the world as the distant source of our own.

Continuing on my course, I will present one or two more essential discoveries made by that ancient civilization, discoveries that, though more or less altered, we can still discern in our own. Again through their mythological and plausible vision, the Mesopotamians greatly contributed to the perfection of one of the essential tools of human thought by providing, in their own way, access to learning, to knowledge—by this I mean the possibility of discovering and knowing things with certainty through the use of one's reasoning alone.

In order to show this I must speak of a phenomenon that to us might appear rather futile, frivolous, and useless: divination—a way of "ascertaining" the future that has interested people throughout time. The ancient Mesopotamians, between the end of the third millennium and the beginning of the second, developed a completely original method for discovering what would happen in the future. This method was logically embedded in their writing system in its most ancient, never erased or forgotten, form, as I have explained; it was also linked to an old conviction, one that existed unaltered in the land, which identified the name of a thing with the thing itself. For us, a name is a sound from someone's voice that arbitrarily designates something but that in itself is by no means necessarily connected to the thing in question. For the Mesopotamians the name was the object being designated, the vocalized thing when the name was uttered and the written thing when it was written. The person who wrote (and this is the evidence that must have leapt to the eyes of the inventors and then the users of cuneiform writing), while he formed the characters that represented and reproduced objects, thus made and produced those objects themselves. Therefore the gods, creators of everything and who, not only in the beginning but each and every day, produced beings and events, thus also wrote, in their own way, those beings and those events. The entire world, the work of the gods, was similar to a written tablet and like the tablet was full of messages. When the gods, who were supposed graciously to condescend to reveal the future, wanted to do so to an individual or to a ruler, they thus created a unique being or event, something unusual, extraordinary, or monstrous to warn those concerned that this creation contained a message concerning their future, which the gods obviously knew well in advance, since they had conceived it before carrying it out. In other words, when things were normal in appearance or presentation, it was, if I may say so, a negative sign: one of a nonmessage, through which the gods were showing that they had nothing to say. But once something unexpected occurred in any realm of real life, since everything and everyone were the work of the gods, that bizarre being or event contained a message concerning the future and a warning from the gods, just as the signs of writing—pictograms and ideograms—contained, enclosed, and expressed a message from the scribe. But that message, like those in writing, was encoded: only those who had learned the many meanings of the signs were able to decode it. Just as there were writing professionals, so, too, there were professionals who dealt with the writing of the gods. These specialists were called *bārū*, a term derived from an Akkadian verb meaning "to examine, to scrutinize." The *bārū*—professional diviners—examined and scrutinized unusual things or singular events, and in them they learned to read what the gods, in "creating" those abnormalities—or in other words, in "writing" them—wanted to teach people concerning the future.

Because of their talents, the *bārū* of Mesopotamia, from at least the beginning of the second millennium, were employed to study and gather, in all the realms of the universe, every unusual situation, unexpected event, and abnormal being, real and imaginary, to decipher them and, facing their description, to translate them with regard to the future. And since the ancient Mesopotamians, or at least their scholars and specialists, were, as I mentioned, intensely curious about their world and capable of relentless research, were methodical and passionate in their quest to put together logically and rationally all things in their world, to classify them and draw up an almost infinite number of lists of them, the fruits of this preoccupation with divination came together in what we might call "treatises"—because they are systematic—specialized in all sectors of the universe: the movements of the stars and of planets (let us say, astrology); the examination of humans and animals as they appeared at birth or during their lifetime; phenomena of all kinds able to mark the course of daily life and encompassing all circumstances in it; but also phenomena caused during various activities, primarily cultual and sacrificial, in particular the observation of the normal or abnormal condition of the internal anatomy of a sacrificed animal.

All of these works are presented as interminable and dreary lists, continued over more than one tablet, of unusual, deviant, unique phenomena, described with their essential characteristics in an initial half-sentence, then with their corresponding oracle: the part of the future, favorable or unfavorable, deciphered in the protasis. For example: a man dreams that he is eating the flesh of a dead person—a third party will take everything that belongs to him. Then, listed in an orderly fashion, are the consumption of dog meat, gazelle, buffalo, monkey. And everything is classified with extreme minuteness while varying the essential phenomenon with details of situation, localization, importance, magnitude, color, and so on. For example, if someone had a birthmark, the variables would be its size, its coloration, its placement (on the face, the forehead, the body, the arms, the legs; on the right, the left). Most of the "divinatory treatises" swell in this way in considerable volume. The one dealing with oneiromancy (divination through dreams) takes up 11 or 12 tablets; the one concerning astrology, 70; the treatise on the chance occurrences of daily life, at least 110—which amounts to more than twenty thousand lines, and as many items to consider, since each one fills up one line. To aid in understanding this system, which is perfectly logical but rather far from our own customs, I will give an example of it. I have taken the following from a treatise on physiognomy in which the message about the future is hidden in the appearance of the body of the person in question:

> If a man has a flushed face—his elder brother will die.
> If in addition to this his right eye is inflamed—his father will die.
> If in addition his left eye is inflamed—what he will have inherited from his father will thrive.
> If in addition his right eye is fixed—in a foreign city dogs will eat him.
> If in addition his left eye is fixed—in a foreign city, or in his own city, he will prosper; or else he will not be stricken by any illness.

We see the system of classification and variation, and we can note (this is a well-known element of the "code" of reading) that if what occurs on the right is generally the sign of a favorable future, and what happens on the left, the opposite, the principle is reversed when there is a defect or an illness: a defect on the right brings bad luck; the same one on the left brings good fortune. In the example above it is difficult to see what authorized the diviner to conclude from a fixed eye in a flushed face that the person concerned, when in a city different from his own, would be devoured by dogs there. In other words, the code that would enable us to decipher and understand these divine writings in large measure escapes us. Sometimes it is clearer, however: for example, the meaning could rest on what we might call a play on words, an assonance, which should not be surprising to us, since to those people, who considered the name of the thing to be the thing itself, nominal similitude implied true similitude. Thus:

> If it rains (*zunnu iznun*) on the day of the festival of the god of the town—that god will be angry (*zeni*) at the town.
> If the gall bladder (of the sacrificed animal) is recessed (*nahsat*)—there is supernatural danger (*nahdat*).
> If the gall bladder is caught (*kussā*) in body fat—it will be cold (*kussu*).

Elsewhere there is similitude not in names but in situations:

> If on the right side of the liver (of the sacrificial sheep) there are two finger-shaped outgrowths [probably what anatomists would call "pyramidal process"] it is the omen of a period of anarchy.

> If on the right-hand side of the gall bladder two clearly marked
> perforations [Akkadian: *pilšu*] are pierced [*palšu*]: this is the omen
> of the inhabitants of Apišal, whom Narām-Sin [226–2223] made
> prisoner by means of a breach in the wall [*pilšu*] [one notes here
> the inverted assonance: *plš/pšl*].²

But more often the "code" escapes us entirely: we did not study
with the *bārū* diviners, and we are much less enlightened than they
were about the complications and the secrets of cuneiform and
other enigmas, and thus are unable to interpret it with the necessary mastery and to derive from their writings all that they were
able to derive from them.

In any event, one thing is highly likely, if not certain: in order to
achieve this method of predicting the future, even though it was
associated with the belief of that time in what I have called "the
writing of the gods" and in the divine creation of things and situations, the Mesopotamians had to have first gone through a period
of what I call empiricism. They had to have observed abnormal
situations followed by events that boded well or ill, and those situations had to have been at least partially repetitive and similarly observed (let's say, the birth of an abnormal sheep came shortly before
the death of an important person, and that this occurred on several
occasions—they noted everything), so that their attention had
been attracted to such sequences to the point of turning them into
laws: post hoc, ergo propter hoc—what follows something is caused
or announced by that thing. They must also have noticed that in
those sequences of events analogous situations (the king who conquered a town by means of breaches in walls, when a sheep that
had been sacrificed shortly before was discovered to have had per-
forations—types of breaches!—in its liver) or assonances (a misfortune brought upon a town by its god, who was obviously angry
with the town shortly following a downpour) could occur. Only
this connecting of phenomena could have resulted in the discovery
of the divinatory process I have presented, a process that henceforth unleashed such interest that people began ardently to research, imagine, study, and classify, in all realms of nature and culture, events that might be indicators of the future, to the point of
gathering and ordering tens of thousands of them.

The proof that the Mesopotamian system of foretelling the future
truly came out of numerous experiments and observations is that
we often encounter, in oracles that detail part of a predicted future,
not only historical items (such as that mention of the war of King
Narām-Sin against the people of Apišal) but a large number of indi-

vidual characteristics that could not be applied to everyone, whereas divination in general and its treatises were a priori written to offer everyone divine messages concerning the future. For example, in the excerpt cited above, one assumes that the person involved had an elder brother, which is not the case for everyone; likewise, that his father was still alive and that the father was expected to leave his son a considerable inheritance; that the son would travel to a foreign town, and so on, facts that are all too specific, contingent, and, as we say, existential for it to be possible to apply them to everyone who read the text, that is, to all the clients of the *bārū* diviners.

I can cite another message concerning the future, a particularly interesting one, but one that is also highly circumstantial, since it concerns only a single type of person, a married woman who had deceived her husband and who was expecting a child from that affair and feared a scene at the child's birth. This is what was "deciphered" from a certain abnormality revealed in the liver of a sheep that was sacrificed so that the consultant could find the future foretold in it: "This woman, pregnant through the actions of a third party, will constantly implore the goddess Ištar, saying to her: 'Please let my child be born in the likeness of my husband!'" We cannot know or understand in the name of which code such a complex and specific situation could be taken from the abnormal condition of the liver. But who cannot see that such a detailed forecast was strictly reserved for an extremely small number of people, whereas divination was for everyone? Therefore, there is the greatest likelihood that for every protasis, whatever the exemplary "oracle" of it cited in the treatise, it was "translated" and applied to each consultant and person interested in what the future held. Briefly, such a disadvantage gradually disappeared from the treatises, and the more recent ones replaced such anecdotal futures with their essential and simultaneously universal characteristic: "favorable" or "unfavorable"—which was in effect supposed to provide everyone with an immediately applicable response. But because treatises contained, at least in the earliest days, a certain number of such individualized oracles—"divine messages concerning the future" obviously taken from daily life, experience, empiricism, historical items—we can only understand such divination by referring to a more or less lengthy period in time during which what I have called "deductive divination" was first formed, through observation and a connecting of successive events, brought together and placed into strict relationships. This divination, unique to Mesopotamia, was thus based on a certain number of accepted mythological "imaginings" that had become accepted axioms in the region but that are, to us, completely fantastic and worthless: in our world, which has been for a long time resolutely disenchanted, we are unable to accept the presuppositions indispensable to the credibility of that divination, in particular, the omnipresent gods and the "realistic" interpretation of writing and language. In our judgment, such a divinatory method—developed and elaborated though a very long work of compilation and reflection beginning at the latest in the second millennium in Mesopotamia, and that throughout the history of the region played a central role in the life of the people (as seen in the thirty thousand documents that have been retrieved)—is thus an arbitrary construction, one of pure imagination and without objective value.

And yet on such a fragile, and to our eyes perfectly frivolous, foundation, the ancient Mesopotamians built something solid and definitive, the essential part of which has continued to the present time. From the moment when they had the idea that a given phenomenon could, with the knowledge and by the decision of the gods, allow them without fail to expect a particular situation to arise, unconsciously, perhaps, obliquely, but no less truly, they established between them a necessary relationship that made it possible to pass with certainty from the first to the second, to deduce the second from the first, through a pure mental operation that caused them to read the second in and through the first, let us say, to conclude unfailingly the second from the first. Thus we see the following proposition taken from a treatise on astrology: "If on the day of its disappearance [the last day of the month], the Moon lingers in the sky [instead of disappearing abruptly]—there will be drought and famine in the land." This implied a necessary connection not between a chance delay of the moon's disappearance but between any such delay and a scarcity of food caused by drought. And this connection was not only necessary, but it was also universal: every time, unfailingly, the delay of the moon's disappearance would precede and announce the halt of atmospheric precipitation, bringing its equally inevitable consequence, famine. Thus, on the strength of their reflections alone they could move with assurance from a known fact (the delay of the moon's disappearance) to an unknown: drought leading to famine, and this without any other undertaking than that operation of the mind which in one thing finds something else that was hitherto unknown and henceforth certain. This was of course not yet our syllogism, the essential instrument of our search for the truth; nor was it yet our logic, our rules of reasoning; it was not yet our science, with its demands, its controls, and its rigorousness but also its known certainties and its indefinite progress; but it was the first step toward all that, all the more rooted in the minds of its inventors in that they increasingly applied it to thousands of problems, as is shown clearly by the existence of many rich treatises on deductive divination.

Thus through the naive and faulty postulations of this divinatory system, the ancient Mesopotamians brought to other minds and cultures something more, which the Greeks perfected and then sent on to us, which we then integrated into our system of thought and made the jewel of our civilization. Not only did they hand down a framework for the universe that has long remained our own and that, greatly revised and improved in the course of scientific progress, is still at the heart of the vision that we have of the universe, but they took the first steps on the path of "scientific" knowledge, which has enabled us, along with other acquisitions, to correct the naïveté of that image and to provide ourselves with a set of rules for the functioning of our minds in our search for knowledge and truth—and no longer simply for the likely.

Have I been wrong to laud the ancient Mesopotamians' intelligence and insight and to introduce them as our ancestors?

CHAPTER FOUR

The Gods: A Reasonable Religion

I have already mentioned the Mesopotamian religion once or twice, and from different angles. I would now like to present it briefly through its essential characteristics and as a complete system. Not only is it, along with Egypt's, one of the most ancient religions known to us, but—and this is another exceptional advantage—we can follow its development over three full millennia. A religion is not transmitted from one people to another: it is not easy to change one's gods. We must not expect to see it spread around elsewhere, like so many cultural traits. But it was an integral part of Mesopotamian civilization, and, at least through its myths and practices, it was able to impress, even to influence more or less profoundly, the ancient cultures that surrounded it, all the more so in that the Semitic character of many of those peoples made them quite open, as I have explained, to such influences, even if in accepting and integrating them, they had to change them more or less in accord with their own way of seeing and feeling. This becomes quite evident when one looks at the Israelites.

When we speak of religion, we have to know what we are speaking about; otherwise we leave ourselves open to mixing up everything and saying whatever comes to mind. What, then, is a religion? This word is most often taken to express primarily a social phenomenon, an ensemble of collective beliefs and practices unique to a given society. But a society exists only through and within its members. Perhaps, then, it is wiser, more "realistic," and more fruitful first to examine religion not in relation to a group of individuals but in relation to each one of those individuals, hic et nunc, not on a collective level but on a concrete, personal, and above all psychological level.

Considered in this way, religion is defined by three essential elements, all of which presuppose the existence in a, let us say, "normal" person of, among other fundamental givens of our nature, a sense that there must exist above us, above all that is visible and tangible, an order of things that goes beyond us and rules over everything. This order is called "the sacred" or "the supernatural," and it is this that explains the existence and the formation of every religion. Indeed, it governs three fundamental attitudes within us. The most profound—because it is irrational and thus spontaneous—is the feeling that the supernatural brings about an attachment of the inferior to the superior. This can occur, if I may say so, in two possible directions: either centrifugally (fear, respect, a distance held vis-à-vis the supernatural—as in "reverential" religions); or by way of the attraction that it exercises over us, the love that draws us to it (as in "mystical" religions). This is called religious feeling, religiosity, and it varies among all religions.

But regarding this same supernatural being, no one—with good reason—ever having encountered it, every religious person has to create an idea of it for him- or herself ("through his very nature, man wants to know"), to define it, to represent it—which is not possible except by resorting to one's imagination. This is the "intellectual" part of every religion, which develops a complete mythology, and even a theology, around the sacred. Finally, as a function of the deep feelings one has toward the figured and imagined supernatural, one feels obliged to adopt a certain path of conduct, rules of behavior, with regard to it: this falls within the domain of religious behavior, which also varies more or less within each religion.

Every religion, thus being necessarily comprised of the three elements that define it, will be of help to us as we attempt to form an idea of the Mesopotamian religion. But we must still take into account an essential distinction that separates religions into two irreducible categories. Those best known to us are what are called "historical religions." They were established at a definite and known moment in historical time (this is the case for Judaism, Christianity, Islam, Zoroastrianism, Buddhism, and a few others that are not quite as old or as historically significant, such as Mormonism), by an identifiable person, someone deeply religious who, after using the sacred and our relation to it to form his own personal convictions, set out to spread them, indeed to propagate and impose them, first by himself, then with the help of disciples, and then through writings, his own or others that contained the essence of his message. The "sacred and normative books" are in fact an inseparable element of every historical religion, as they are always organized around a tradition, above all a written tradition, which sets down and imposes its meaning and spirit, in one place and for all, even if, as with all that exists here on the earth, that meaning and spirit are subject to subsequent developments or even changes.

The Mesopotamian religion is not one of the historical religions: it has no known or knowable historical beginning, nor a founder, nor any holy books, nor any rigorous and normative religious tradition. It is one of the "prehistoric" or "popular" religions—as they are called—that is strictly a part of the cultural baggage of a people (the Mesopotamian people), their civilization, of which it represents the face turned toward the supernatural, the sacred. It evolved, at the same time as that civilization, without ever being maintained or led onto a determined path—as by means of a sort of balancing gyroscope—by holy books, which might have contained and codified its beliefs, its emotional attitudes, its sacred rituals, or by religious authorities, who would have controlled them and forced them to be applied in a given direction, intended or presumed to conform to the vision and the will of the founder, as happens in historical religions. This is a point of supreme importance that should never be forgotten, at the risk of forming a completely false idea of the religion of ancient Mesopotamia based on the model of religions that are familiar to us.

Let us now take a quick look at the three basic elements that define every religion in its profound and essential reality: the psychological, the concrete, and the individualized.

In Mesopotamia religious feeling was in no way mystical. One can read the entire collection of prayers, hymns, pleas to the gods, all the great many myths relating to them whose content is most likely to reveal the tone of people's relations with the gods, and one finds only signs of respect, veneration, deference, submission, and admiration, a feeling of the greatness of the gods and of the uncrossable distance that separated them from humans, at the very most servants to their awe-inspiring masters. There is not a single impulse of attraction, of fervor, of the desire to approach them, of tenderness or of love, of an impression of finding in them something like an indispensable part of oneself. As the myth of the Supersage emphasizes well, humans were created by the gods to serve them: their basic cordial attitude was thus that of servants before their very lofty masters: they respected them, venerated them, and had only one true obligation toward them—to work in order to provide them and offer them everything they might need—this was the essential nature of their relationship. Mesopotamian religion was of the "reverential" type: just like hierarchical superiors, the gods were respectfully served but not loved, not at all sought out as essential complements to the lives of each of the faithful.

The realm of concrete religious representations is necessarily more complex and cannot be dealt with hastily, as could the preceding one, in just a few words. I have already explained a few basic parameters of this area in speaking about the Mesopotamian vision of the universe, in which the gods played the primary role. The ancient Mesopotamians, in an attempt to understand something about that universe, felt the need to ask, assume, and perhaps infer the existence of a complete supernatural society: they were polytheists. With their mania for classifying, they ordered their gods into a hierarchy, a transposition of their earthly kingdom's. It was that hierarchy that provided them the best image to represent their divinities, for it played the same role with regard to the world and mankind as that of the king and his high functionaries with regard to the subjects of his kingdom, but on an even more grandiose and more powerful scale. At the head of the gods' society there was therefore, as among humans, a ruler, a king. But this pyramidal vision never developed into a strictly monotheist tendency. The Mesopotamians sometimes exalted one or another of their gods to such an extreme degree that one might think, at first glance, that they had turned that god into a divinity so superior to the others that he was believed to possess more of a divine nature than the other gods. But the others still existed, and they, too, were gods, a fact that could not have been upheld in a monotheism.

Furthermore, the ancient Mesopotamians were anthropomorphists, that is, to represent their gods they had chosen the human image as their model: the gods had the same appearance, the same sexual division—there were gods and goddesses, most often paired up in couples, like humans; they had children, like us; and they lived in society, as we do. They were driven by the same needs as we are: to eat, to drink (in the tale of the flood the poet describes them as ravaged by hunger and dying of thirst, since the cataclysm had wiped out their providers and servants). Obviously, the very grandeur of the gods meant, as I have already implied, that in creating an image of them, one had to use not the image of the man on the street, of the poor, unsophisticated peasant, of the most ordinary representative of humanity, but that of the highest figures in the land: the king, the queen, their children, and their magnificent court. In providing for the needs of the gods, humans therefore were expected to behave accordingly, but in a better, richer, more elaborate and more splendid way, as they did with regard to their rulers: the gods were to be lodged in the most splendid palaces and temples, adorned with rich clothing and the most costly jewels, and one was supposed to ensure them the most pleasant and leisurely life possible, with outings, in carriages or by boat, as well as with frequent festivals. We will discuss this again with regard to the Mesopotamians' religious behavior.

I must again say, at least briefly, that the very notion of divinity did evolve in a certain way in Mesopotamia. In the third millennium, most likely under the dominant influence of the Sumerians, there were a great many gods, each believed to be behind or inside the infinite natural phenomena that people tried to explain by the gods' intervention (even their names reflect that role: Ninurta, "Lord of the Arable Land," was the god of agriculture; Nin-kilim, "Lady of the Small Rodents". . .): we can count several hundred of these. But also, and most certainly for the same reason—the predominance of the Sumerians—the gods were very often depicted as being quite down to earth, indeed, too "human": for example, the most dignified of the gods indulged in rapes, incest, and amorous excesses. Depending on the size of the Semitic portion of the population, and in accord with a more elevated idea that the Semites had of their supernatural world, the gods became very lofty and magnificent lords, and their numbers diminished: religious attention was turned toward and concentrated on a handful among them, around thirty at the most, whose names constantly recur, while the others no longer played much of a role except, as in the Christian memory, in the manner of our obscure and picturesque medieval saints.

The Mesopotamians had only a vague and truly imaginary and mythological notion of where the gods actually were, a difficult issue that was never really resolved. Sometimes they were seen in or behind the phenomena of nature, whose existence and functioning were explained by their "management" (the sun, the planets, fire); sometimes they were gathered together, as in a court, on high, in the celestial residence of the king of the gods. In any case, they remained, even if in a rather mysterious way, inside the statues and images people created of them, out of stone or wood, or—this was the case with the "statues for worship" that were placed in temples and were the objects of everyone's veneration—out of sheets of precious metal stamped and pressed over a core of equally precious wood: with these representations the gods were truly present in the "houses"—the temples—that had been prepared for them, houses that were like true palaces.

After the gods had created the world, they governed it, as I have explained, from their headquarters: nothing that happened on earth escaped their vigilance, their will, or their intervention. Of course, the Mesopotamians were not so naive as to be unaware of the immediate and "natural" causes of things and events. But behind them, mysteriously directing and moving them, they saw their gods at work: they were the masters not only of nature, but also of culture, and no less of history. It was because nothing that appeared or happened on earth was unrelated to the gods that people believed that the unfolding of things, of life, of history, was all part of a general plan that the gods had devised—like a ruler in his governmental councils—that the gods knew it in advance and could reveal something to those concerned, as I have explained, through "deductive divination." This divination presented oracles, unveilings of the future, as so many decisions taken, almost as "sentences" passed down from the gods concerning the destiny of concerned individuals or of the entire land and its king: again based on the model transposed from the royal government on the earth, the people even imagined periodic meetings of the gods gathered around their lord, during which they made decisions (as kings did) that they considered useful or necessary, relating both to the general functioning of the world, nature, and history and to the destiny of each individual; and these decisions (again, just as was done at the palace) were expected, once they were made, to be set down in writing on a specific tablet, the "Tablet of Destinies," kept as a token of his supreme power by the ruler of the gods. And yet, again in the manner of earthly kings, these decisions were not absolute and definitive but subject, we might say, to appeal and to reformation, because the freedom to change one's mind was recognized as an essential privilege of power. In his "code" Hammurabi ordered that a married woman who was caught with her lover should be condemned to death along with him, but the text adds, if the husband wants to keep his wife, the king must also pardon her accomplice. In other words, it was possible, through pleading, supplication, or a request for grace, to obtain from the king, as well as from judges, that a sentence be commuted or repealed. We will see later how such a possibility of escaping one's destiny, once it was decreed by the gods, was in fact offered to everyone.

We must now look at an issue central to every religion—each one dealing with it in its own way—the issue of evil. By this word I mean "suffered" evil, everything that thwarts our desires, darkens our lives, forcing us to suffer what we do not want to suffer or depriving us of that which is important to us: evils such as illnesses, accidents, thwarted loves, losses of jobs or fortunes, sadness, and misfortunes of all kinds. Most often the immediate causes of such bad fortune were known: a certain lack of caution provoking a certain illness, and ill-considered expenses, financial ruin. But from the moment one considered oneself governed by absolute powers and totally dependent on them, as is the case in many religions, beginning with that of Mesopotamia, how could one not see in a misfortune, even if the direct cause of it were known, the effect of a more distant supernatural cause, of a decision made by divine beings in whose hands one existed? I well know that if I suffer from a sunburn, it is because I stayed too long in the sun. But why did that misadventure happen to me, *to me?* Why did the gods send it my way? Why did it have to be a part of my destiny, decreed and desired by the gods alone? Such was the problem posed by evil. How did the ancient Mesopotamians resolve it?

First, since they considered their gods superior to them in all things, and consequently necessarily just and reasonable, it would have been repugnant to them to imagine the gods as being sadistic or mean in any way, finding enjoyment in persecuting humans without any reason. Moreover, because humans were above all their servants and their providers, shall we say, their workers and domestic employees, the gods would not have been very wise to poison their existence without a serious reason and thus diminish their "yield." Each decision for evil or misfortune that they brought against an individual or the entire land thus had to have been done with a motive. Here, too, the ancient Mesopotamians appealed to the fundamental metaphor that governed their entire mythological concept of the organization, the role, and the behavior of their gods: the transposition on high of the government of the state and of royal power.

It was the duty of the king to carry out the perfect administration of his land, to set forth a certain number of statutes intended to define the obligations of his subjects and the bans he imposed on them so as to ensure the maintenance of public order and the prosperity of the land. If any contravened his will thus expressed, the king would normally punish them (even if it happened that he did not do so) with dishonoring or corporeal punishments, which were inflicted on the guilty by the "forces of order" that were in the king's service. Such a schema was mythologically transposed to explain the behavior of the gods in the face of people's misfortune, of which the gods were necessarily the cause.

It was clear that everything on the earth that dictated human beings' behavior either positively or negatively, all the innumerable obligations and prohibitions that arranged their lives, as emanated from the express will of the gods, had been desired and ordered by those gods, just as the sovereign set forth his decisions to force his subjects to behave in a way that was favorable to the land. It was not only a matter of great juridical rules against stealing, killing, lying—crimes that were related to common justice and were judged and punished in their own right by the public forces, but (and we have a few lists of these, sometimes highly detailed, and of the greatest interest) there were also strictly religious constraints regarding ritual (for example, washing one's hands before taking part in a worship ceremony) and obligations or prohibitions in the realm of individual morality (do not trouble others; strive to help them) or linked to a folkloric tradition of immemorial origin comparable to the one that causes us to express wishes when someone sneezes (do not pull a reed from the reed-bed; do not urinate or vomit into a stream). Since all of these positive or negative constraints emanated from the single and same governmental will of the gods, they were considered equally worthy of respect and obligatory, and to ignore them constituted a grave offense, since it was to scorn the decision of the gods and thus to lay oneself open to their punishment, a punishment similar to the one ordered by the public powers on earth to correct and discourage fomenters of disorder.

This sentence was precisely the "suffered" evil mentioned above. Just as the king did not punish in person those who had contravened public order—it was beneath his dignity—neither did the gods intervene themselves to punish those who did not follow their precepts: for this purpose they had auxiliary forces that were inferior to them and obeyed their wishes, what we would call demons, supernatural beings, which the mythology had imagined to fulfill the role of "policemen of the gods," executors of their high and low works. These demons, to our knowledge, were never made the object of a developed mythology or of an attempt at organization and unification: we find them under various names, mysterious and imaginary beings whose origin and composition escape us, simple sublimations of public forces, usually depicted as being frightening and formidable. They sometimes bore the names of illnesses or hypostasized misfortunes that were no less fearful: Fever, Jaundice,

Cough, Shivers—somewhat in the way we speak of Death as a person. Each one of them seems more or less to have had its own harmful specialty—for example, there was a female demon called Pashittu, the "Extinguisher," in charge of bringing about the death of small children, and a demon called Namtaru, something like "(Bad) Destiny," who was the patron and cause of epidemics. And it is thus that the gods used them, commanding them to punish severely, each according to their powers, those who had not followed the gods' orders.

It must be said that such a simplistic concept—evil as the repression of "sin," of the disobedience of divine will, which implied a scorn of the gods and a revolt against them—was not without its difficulties. The main difficulty came from the fact that the local "theologians" never sought to set forth a rigorous and absolute construction of the justice of the gods, one which in a certain sense would have forced the gods to punish systematically all those who committed "sins" in such a way that from the moment when a person had committed one, he would have without fail expected to have some bad thing happen to him, at least something bad in proportion to the act he had committed. First of all, all sins carried the same weight, since they were all equal acts of disobedience against the gods and a scorning of their orders. And above all, people did not reason a priori (I have sinned, therefore the gods are going to punish me), but a posteriori, starting not with the sin but with the misfortune that was supposed to have been the punishment for an infraction (I'm experiencing some misfortune, therefore I *must* have sinned). Such a conclusion was easy to draw when the unfortunate one was aware of or remembered having done something wrong. But what if he didn't remember doing anything? In that case it was adamantly held that he must have sinned; otherwise the gods would have been unjust. And since, as I have just said, the obligations and prohibitions of all sorts that governed human life were innumerable, there was always the chance that knowingly or not, voluntarily or inadvertently—it didn't matter—the one concerned, the victim of the evil, must have infringed on one of those laws. In any event, in order to save the justice of the gods at all costs, one could always appeal to familial responsibility: if it wasn't the person himself who had sinned, then it was his father, his mother, or his brother. Such was the Mesopotamian solution to the problem of evil, a solution that to us appears rather naive and simplistic.

Moreover, not everyone seems to have been completely satisfied with it. Why did certain sinners, indeed, true evildoers or criminals, escape divine prosecution? One could always attribute such an anomaly to the sovereign freedom of the gods: just as the king, for his own reasons, since he was sovereignly free, could quite easily refuse to punish a recalcitrant subject, so too could the gods. But what if an individual who was suddenly plunged into misfortune, all the while aware of the fact that he had always respected at least his major obligations toward the gods, as compared to notoriously impious types—libertines and public sinners, as we would say, who themselves prospered—complained of such an anomaly? In that case the theologians had perfected another solution, one that to us seems rather absurd, even if it appeared, like other solutions, irreproachably logical within the religious perspective of the land. It was also based on the sovereign freedom of the gods, copied from the freedom of their earthly models, the kings. A text written during the second half of the second millennium reveals that it was in the nature of the gods to change their minds and speech: they passed unpredictably, like humans, from malevolent and irritable moods to moments of pardon, to such a degree that hostility—in other words, the arrival of evil—surely announced an ulterior sudden change, a return to good fortune. It was therefore necessary for the afflicted one to wait: tomorrow all would be well! After rain (they always began with this: it is the anomaly) comes good weather: be patient and have confidence! Clearly such a response to the problem seems to us rather an evasion. But we must recognize that with their religious presuppositions the Mesopotamian thinkers could hardly go any further.

This was all the more true in that the gods themselves, in dispensing evil, had prepared the remedy for it: exorcism. This has also been referred to, but wrongly, as magic. In reality, although it was obviously inspired by magic, it represented something that was oriented differently, something truly religious, which magic, as such, is not. What did it involve? We possess roughly thirty thousand tablets that are devoted to exorcism, which indicates a universal usage throughout the history of the land. They record procedures for getting the gods to relax the misfortunes inflicted by them as punishments for sins and mistakes, as I have just mentioned. Each text is a mixture of gestures and prayers, prayers through which the unfortunate one told the gods of his sad condition, recognized the mistakes responsible for that condition, and asked those same gods to pardon him and to reverse the sentence they had pronounced against him—and that, as we have stressed, could be changed if one used the means to bend one's judges, that is, if one resorted to exorcism. The condemned person therefore asked the gods to order the demons who, in obeying the gods, had brought misfortune on the person to withdraw and to leave him alone, thereby ridding him of the evil that had stricken him. These prayers were always accompanied by actions that were supposed physically to suppress the evil by using, when needed, schemes or substances presumed to be efficacious: for example, to eliminate the serious threat represented by the birth of a premature baby or a deformed stillborn baby in the house of the marked person, the baby's body was placed on a little board and a sort of small boat ramp was prepared before placing the body in the water, while the gods were asked to command the river to make it sink like a stone.

In this way the gods offered the remedy as well as the misfortune. And since, moreover, they often arranged to reveal to their "servants" the future they were reserving for them, one can see through this double advantage (complementary, since for each bad future decoded by the diviners and announced to the intended victim there existed an exorcism able to eliminate the bad future) that the gods were considered to be rather benevolent with regard to their workers. They were, as we would say, good bosses.

This was on the condition, of course, that people applied themselves to fulfilling their destiny, to undertaking the work needed to provide their masters with everything necessary for the altogether leisurely and opulent life that befitted them. Everything humans produced, the issue of their universal and multifarious work, was presented to the gods through the humans' religious behavior, the third and final part of the religious system. The king was primarily responsible for overseeing religious activities, and, in their dedicatory inscriptions, throughout the history of the land, rulers were always listing their own merits in this regard: the construction of magnificent temples or the restoration of sanctuaries that threatened to fall to ruin; repeated offerings of the richest furnishings to fill these splendid residences, which were even more lavish than those intended for earthly rulers; offerings of the most precious statues and images of the cult, which represented and, in a mysterious way, were supposed to contain the divinity they represented; offerings of extremely lavish clothing and jewelry with which those images were covered; and solemn and ostentatious feasts that were held amidst the divinities and were dedicated to their honor, and involved taking the images around in a cart or by boat, from one part of the temple to another, from one temple to another. During these festivals, but also every day of the year, the temple kitchens and their officiants prepared lavish and copious meals using techniques that were simultaneously opulent, rich, and complicated. We have found about thirty of their recipes, the study of which has forced us to admit that the ancient Mesopotamians had already developed, at least for the great of this world and of the other, a refined and knowledgeable culinary art: a true gastronomy! For example, illustrating the amount of food involved in these meals, we possess a list of the supplies that the temple cooks of Uruk were to use in order to prepare the "four daily meals" for only four of their principle divinities: two meals in the morning—"a small and a large"—and two similar ones in the evening, "every day, all year long." The numbers are impressive, and I am citing them just as they were discovered: 800 hectoliters of fine beer; 2,500 hectoliters of flour for bread; 18,000 sheep; 2,580 lambs; 720 cows; 3,300 fattened geese and ducks—a frightening carnage and a rather stupefying amount of food! All of this was prepared not as a sacrifice in the mystical sense of the word—to lose it, to deprive oneself of it in the name of the gods—but as literal, material sustenance to feed those gods and to assure them, even while they ate, a rich and festive existence, at the level appropriate to the owners and masters of the world of human beings.

As was fashionable at the time, such meals included fragrant fumigations and songs, most often accompanied by instruments. We have discovered a large number of religious hymns, in all evidence composed for this purpose, in which the divine receivers are glorified, magnified, praised, admired, and flattered in every way, and their goodwill praised and invoked on behalf of their servants, who were carrying out their tasks just as perfectly and were fulfilling with just as much conscientiousness their service to the gods: their primary vocation, which had earned them their existence.

Such was the magnificent and lavish service that unfolded in the ancient temples of Mesopotamia. It was here that human beings' duties to their gods ceased. For unlike our own way of seeing and behaving—the direct issue of biblical religiosity, the obeying of a certain number of ethical precepts—a moral life did not enter at all into religious obligations in Mesopotamia. There was no Decalogue in Mesopotamia. Once the ceremonies of this, shall we say, "material" form of worship were carried out, and thus once their function as servants of the gods was duly accomplished, those servants could count all the more on the favor and goodwill of their masters since they had served them well, and people no longer owed them anything else. The basic religious sentiment that guided the Mesopotamians was reverence, respect, that kind of fear experienced by very low-level workers vis-à-vis their sublime and very highly placed bosses.

Of course, in Mesopotamian civilization, as in all other cultures, there was certainly an ethical dimension, as well. Even if, as their primary ideal in life, those people appear to have had a great desire for material success and happiness, which never goes very far, they had a traditional morality, the commandments and restrictions of which come through more than once in the documents we possess: honesty, dignity, helping others, for example. But in itself this morality had no religious significance, and it was not to honor the gods that people followed it, but only in order to insure a bearable, if not pleasant, life in a community, and a successful, that is, tasteful, personal life, without harming anyone else and with all the desirable advantages and pleasures. If one fell short in any of this, that is, if one ignored a ritual, the laws, traditional obligations, one was exposed, of course, to a vindictive reaction by the gods, who wished to insure the observance of the innumerable obligations and restrictions—including those concerning "morality"—that they had instituted and decreed for the smooth running of the world and of human society. But one did not honor the gods any more by obeying them on that point: one only avoided serious disadvantages that could easily compromise one's success in life.

A sign that the observance of morality was not of particular importance, at least insofar as the gods were concerned, is that in that land no one ever expressed the notion that at death people received different judgments according to whether they had lived their lives in conformity with or against morality, that people might expect a different existence after death. All the ghosts of deceased persons, taken to an immense and dark infernal cave, were forever destined to endure the same depressing and melancholic torpor. Everyone knew the story of that great man from the past, Gilgamesh, who, at the price of superhuman efforts, had attempted in vain to escape death and the sad perspective it offered everyone. And everyone remembered what was said to him, to warn him of the futility of his efforts, by a mysterious figure he encountered on the way. This warning defines perfectly not only human beings' place on earth but the limits that the gods had assigned to their ideal in life:

Figure 2. A fragment of a clay tablet inscribed with the Assyrian version of Tablet XI of the Gilgamesh epic. The fragment contains lines 55–106, 108–269. Copyright © The British Museum.

> Gilgamesh, where are you hurrying to? You will never find that life for which you are looking. When the gods created man they allotted to him death, but life they retained in their own keeping. As for you, Gilgamesh, fill your belly with good things; day and night, night and day, dance and be merry, feast and rejoice. Let your clothes be fresh, bathe yourself in water, cherish the little child that holds your hand, and make your wife happy in your embrace; for this too is the lot of man.[3]

Not only was such a destiny comprised of advantages and joys, at least during one's lifetime, but it had also been assigned to humans by the gods, and thus one could do nothing about it; and the ancient Mesopotamians knew how to resign themselves, how not to fight against someone stronger than they.

JEAN BOTTÉRO

This is why I contend that even if we don't see any great drive, any vehement enthusiasm, a bit of that flame, of that passion with regard to the supernatural world, of that sort of "madness" that we are forced to admire, even if we see the dangers of it, their religion was an intelligent and reasonable system. This is first because of its, shall we say, intellectual construction, its mythology, and, if we wish, but in quotation marks, its "theology," in which that knowledgeable vision of things that is one of the characteristics of their minds shone through. In short, everything rested on a metaphor, a transposition: the gods, sovereign, were, in and for the world and human beings, like the kings on earth, for their land and for their subjects, infinitely more lofty, more intelligent, more irresistible, immortal. The supernatural world was considered to be a magnified reflection of the earthly world. Like royal subjects, who were exploited by their king and available for forced labor at his mercy, humans were the "employees" of the gods, servants whose role was above all, by providing the goods they needed, to leave the gods in peace so they could concentrate on their governmental duties. It was with this purpose in mind that the gods had imagined and created humans, with at the same time enough know-how, abilities, and energy to carry out such a role wonderfully and incapable ever of climbing higher than their nature and destiny allowed, incapable of reaching that immortality that would have made them the equals of their masters. As long as humans were alive, they therefore worked in the service of the gods. After death they remained immersed forever in indefinite somnolence, replaced on earth by their descendants, who continued the work they had done. And this system, intelligent in itself, since it was based on an objective vision without any illusions about the world, completed by mythological explanations, all calculated for their plausibility and likelihood, at the limit of what one might hope for at the time in a search for the truth, this system was accompanied in the minds of the ancient Mesopotamians not by what we would call resignation, since that implies a way of regretting what one does not have, but an acceptance that really should be considered reasonable.

There is a possibility that the reader of this brief summary of such an ancient religious system has been struck at one time or another by characteristics that, without any longer belonging as such to our own religious vision, nevertheless seem to be a distant rough draft of it. For example, to mention at least these: the notion of sin; of evil, punishment for sins; of prayer and rituals through which we can hope to be both absolved of those sins and freed from misfortunes; or even the very framework of the afterlife and the condition of the deceased.

In realms other than the religious, the general Mesopotamian tableau of the universe, as I have sketched it here, is not very far from the traditional and prescientific conception that we inherited from our ancestors, who had inherited from their own. And although our intellectual methods of research for the truth, for analyzing ideas, for finding the necessary links between the one and the other—which are capable of leading us through reflection alone from the known to the unknown—were developed and perfected after the Mesopotamians and beyond them, it should be no less clear, as I have attempted to show, that the Mesopotamians took the first steps on the long road that has led to those methods, to our own way of reasoning and our rigorous and objective procedures of investigation.

In the final analysis it is again to the Mesopotamians that we owe that incomparable instrument of knowledge—writing. Our own writing system is extraordinarily simplified, if we compare it to theirs; it is practically accessible to everyone. But they were the first to teach us that one could concretely set down thought and in that way distribute it through space and time, along with all the prodigious changes in our reasoning and the progress that such a possibility has offered and continues to offer us.

To draw up and catalogue our heritage in full would be an infinite task, impossible for one person and in any event extremely difficult, since it would be necessary, while journeying back in time, to reconstruct its entire history, which is neither simple nor rectilinear. However, and this is at least what I hoped to suggest here, at the end of the journey one would most often end up at that venerable mixture of ancient Sumerians and Semites, who, for four or five millennia, at the very beginning of history in the strict sense (which they inaugurated, moreover, through their writing), gave birth to that imposing and precious construction—Mesopotamia—and to its exemplary civilization.

TWO

Writing between Visible and Invisible Worlds in Iran, Israel, and Greece

CLARISSE HERRENSCHMIDT

CHAPTER FIVE

Elamite Civilization and Writing

Of course there is a radical difference in dealing with the living and with the dead. A dialogue between the living takes place through questions and answers, out of the strength of being a self that allows each person to connect with the other. But there is an analogy to this in dealing with the dead. I bring this one equally to life in the dialogue.

—Karl Jaspers

The name Elam, as it is currently used in Oriental studies, comes from the transcription of an old Elamite word, *Haltam* or *Haltamti,* which corresponds to Sumerian *Elama,* Akkadian *Elamtu,* and biblical Hebrew *Elām.* In this case, as in many others, Western tradition adopted the Hebraic transcription.

Elamite civilization extended over a portion of what is now called Iran. Two principal zones marked its entire history: one was Susiana, the plain around the city of Susa, in southwestern Iran, slightly to the north of the large oil-producing modern city of Ahvaz. Situated next to Mesopotamia, Susiana sometimes participated marginally, sometimes intimately, in Mesopotamian civilization. Then there was Iran of the plateau, with central and southern Zagros, Persis, and Kerman, where several centers of Elamite culture flourished; the best known, Anshan (its modern name is Tall-e Malyān), in the Shiraz region, was the heart of Elam strictly speaking. Recently discovered and excavated, this site has provided texts from all periods, revealing traces of an original culture. Other Elamite centers are

I wish to extend my heartfelt thanks to all those who have encouraged me or who read and corrected the text of this essay: J. Bottéro, H. Clastres, F. Fabre, M. Gauchet, J.-J. Glassner, V. Hachard, M.-J. Imbault-Huart, F. Schmidt, F. Smyth-Florentin, L. Tournon, L. Verlet, and P. Vidal-Naquet. I also want to express my deep appreciation for the help of Prods Oktor Skjaervo with the preparation of the English version of this text; my thanks also to Rahim Shayegan for his insights.

now scarcely more than names: Awan, perhaps in the Zagros near Hamadan, and Simashki, perhaps in the Kerman region.

Western and central Iran were inhabited by Elamite populations that, from our point of view, were autochthonous, that is, they were already there when history begins. Their language, Elamite, has no genetic ties either with another ancient language (it does not form a linguistic family along with Sumerian, Akkadian, or Hurrian) or with any modern language, since no known spoken language is descended from it. Our knowledge is limited by this isolation. Although linguistics enables us to describe the Elamite syntax, it is difficult to understand its lexicon, for there is no point of comparison; thus progress is made at the whim of hypotheses put forth by a few Elamologists. In the middle or at the end of the second and especially of the first millennium B.C., Iran was gradually invaded by the populations who gave this region the name of Iran—a word that means "land of the Aryans"—who spoke an ancient Iranian language, a first cousin of Vedic Sanskrit, both members of the Indo-European language family. Linguistically, politically, and culturally, the Iranians in the strict sense—whom one ought to call Aryans—overlaid the ancient Elamite civilization.

Elamite civilization did not have the same impact on human history as Mesopotamian and Egyptian civilization, both of which also disappeared; on the contrary, it was even more discrete than the Hittite civilization, which lasted an even shorter time. Its unassuming character is caused by the poor documentation, which is much more sparse than that of Mesopotamia, for the Elamites were little concerned with writing down their mythology, theology, literature, and mathematics, and so we possess very few Elamite texts today. In Elam, writing above all served for administration and to commemorate kings and their works of piety.

But in spite of this small amount of documentation, the history of writing in Elam is complex and fascinating; it highlights the geographical location of Susiana and its inhabitants, who were sometimes drawn toward Mesopotamia and sometimes toward the Iranian mountains and the plateau. It typifies the difference between writing and language, for although Susa was geographically part of Mesopotamia, the Elamite language came from the Iranian plateau. As we shall see, the history of writing in Elamite Iran can provide an excellent historical background for a more general reflection on writing—its relation to history and culture, on one hand, and to language and speech, on the other.

It is appropriate to begin with the first steps that led to the creation of writing: from around the middle of the fourth millennium we find bullae, calculi, counters, tablets; then we take a large step from around 3000 to around 2000, when we encounter the writing system called Linear Elamite, still undeciphered; and finally, in the last third of the second millennium, we see that among these Elamites who wrote so little, writing had become a major medium of communication between people and the gods.

The city of Susa, where excavations have been going on for more than a century, was excavated by the French Archeological Delegation in Iran. The excavators uncovered the acropolis, the main city, and, in the ground of levels 18, 17, and 16, perfectly stratified (which means that there is no question about the material succession of these layers and thus their relative chronology) objects that illustrate the invention of writing. These levels date from the second half of the fourth millennium, a period when Susa was an important city and belonged to the same civilization as southern Mesopotamia. Mesopotamian writing, as known from Uruk IV, probably preceded Elamite writing, but the path toward writing is more clearly illustrated in Susa than in Uruk. The clear chronological succession within one and the same area is of capital importance, for, in order to describe the path that led to putting speech in writing and in order to try to understand the mental processes that people realized more than five thousand years ago, we need a concrete, even if imperfect, description of what took place in history, not just an intuitive reconstruction.

The first stage of the investigation consisted of the following: on level 18, objects called bullae were found. These are fairly round, hollow clay vessels that contained what are called calculi, from the old Latin word *calculus,* which is at the origin of our *calculation.* These calculi are small man-made objects fashioned out of soft clay, modeled into various shapes: little elongated sticks, little balls, disks, large and small cones; the use of calculi for counting is quite ancient, for calculi have been found in sites from the seventh millennium B.C.E.

On the rounded surface of these bullae are impressions of cylinder seals depicting scenes from economic life (the gathering of harvests, weaving and pottery workshops) or from religious life. The cylinder seal was a personal object, and the impression, produced by rolling the seal lengthwise onto soft clay, identified its owner, either a notable or a functionary; the cylinder seal represented social status and bore testimony to a central authority. All of these

Figure 3.   Bullae. Courtesy of Musée du Louvre. Département des Antiquités orientales. Reproduction interdite sans autorisation. Copyright © Pierre et Maurice Chuseville.

items—bulla, cylinder seal, calculi—were a means of recording a transaction, a transfer of goods. It is likely that identical bullae were made in two copies, one kept by the private individual who participated in the transaction, since bullae were found in private homes, and the other by the administration. In the event of a dispute, those involved could refer to this administrative record.

In the second stage we still find calculi inside the bullae; on the surface, along with the impression of the cylinder seal, appeared new markings: either a long, thin indentation, a small circle, a large circle, a large indentation, or even a large indentation along with a small circle. A bulla with calculi and markings impressed on its surface could be broken, and this made it possible to see whether the quantity indicated by the calculi was reproduced by the markings on the bulla. For certain scholars there is a direct formal relationship between the calculus and the impression: thus the calculus in the shape of a small stick would be represented by the long, thin notch, the calculus in the shape of a marble by the small circle, whereas the large circle would represent the disk-shaped calculus, and so on. According to others, "different calculi sometimes correspond to similar numerical marks. This may suggest that the calculi might have specified countable commodities, for which the notches

CLARISSE HERRENSCHMIDT

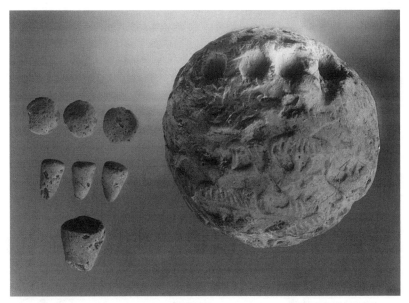

Figure 4. Bullae and calculi. Courtesy of Musée du Louvre. Département des Antiquités orientales. Reproduction interdite sans autorisation. Copyright © Pierre et Maurice Chuseville.

gave the abstract number. In fact, other bullae held different calculi."[1] Signs and calculi referred at the very least to quantities; if the numerical value of the markings and the calculi is disputed by specialists, the principle is not; there is agreement at least that the long and thin notch, identical to the small clay stick, referred to one unit.

The next stage, established through archeology, is defined by pillow-shaped, rounded, and oblong tablets—the old bullae, now become solid. Quantities are indicated on them by impressing the same markings, which, from then on without any connection with the calculi, became numerals, that is, signs that conventionally served to indicate numbers. The pillow-shaped tablet also bore the impression of a cylinder seal. Along with these first accounting documents, they also made "tokens," small objects of baked clay, some with recognizable shapes such as the head of a bull or a jar (most likely a measure of volume), whereas others are triangular in shape. These tokens also referred to a transaction, as is proved by certain markings: three or six dots impressed on the bowl-shaped tokens, six dots on a token with the head of a bull, lines that perhaps symbolize fractions of indeterminable quantities on the triangular tokens. The shapes of these tokens, which do not bear any seal im-

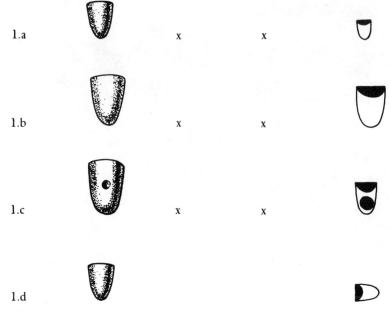

1.a   x   x

1.b   x   x

1.c   x   x

1.d

Figure 5. Four first tokens and signs impressed on tablet. From *Before Writing: Volume I; From Counting to Cuneiform,* by Denise Schmandt-Besserat, copyright © 1992. By permission of the author and the University of Texas Press.

pressions, herald the pictograms. We know nothing about the different ways bullae and tokens were used for recording purposes. From a formal point of view, the invention of writing is based upon bullae bearing the marking of a seal on their surface and with calculi inside them.

The tablets that came immediately afterward were rectangular and flatter, and so were true tablets, as they would later be used in abundance, bearing numerals and pictographic signs, whereas cylinder seal impressions became more rare. These signs—the drawing of a jar, for example—represented things that were exchanged, delivered, or warehoused, in short, the objects of transactions or of recording, which we can from now on say were "written" down.

Such would have been the modest beginnings of writing. First bullae, then tablets, which preserved the terms of a transaction in clay; all of this was in a very official form, that P. Amiet has called a contract and others call a commercial exchange, a term that does not appear convincing. In fact, by *commercial exchange* we understand "exchange between two private individuals," while here, even if it was a matter of goods that had circulated over a long distance, from the Iranian plateau to Susa, for example, the transac-

     CLARISSE HERRENSCHMIDT

Figure 6. Numeral tablet. Courtesy of Musée du Louvre. Département des Antiquités orientales. Reproduction interdite sans autorisation. Copyright © Pierre et Maurice Chuseville.

tion took place within a state administration and cannot be identified with an exchange.

Writing therefore did not begin with a graphic representation of the objects of a transaction—whether those were jars or goats—but with their quantities. The recording of the quantity brought about the representation of numbers by numerals. But what is a number? A number is not something in the visible world but an act of the human mind. Saying that there are three apples on the table says nothing about each apple and nothing about apples in general; if one were to add one or twenty thousand more, the first three would in no way be changed. It is the human mind that is capable of the activity of numbering and that imprints it on reality. There is nothing immediate about the invention of writing, for humans did not begin writing by naively drawing things in the world around them. In the writing of numbers, the first operation consisted of thinking a number, the second of representing the number by a calculus. Once the products of human mental activity were made visible—

Figure 7. Tokens from an archaic recording system in the Uruk-Jemdet-Nasr period. Courtesy of Musée du Louvre. Département des Antiquités orientales. Reproduction interdite sans autorisation. Copyright © Pierre et Maurice Chuseville.

numbers by calculi—writing, duplicating that first representation in signs, unfolded.

Pictograms, signs that represent objects in the visible world, are the "writing of things," as Jean Bottéro calls it; although pictograms have no graphic relation to language, since there seems to be no expression in writing of sounds or of grammatical elements, still, they are based on the process of naming—after all, the goods involved in a transaction had to be named. Pictograms are portraits of things in the world, which are already represented by their names: here, too, as with numerals, we are dealing with a representation of the representation, but this writing of things appears with an innocent face, one that has perceived for the first time. The writing of numbers, like the writing of things, through its reference to calculi, on one hand and to the shapes of things, on the other (tokens and pictograms), hides the first mental creations: numeration and naming. At present, our documentation allows us to say that it was the stage of the writing of numbers that led to the written representation of things.

At the very end of the fourth millennium, Susa and Susiana were cut off from Mesopotamian civilization, most probably owing to a

CLARISSE HERRENSCHMIDT

military conflict. From that time the graphic traditions of Iran and Mesopotamia diverged. Jean Bottéro has explained how writing in Uruk and Jemdet-Nasr was born and developed at the end of the fourth millennium and how the history of the signs unfolded out of pictograms, with cuneiformization and syllabic phoneticization, that is, the expression of sound in writing.

The writing civilization of Susa, Susiana, and Iran continued until around 2800, providing a rather large number of tablets called "proto-Elamite," discovered at Susa and in other places, sometimes very far to the east. All of these tablets are accounting documents that contain numbers and pictograms. It appears that these texts sometimes refer to the provision or to the delivery of the goods that are shown pictographically and sometimes to the inventory of the supplies of an administration. In addition, there are signs that certainly represent proper names. Nothing more can be suggested: the signs have not been deciphered and are indecipherable in the current state of our knowledge. Among the pictograms we can recognize animals: on a remarkable tablet in the Louvre there is the head of a horse without a mane, which would be a colt; another with a raised mane, which has been interpreted as referring to a stallion; and another with the mane lowered, which would represent the mare. These interpretations remain hypothetical, of course. There are also pictograms representing grain, which differ from each other in the number and variety of ears attached to the main stem, but it is impossible to recognize which grain they represent. But most of the numerous proto-Elamite signs, apart from a few that are the same as those in Mesopotamia, portray nothing familiar.

These texts, which are somewhat too quickly called proto-Elamite, are no doubt in Elamite language, but we can know nothing about it, since we can in no way read the drawings, that is, attach words and sounds to them. The difficulty of reading rests on two facts. First, in order to recognize the pictograms of a civilization that writes only pictographically, one must belong to that civilization, be immersed in its technical and symbolic milieu, and recognize things through experience. Vincent Scheil, pioneer of Elamite studies, wrote: "Without being familiar with the practical life of the ancient Elamite world, how can we identify signs with the objects they originally represented? Let us recall Egyptian writing: in spite of the scrupulous precision of the images, in spite of the unheard-of richness of the paintings and reliefs, in which a thousand and one scenes from public and private life are reproduced, which enable us to grasp as they were all the accessories of rural and industrial activity, in the pharaonic repertoire identifications of sign with object have, for the most part, still to be determined."[2]

On the other hand, proto-Elamite signs differ from Sumerian signs in how they are written. Whereas certain Sumerian signs contain something concrete that enables us to recognize what they are about, Elamite signs are considerably more abstract. This is a basic fact: the Elamites liked very stylized, very artistic drawing, and, while they were wonderful at portraying animals, they did not attempt to reproduce the shape and contours of the human body. They preferred the emblem to the portrait, made from the signs that resembled the imaginary and abstract idea they had of things and not the concrete model. By contrast, the Sumerians had chosen a less free style of representation, a more modest, but more realistic, style. In proto-Elamite writing, there is not a single part of the body that is clearly drawn and identifiable, whereas among Sumerian pictograms one finds hands, heads, legs, and so on. One might expect, however, that the Elamites, in recording their economic transactions, would have needed to refer to these things that are so highly symbolic, that is, the human hand and head; in fact, in the Achaemenid Persepolitan administration (twenty-five hundred years later, in large part in the hands of the Elamite scribes), the responsibility of a functionary over a shipment was expressed with the word for hand. If the Elamites created pictograms with representations of parts of the body, they transformed the object so profoundly that it is no longer recognizable.

In addition to the difficulties inherent in the abstract form of the drawings, the main reason proto-Elamite is not read is because nothing came after it, unlike the earliest Sumerian writing. Indeed, proto-Elamite civilization toppled between 2900 and 2800. For archeology the writing disappeared, but it is not impossible that new discoveries will change our knowledge.

The disappearance of this writing system is to be linked to the political conditions of its appearance, which can be assumed without too much uncertainty: we are dealing with the city-state, an urban establishment with an agricultural hinterland to support it in which an economy of redistribution encompassed all the inhabitants. Land and livestock belonged to the centers of power, the royal palace and the temple, which were sometimes combined into a single location of authority; each person worked and, depending on his social level, type of work, age, gender, and abilities, received enough to be fed, clothed, and to live. These conditions are most probably the ones that existed at the time of the invention of writing with bullae and calculi.

Furthermore, the geographical distribution of proto-Elamite shows that writing served to record the movement of goods beyond the limits of the city. Susa maintained political relations with various regions on the Iranian plateau, and "gifts" (livestock, slaves, valuable objects) seem to have circulated between Susa and the plateau, these "gifts" of course being the expressions of relationships of alliance and dependency.

Writing disappeared—inasmuch as we can judge from our sources—from the daily life of Susa because the political system of the city-state with its integrated economy, a well-known system in Mesopotamia, had collapsed. One can therefore assume that the economic units of production returned to a relative autarchy. Writing no doubt ceased to be necessary when the political power no longer had the means to force those it conquered to pay tribute and when the economy of redistribution became fragmented once the pole around which it centered had disappeared.

But such a portrayal of the facts, if one were not careful, could introduce a dizzying and ethnocentric misunderstanding, namely the belief that in ancient societies, economics and politics were independent of religion. In the city-state, however, economic relationships were the visible signs of the political and hierarchical relationships between people and of the relationships of dependency of people vis-à-vis the gods. We must not imagine that it was only because there was a need to know what quantity of grain was in the silos or how many horses were in the stables of the master, whether a king or a priest, that writing was introduced. Insofar as a cylinder seal impression on a bulla was the signature of a functionary, indicating an administrative action and therefore, in the event, a repression, it is possible to say that people began to write because written accounts maintained social order. Accounts situated each person in his place—he who brought a harvest, he who stored it, he who redistributed it, and the functionary in charge—they allowed relationships between people to be seen, then, beyond that, the relationship between human beings and the gods as well.

On earth, among humans, the gods were represented by the kings and priests who transmitted the divine messages, carried out the contact between the visible living beings and the invisible, testifying to the gods' interest in humans. The other members of society were therefore the debtors of the kings and priests, and their debt had constantly to be paid through gifts, that is, tributes, tithes, and corvées. The maintenance of world order, desired by the gods and guaranteed by their representatives, had to be paid for endlessly. For, while the economy of redistribution situated each individual in his place, the entire arrangement thus worked out and maintained was for the ancients the likeness of the order desired by the gods, they who granted mortals their lives.

True, we lack theological and religious texts describing the social state in 3000 B.C., but the rest of ancient Oriental history proves abundantly to what extent religion saturated all of life. For our purposes, it is essential to know that although the first texts were economic in nature and although the invention of writing in Mesopotamia and in Elam occurred within an economic context and pursued an economic goal, it was in no way isolated from the political and religious realms. Writing began long after humans had established a political and sacral hierarchy,[3] which happened in the ancient Middle East around the sixth millennium. This social hierarchy, causing a severe rupture with the egalitarian societies that had preceded it, implied that legal violence was in the hands of a single chief and that that ruler concentrated in himself a quasi-supernatural quality and essence that came from the gods, the natural consequence of which was an inexhaustible political, economic, and symbolic debt on the part of the subjects. Indeed, one might say that the purpose of writing was in fact to record that debt. Although the art of writing did not appear wherever state societies developed, with kings, priests, gifts, and tributes, it nevertheless remains true that it could not have appeared except in such environments.

It must therefore be understood that the most uncertain, the least discernible pictogram, bursting with its infinite number of possible, very valuable meanings, the one most likely to enrage the often disappointed decoder, in its basic function of a spark of meaning, serves as a mirror in which the relationships between humans and human beings' relationships with the gods are expressed, through things and speech. There could only have been writing, a visible representation of those invisible mental acts of numeration and naming, to the extent that the representatives of the invisible gods had already imprinted their order among humans, in a place where visible, living beings were already representing invisible ones.

Before continuing, let us recall what the history of writing in Iran has taught us.

　　　　　　　　　　　　　　　　　　　　CLARISSE HERRENSCHMIDT

The first experiments in writing were with bullae, showing a seal impression and enclosing calculi; only the state can be seen in the impression of the cylinder seal, since it belonged to one of its agents involved in the transaction. Writing began once the shapes of the calculi hidden inside were made visible, pressed into the surface of the bullae; the presence of the state and the enumeration of the goods in the transaction were then placed side by side on the bulla.

In the second phase, writing captured things and their names through pictograms, which appeared following numbers. This constitutes one of the most stupefying aspects of the history of writing: it did not suddenly come to the minds of human beings to write down their linguistic exchanges; they only discovered the possibility by chance, by recording quantities. But once writing was invented, people never stopped, up to radio, television, and computers, transcribing recordings, taking hold of this human speech, which disappears the moment it is born. Writing could only be maintained, in these its fragile beginnings, with a certain political, sacral, and economic structure: the city-state and its extensions.

The great Sargon I of Akkad (2334–2279) founded the first Semitic Empire in Mesopotamia, known by the name of the Old Akkadian Empire. He put Susa and Susiana back into the Mesopotamian political and cultural orbit, and they were henceforth governed by representatives of the king. In the final decades of the twenty-third century, Sargon's grandson, Narām-Sin, who was very busy waging war in the northern regions of the empire, signed a treaty of alliance with Susa to ensure peace in the south. We do not know who the representative of Elamite power was or where this treaty took place. Fortunately, it was piously preserved in the temple of Inšušnak, the great god of the city of Susa during the second millennium. This very mutilated text, difficult to read, begins with a list of close to forty gods; a single sentence is more or less legible: "The enemy of Narām-Sin is my enemy, the friend of Narām-Sin is my friend." This is the first text in which Elamite is written with cuneiform signs.

Elamite was written in cuneiform owing to the progress made by the Mesopotamians, that is, syllabic phoneticization: the signs represent syllables (consonant-vowel, consonant-vowel-consonant). We already find certain peculiarities in it of the Elamite way of writing that later became well known: hesitation between the voiceless and the voiced consonants having the same point of articulation (between *p* and *b*, for example), the irregular presence of the implosive nasal consonant before a stop having the same point of articulation (for example: *m* before *b* or *p* is not always written).

How was this borrowing of syllabic signs possible? All syllabic writing reproduces the sounds that are heard by the listener, notes the sounds that strike the eardrum and penetrate within the subject. The Elamites analyzed their syllables and from the stock of syllabic values of the Mesopotamian signs chose those that they needed, those that came closest to the phonetics heard in their own language. Cuneiform writing spread because of the universal nature of the syllable, and it spread over an immense area.

But from the twenty-first century the Elamites of the Iranian plateau and of the Zagros became independent of Mesopotamia, and Susa became autonomous once again. The history of Elam, and that of Susa in particular, is characterized by this swinging movement, marked sometimes by the Mesopotamian stranglehold and sometimes by its rejection by the Elamites, who waged war on Mesopotamia. The king of Awan—a region of Iran located on the slopes of the Zagros—Kutik-Inšušnak, the liberator of Susa, published a number of texts in Akkadian written in cuneiform, along the lines of the formula of Narām-Sin, as well as a number of texts written in a specific script called Linear Elamite.

This script does not resemble Mesopotamian cuneiform script in any way. Rather awkwardly traced, "linear," since its technical basis is a line incised by a point in soft clay, thin, without clear dimensions, these signs seem to represent objects. But the Elamites liked abstract representation, which makes the identification of the objects impossible.

Linear Elamite has special connections to proto-Elamite. First, it borrows a number of signs from it, which seems extraordinary since there is no trace of writing between the two scripts, that is, for more than seven centuries. What were the channels of preservation of these signs? There must definitely have been some, but we know nothing about them. Moreover, unlike proto-Elamite, which contained close to a thousand signs, Linear Elamite contained only about eighty. The number of signs in proto-Elamite brings to mind a system of logograms (a *logogram* is a symbol that represents a word); that of Linear Elamite, similar to the number of signs of Linear B of Crete, leads us to suppose that this script constituted a syllabary. What we have would therefore be schematized drawings of things used to write syllables, perhaps the first syllable of the name of the thing represented; thus, for example, a drawing of a building allowed them to write and read the first syllable of the word: "buil." It is nevertheless likely that, alongside these syllabic signs, logograms were also included in the repertoire of Linear Elamite.

Lastly, while Linear Elamite is mainly found in roughly twenty inscriptions from Susa, on statuary, stair steps, vases, and large clay tablets, it seems that this second Elamite script followed channels of dissemination similar to those of proto-Elamite. Indeed, recent discoveries have revealed documents with Linear Elamite signs from eastern Iran, central Asia, and the Persian Gulf. While the need for writing was reborn during the time of Kutik-Inšušnak and within the political sphere of Susa, yet the spread of writing toward Elamized zones was immediate.

Finally, like the proto-Elamite tablets, Linear Elamite texts have not been read—a vexing but not very serious situation, for this script had very little success and went out of use rather quickly. Insofar as we don't read it, we cannot even be sure that the language written in them is indeed Elamite. Recent attempts at deciphering have failed, because the state of the Elamite language in that period is too little known. In fact, the treaty of Narām-Sin, a bit older, is in such poor condition that it does not allow us to describe the nature of the language at that time, whereas the Elamite texts that we understand fairly well are later, dating from the thirteenth century. But the language changed between the twenty-second and the thirteenth century. When one doesn't know the meaning of signs and must read a too little understood language, reasoning based only on the combination of signs is destined for failure.

All hope then rests on bilingual texts whose contents are identical. Several texts of Kutik-Inšušnak have Elamite and Akkadian versions, but as far as we can tell their contents seem to differ. The following Akkadian text, recently published by B. André and M. Salvini, cannot be superimposed as is on to the Elamite version:

> For his lord = the god Inšušnak, the mighty king of Awan, Kutik-Inšušnak, son of Shimbishhuk, built a staircase of stone, the year when the god Inšušnak looked at him and gave him the four regions to govern. He who erases this inscription, may Inšušnak, Shamash and Nergal uproot his foundation and erase his descendants. My lord! stir up trouble? in his mind![4]

If the contents were identical, we could at least transfer the royal titles from Akkadian to Elamite. But these inscriptions are not real bilinguals, for the king did not say the same thing in his language and in the language of others.

After the time of Kutik-Inšušnak, Susiana returned into the Mesopotamian orbit, during the third dynasty of Ur, the final Sumerian Empire (2094–2004). Thus Sumerian was written in Susa, and the sources bear witness to connections with all the regions of Iran. Then, around 2004, the Elamites themselves put an end to the Sumerian Empire.

From 1900 to around 1500 Elam was a rather important political power. This was the period of the Sukkalmah, "grand regents," which is well documented—but everything is relative with the Elamites!—through foundation inscriptions, dedicatory inscriptions, seals, and a number of economic and legal texts. Most of the texts are written in Akkadian, a few in Sumerian. Only two royal texts are written in Elamite with the cuneiform syllabary. They come from King Siwe-palar-huhpak, who ruled around 1765. Here is one of them in a free translation:

> Oh god Inšušnak, master of the Acropolis, I, Siwe-palar-huhpak, I am the enlarger of the kingdom, the prince of Elam, son of the sister of Shirukduh.
>
> For my life, for that of Ammahashduk, of her family and her offspring, I have [built? a temple?].
>
> Oh Inšušnak, great lord, I, Siwe-palar-huhpak, implore you through the offering, listen to my prayer for days and nights a favorable length of time.
>
> I devote the populations of Anshan and Susa to your worship; let me obtain that they . . . [what follows is incomprehensible].
>
> Let fire burn my enemies, [let] their allies be impaled, burned, and bound under me!

The two Elamite texts known from this period have the same titles, as was the custom. The signatory king then calls on the protection of Inšušnak—the god of Susa—over his life, that of his wife and her family, in exchange for the construction of a holy building; he then affirms that he has made Inšušnak the god of all Elamite populations, both within Susa and without. In place of that, the other text gives an impressive list of the lands subject to the king—and thus to Inšušnak. The Elamite texts say what the connection is between the king, the god, people, and the world.

If we look at the policy of writing of the Elamites between the reigns of Kutik-Inšušnak and Siwe-palar-huhpak, it appears that during that time the Elamites progressed toward an essential conceptual operation: they separated the language from the writing that recorded it. Let us follow the process step by step. In the first stage, at the end of the third millennium, Kutik-Inšušnak created, or more exactly, had his scribes invent, Linear Elamite to transcribe the Elamite language, although the major part of his texts were written in Akkadian. The scribes drew upon the old inventory of proto-Elamite signs, some of which they simplified, and they created other ones with what they had learned about the syllabic phoneticization that came from Mesopotamia, and they endowed Elamite Iran with a modern script. In the time of Kutik, the language was not separate from the writing; it was all as if the signs belonged to the language and the language to the signs, as if the writing down of the Elamite language was to be done with its own ancestral signs. One might argue that Kutik-Inšušnak had the political wish to possess his own script to write his own language, which is perhaps true but is not sufficient to explain his policy. In fact, a political will in the language allows us to see the representation of the language and goes far beyond politics.

Siwe-palar-huhpak had texts written in the two languages, Elamite and Akkadian, using the same cuneiform script. He thus found himself able to write his own language with a borrowed syllabary: the language was separate from the writing of it. A more abstract conception was born, namely, the universal syllabic division of languages, meaning that the Mesopotamian signs used to write the syllables *gi, ir,* and *gal,* for example, could in fact be used to write the same syllables in Elamite. But, the syllable is the minimal unit of perceived sound. According to the work of cognitivists, who seek to establish a relation between the mind and the brain, it would seem that the human ear and brain deal with the flow of sounds of perceived speech by dividing it into syllables.

This separation of language and the signs used to write it, this independence between the sign and the syllabic unit, brought about an irreversible movement toward the appropriation of language by people. In fact, human beings did not always believe they were the masters of language. While all cultures and civilizations have a theory of language—for language is a pure given that must be symbolically dealt with and integrated into the social, like birth, family ties, and death, yet few among them believe that language is something created by humans. Therefore we find myths about language everywhere, myths that do not appear as such but that combine an explanation of the nature and the origin of things with the nature and the origin of their names; the myths of the origin of language concern the names of things—thought and perceived as the proper names of the things.

Reading the myths of ancient societies reveals that people have long thought that a thing is identical to its name and that it fell to humans to capture, grasp, go and seek, and sometimes see the name of the thing as the thing itself indicates, reveals, implies, or delivers it. The Cashinahua—an Amazon people of Brazil living midstream on the rivers of the state of Acre—have a myth of the flood and of the reinvention of life in which the cultural hero is a woman, Nëtë, who survives the flood and provides herself with children by crying into a gourd.[5] Her too plentiful tears wear out her eyes, and Nëtë becomes Bwëkon, "blind"; since she wishes to teach her children everything they must know to feed themselves, they place in her hands a few leaves from a plant, which she sniffs, feels, and names: "This is manioc." Since she is blind, she no longer grasps anything of the outside world, but her body unites with the things she touches and smells, and in this fusion she produces the names of things, lending those things her human voice separate from all sight. If knowing the name is nothing more than knowing how to handle the object that bears that name, if "it is manioc" denotes an agricultural mode and a cooking recipe, yet knowing the name comes from Nëtë Bwëkon's ability to remove herself and to allow things to speak through her; and so language is indeed knowledge and know-how, but only if the human body vanishes. This myth, itself told, says that the names of things are not man-made: language is the condition of the myth, the myth of the myth. Even if we do not know the Elamite myths, we can imagine that it was approximately this representation of language that enabled the invention of pictograms: writing amounted to portraying an object, which amounted to exposing its name, for the thing and its name were identical.

This idea of language—a self-referred condition of myth—which formed the linguistic theory in which mythical thoughts have blossomed, is eroded and destroyed by writing. The primary victim of writing is the myth.

In the second millennium, when the Elamites separated their language from the signs that were used to write it, when Babylonian scholars were making their mathematics shine in all their brilliance, when, in Mari, prophets appeared who spoke in the name of the gods, things of the world tended to be dissociated from their names. Names began to lose their absolute value, being divided into syllables, which could be the same in Elamite and in Akkadian. In short, the bodies of humans no longer vanished between things and their names; they seemed to integrate this strange relationship, and people gradually appropriated the language.

Let us return one last time to Elam.

Between the thirteenth and the twelfth centuries, Elamite civilization experienced a relative splendor. Kings produced a number of texts in the Elamite language and in cuneiform script, the adoption of which became definitive. Elamite was still written under the Achaemenids (550–330), then it disappeared.

The Elamites reduced the 600 signs in the Sumerian syllabary to 150 or 160, and simplified the script by attributing approximately only one value to each sign and only one sign to each syllable. The syllable was formally variable and could represent the following sequences: consonant-vowel, vowel-consonant, consonant-vowel-consonant. Nevertheless, two phenomena took place: (1) the reduction of polyphony: the sign *ri*, for example, only had the value *ri* in Elamite, whereas in Mesopotamia it had the values *ri, re, dal*, and *tal*; (2) the limitation of homophony: the syllable *ri*, for example, could be written using two and not a half dozen signs. The Elamites began by eliminating a great number of logograms, the signs created by the Sumerians to represent words but that the Elamites read in their language, keeping only around thirty of them. All the same, the movement was subsequently inverted, as Marie-Joseph Steve explains: "The later system was, on the whole, not the most simple overall,"[6] for the Elamites, like the Mesopotamians and the Egyptians, increased the number of logograms as time went on. Here is an approximate count: in the year 1400, one sign in six was a logogram; in the year 600, one sign in two was a logogram. That certainly had something to do with the status of the sign: if writing with logograms was the harnessing of things in the world and of their names through their representations—even if it was a completely abstract portrait—the increasing number of signs protected people from a radical desymbolization.

If humans appropriate language in a writing system that divides words into syllables, they refuse to go any further and allow the words of their language—the names of things—to keep their ability to represent the thing itself.

Elamite cuneiform writing, like that of Mesopotamia, has signs that represented vowels without accompanying consonants, such as *a, i, e,* and *u;* it had no punctuation or capitalization and it separated neither words nor phrases. It used a few signs, called determinatives, which had no meaning in the language but only in the writing, since they were not pronounced but facilitated reading: they indicated in fact that the word that followed was characterized either by its divine nature (thus the names of gods and the names of the months were preceded by the determinative *dingir:* 𒀭), or by its matter (thus the determinative *gish:* 𒄑 was found before the names of things made of wood), or by its nature of being a male human being (determinative 𒁹 before proper masculine names, names of professions); there also existed the determinative *mesh* 𒈨𒌍 indicating that the sign that preceded it was to be read like a logogram and not as a phonetic sign, and so on.

As far as I can tell from our practices, the process of reading a writing system such as Elamite consisted of a synthetic mental apperception: the reader assembles the signs in his mind in the course of reading in order to compose words and phrases; he performs relative differentializations. Confronted, for example, with the symbol 𒁹, which represents the number 1 or the determinative "male human being," the reader had to go on to the next symbol to know which meaning was the correct one. Reading was not linear but global: it involved the groups that the signs formed among themselves. Reading and understanding were mixed together in a single operation of recognition, of choosing, and of forming groups.

Most of the texts of the Elamite kings from the second millennium are texts for the foundation or dedication of religious buildings. There are few long texts, barely a detailed report on military victories. What was important was to state that such and such a king, the son of a certain king, built a certain temple, sanctuary, or chapel for one or another of the Elamite gods. When the modern reader reads that an Elamite king built for Inšušnak, or Napirisha, Humban, Shimut, Nahhunte, Pinigir, Kiririsha, Upurkupak, Ishnikarab, Manzat, or for the couple Hishmitik-Ruhuratir a temple or an enormous city-sanctuary such as Choga Zambil, he does not have the impression of being in the presence of a theological and religious text, for he sees political calculations and interests throughout. These texts, in their short form, express the essence of the religious content, namely, the presence of the gods, the repetition of rituals, the dependency of humans, and the role of the king as an intermediary between the gods and human beings.

In the thirteenth century King Untash-Napirisha built Dur Untash, "city of Untash" (in modern Persian, Choga Zambil), several dozen kilometers from Susa. Three concentric enclosures surrounding the temples and an enormous tower were built there, but Dur Untash, the holy city, was soon abandoned. Three-quarters of the bricks that were used are inscribed, in Elamite or in Akkadian, with approximately the same content—even if the intended god changed:

> I, Untash-Napirisha, son of King Humban-numena, king of An-shan and Susa, for Nahhunte who fulfills for me what I seek through prayer, who accomplishes that which I express, I have built in colored [?] bricks his temple right in the middle of the enclosed sanctuary. Nahhunte in gold, I have made him, the lord of the temple in the walled precinct of the sanctuary, I have installed him. May my work be dedicated as a gift to Nahhunte of the walled precinct of the sanctuary. May he allow me to have many days for many years, as well as a kingdom with a fortunate reign [?]."[7]

Writing showed piety toward the gods, extended the ritual, and rendered them everlasting.

The ancients believed that writing partook of the invisible. In fact, language, which is itself invisible, shows that which is beyond our sight, it names the invisible. The written word, which captures language, reveals the invisible and becomes the eternal meeting place between the visible living and the invisible eternal. In writing, these two invisible things—language and the gods—are present, visible, immobile, knowable.

CHAPTER SIX

Consonant Alphabets, the Greek Alphabet, and Old Persian Cuneiform

Pharaonic Egypt, Mesopotamia, and Elam represent absolute antiquity, that of the writing civilizations born in the fourth millennium, but now extinct. The period that began in the second millennium, however, and continued into the first saw the flourishing of literary civilizations that are still alive: Iran, Israel, the West by way of Greece and Rome—but also India and China. This antiquity, which appears so distant, is not really that far away in the matter of writing systems. This antiquity, which informs us directly, is in this sense not absolute but relative.

With our overview of the graphic history of Elam, we have seen that the logographic systems and the syllabaries shared the characteristic of writing natural languages as if external to them. Whether a drawing evoking an object in the visible world and its name or a syllabic sign expressing in writing the minimum unit of sound perceived by the human ear (the syllable), these signs referred to the external world, something perceived by sight or the sound of the word captured by the ear. By contrast, with consonant alphabets, such as Phoenician, Hebrew, Aramaic, Nabataean, and Arabic—to mention only these languages—systems used to write Old Persian or even the languages of India, and finally the Greek alphabet, we are in the presence of writing systems that express in writing a sound from the point of view of the person who is speaking.

Certain great civilizations with writing systems alive today thus plunge their roots deep into a distant past. Is it to the exactitude of their systems of transcribing their languages that they owe their longevity? This seems quite doubtful, since languages change. We must go beyond a linguistic analysis to understand, insofar as it is possible, what these writing civilizations were at their inceptions, during their development, then during their existence to the present time; we must discover what writing in itself meant for the people of those civilizations. Once writing systems expressed sounds from the point of view of the speaking, reading, and writing subject, the sign left the external environment, perceived by sight and hearing, and showed humans as thinking and speaking. Its point of application, from being outside of the person, came to be lodged inside him. In the civilizations of absolute antiquity, writing was the eternal meeting place of humans and the gods, yet in relative antiquity it partook even more of the religious and political foundations of the writing cultures and became the mold into which people poured their own thoughts.

But before continuing, let us look at three graphic systems in the chronological order of their appearance: the consonant alphabets, the Greek alphabet, and Old Persian cuneiform.

Consonant alphabets have all functioned following the same model ever since their inception up to the current way of writing Hebrew and Arabic. They do not include logograms and do not note the syllable of the word heard in its varying forms. The alphabetic rule prevails in them: one sign equals one sound. The number of signs was established in antiquity and ranges between twenty-two characters in Phoenician and Classical Aramaic to twenty-nine or thirty signs for the cuneiform alphabet of Ugarit or the Old South Arabic alphabet. On the whole these writing systems are linear, drawn with a pointed implement or with a plume onto very diverse media: stone, metal, shards of pottery, probably leather; but it was papyrus, which was light and transportable, that assured their success.

The first characteristic of these alphabets was their small number of signs; the number of signs in the Mesopotamian syllabaries was around 130, to which were added logograms and determinatives. The second was that consonant alphabets wrote only consonants; vowels had no autonomous signs. The third was that in general words were separated in writing by a vertical bar, by one or more dots, and later by a blank space. In contemporary Arabic script, as in the case of certain letters in Hebrew (*kaf, mem, nun, pe*) the separation of words is assured by the specific shape of most of the letters in final position; the long, vertical, and thin bar of *mīm*, the elegant curving of *het, ayin,* or *sin,* for example, which blossom in final position, was reduced to a smaller shape initially and in the middle of a word. In short, in the absence of a duly recognized word separator, the shape of the letters indicated the end of a word while it also embellished the graphic appearance.

How can we characterize these writing systems, which were immensely successful in time and space, since they no doubt gave rise to the scripts of Iran, India, and central Asia, not to mention the Greek alphabet, as well? The question is not a simple one and it requires a double approach; it is fitting, on one hand, to evoke the absolute beginnings of these systems and, on the other, to recall the interpretations of them that Ignace J. Gelb and James Février have suggested.[8]

The beginnings of the consonant alphabet are very unclear and very contested. The first texts date from between 1800 and 1500; the inscriptions found on the site of Serābīt el-Hādem in central Sinai, where the pharaonic state was exploiting turquoise mines in which workers who were fairly Egyptianized but who spoke Semitic languages labored. The only deciphered texts are two inscriptions found on a statuette of a sphinx representing the Egyptian goddess Hathor, the protectress of mines, in which is written the name of the goddess Bʿlt, "the Lady." It is therefore believed that the scribes employed there recognized in the Egyptian Hathor their own goddess Baalat, and honored her name by writing it with alphabetical signs. On the edges of the great Egyptian Empire a universe of new thought was being born, one that was borrowing symbols and shapes from its master but was creating its own system of references and signifiers.

What followed is very unclear up until the consonant alphabet of Ugarit, which had thirty cuneiform signs written on clay tablets following Mesopotamian tradition. This alphabet is in fact a cuneiform reinterpretation of the linear signs of the very first consonant alphabets, a curious fact that we shall find again in Old Persian. The texts date from the fourteenth century and have provided us with a vast literature.

The cursive Phoenician alphabet was born in the region of Byblos during the twelfth century; in the eleventh century it was fixed with twenty-two signs. It was soon followed by the Moabite, Edomite, Ammonite, Hebrew, and Aramaic alphabets—variants of Canaanite—and much later by Nabataean, and finally by Arabic.

In his strange and stimulating book, Ignace Gelb vigorously maintains, without truly proving it, that consonant alphabets are syllabaries that include a limited number of signs (twenty-two to thirty) that transcribe the consonant but do not indicate the vowel. Gelb's idea has aroused violent reactions and has continued to preoccupy scholars, which shows that he has perhaps aimed correctly, yet his arguments remain weak. His primary argument is as follows:

After the Hellenization of the East, diacritical marks were invented in consonant alphabets to express vowels (*a, e, i, o, u*), as well as a mark the moderns called *shᵊwā*, which characterized the sign to which it was attached as a pure consonant or as a consonant followed by a small neutral vowel (like the French *"e muet"*); for Gelb, "the fact that the Semites felt the necessity of creating a mark showing lack of a vowel means that to them every sign originally stood for a full syllable."[9] This argument highlights the tangible and linguistic value that the people of the time attributed to the signs in their writing systems; and structurally it does have its merits.

According to James Février, the reason why the Semitic civilizations were reluctant to note vowels is because the reader of a Semitic language could easily interpret the consonantal skeleton of words. Every speaker of a Semitic language who hears a spoken word breaks it down mentally into its consonantal root and its vocalic inflection. The root bears the basic meaning; the additional elements—the affixes (prefixes, infixes, suffixes) that are placed in front of, inside of, or after the root—do not change the meaning but determine the grammatical nature of the word as a conjugated verbal form, a nominal form of the verb, an adjective, or a noun (masculine, feminine, singular, plural).

Take, for example, the Hebrew root QṬL, "(idea of) to kill" (whose consonants are traditionally represented by capital letters, whereas the vowels and the consonants of the affixes are represented by lowercase letters). One forms a singular masculine present participle, "killing," by adding an *o* between the first and the second radical consonants and an *e* between the second and the third: *QoṬeL;* one derives the past of the third-person singular, "he has killed," with the vowels *ā* and *a: QāṬaL;* the absolute infinitive is *QāṬōL;* the imperative requires only one vowel: *QṬōl,* "kill!"

For certain forms one adds not simply vowels but also consonants; for example, *yiQṬōl,* "he kills or will kill," and *tiQṬōL,* "she kills or will kill," both denoting uncompleted action, *QāṬaLnū,* "we have killed" (completed action), and so on.

In a sporadic fashion, but at least from the end of the first millennium, certain so-called weak consonants were used as *matres lectionis,* that is, indicators as to the nature of the vowel. For example, in Hebrew, the *he* at the end of a word indicated the back vowel *a;* the *yod* (the English *y*) indicated the front vowels *i* and *e;* the *waw* indicated the rounded vowels *u* and *o;* and *aleph* (glottal stop) all long vowels.

Insofar as only consonants are written, QṬL could be read "he has killed," "killing," "kill!" or "to kill" (if preceded by a preposition)—which are not all the same thing!—and we can understand that there is a fair amount of ambiguity in these writing systems. But the reader, aided by the separation of words, recognizes a root in the basic consonants of any derived form. He then restores the right vowels to read the true meaning of the word he has in front of him by relying on the syntactic order of the sentence, which guides him by its regularity, and on the overall meaning of the text. In order to read, it is necessary to know the grammar of the language and be familiar with the context.

It therefore appears that consonant alphabets have traits in common with logographic systems, complete alphabets, and syllabaries. Their alphabetic nature is the most obvious, because one sign equals one sound. But these facts are perhaps misleading, for the absence of any signs for the vowels presents a problem. How does one define an alphabet, after all? For the linguist Henry Allan Gleason, no alphabet in the world truly expresses in writing "all the phonological sub-systems of the language upon which it is based," for example, stress or intonation.[10] But this extreme position is logically arguable, if no alphabet expresses all the phonological subsystems of the language it describes, then there is no real "alphabet." If we limit ourselves to a less extreme definition based on acoustics, according to which an alphabet would be a system that has autonomous signs for sounds in the language with "formants" (vowels and liquids) and sounds without "formants" (consonants and semivowels),[11] then we can conclude that consonant alphabets are not alphabets, whereas the Greek alphabet is one.

But this negative definition of consonant alphabets cannot be used as a basis for what concerns us here: a comparative history of writing systems and of civilizations with writing. We must go further than the concept of "alphabet." Gelb's arguments, which propose seeing syllabaries in consonant alphabets, are weak, but, paradoxically, his opinion can be strengthened by the arguments of Février and other scholars. As Février has written, the reader recognizes the root; when necessary he sorts the consonants and establishes a semantic hierarchy between the consonants of the root, those of the affixes, and, if there were any, the so-called *matres lectionis*. The reader compensates for the absence of vowels with his knowledge of the grammar and the context that enable him to read, that is, to mentally supply the right vowels in the right places. In the process of reading, he goes through the mental formation of the syllables of the word, reassembling the syllables. If reading is

CLARISSE HERRENSCHMIDT

vocalizing, as was believed by the Masoretes, who fixed the text of the Bible noting the vowels, vocalizing is reassembling syllables.

In the act of reading, a sign in the consonant alphabet has the value of a virtual syllable, still in the form of the consonant-vowel sequence. This has a major implication: the sign does not typify a consonant as opposed to a vowel, instead it evokes a matrix of speech in which vocalic color is undifferentiated and the primary articulatory support (the consonant) is well indicated.[12] Whereas the phonetic sign of the Mesopotamian cuneiform referred to the syllable that was heard, that of consonant alphabets refers to the syllable as it is produced by the speaker. And this presents a paradox, for this uttered syllable, which necessitates (a minimum of) two articulations, should have been written with (at least) two signs.

Like logographic writing systems, consonant alphabets are inseparable from the writing of the word: the word, graphically separated from those that surround it, is the basic unit of such a system. In addition, in the fifteenth century B.C.E. certain signs were recognizable portraits of objects, pictograms, which were used to write the first consonantal articulation of the name of that object. For example: the symbol ⊏⊓ represented a house (a sketch of a house), and *house* sounded something like *bayt,* therefore this symbol ⊏⊓ was used to write the sound *b.* In the course of the evolution of writing, the shape of the symbol lost its realistic character, but the name of the letter, *bayt,* remained concretely anchored to the value of the sign. Thus for a small number of signs, the relation between the sign and the sound was not arbitrary. With consonant alphabets the pictogram was not very far away.

It seems even closer when one looks at the act of reading, which, in the case of a logogram, is a recognition, the reader has a global perception of what is at issue. But, in order to read a word formed through grammatical derivation from a verbal root and written only with its consonants, the reader has to see the root by sorting out the consonants. This act of reading necessitates the restoration—a sort of vision, in fact—of the semantic core, which is then separated from what surrounds it. The presence of other letters also renders necessary a backward movement in the text, sometimes several, as in writing systems in which logograms, determinatives, and syllabic signs are combined.

Consonant alphabets are writing systems in which the unit of sound analysis is the syllable but the writing units are simultaneously the word and the consonant phoneme. Therefore the unit of sound analysis and the graphic units do not overlap. Consonant alphabets are neither complete alphabets, nor syllabaries, nor logographic systems, but all three at the same time. They are, however, alphabets, for they are ruled by the rule that one sign = one sound.

They are a sort of condensed version of the Mesopotamian and Egyptian writing systems—Egyptian most assuredly participated in their births. With their small number of signs, they represented an immense progress as well as a true paradox. In fact, through the shapes and the names of the letters, they prevented the separation between writing and language; by writing consonants that could only be read by being mentally transformed into syllables and through the absence of contrast between the consonant and the vowel, understanding became blended with reading. Because the root was the hidden semantic core, which had to be grasped and understood before reading, this grasping process became the condition for reading.

Pictographic or logographic and syllabic writing systems reflected the thought that things in the world, their names, and their signs are all three identical and treated the syllable as something in the external world, bound to objects in the visible world, since the syllable was by definition the heard syllable; and these collected entities established a continuum of signs in which people found themselves included, as in the midst of a forest of symbols. In consonant alphabets the disjunction between the unit of analysis of the language (the syllable) and the graphic units (the consonant and the word) and the fact that the syllable was no longer expressed in writing established another world-language-subject continuum, which went from the name of things to the human psychic activity and the mental assembling of syllables, but at the same time removed the objective support of the syllable in the writing.

Consonant alphabets meant significant progress in humans' appropriation of language, but they did not inscribe the sounds in the body of the speaker, but halfway between his body and his speech.

With the Greek alphabet things are a bit simpler, but not as simple as is claimed.

The Greeks seem to have lost the use of writing—but not their memory of it—at the end of the Mycenaean period, and the return to the practice of writing necessitated a transfer of the Phoenician alphabet to the Greeks. The signs of what would become the Greek script were borrowed by the Greeks (or possibly the Cretans) from the Phoenicians, perhaps in the ninth century or, at the latest, in the middle of the eighth century, and the first text known to us

CLARISSE HERRENSCHMIDT

dates from 730. The Greeks preserved more or less the Semitic names of the letters: what they called *bayt* became *beta, dalet* became *delta, nun* became *nu.* They also preserved the order of the letters: *aleph-bet-gimel* became *alpha-beta-gamma,* which gave us our "alphabet." They transformed the shape of the letters by rotating or inverting, thus marking their appropriation of the signs. Herodotus knew that the Greek letters came from the Phoenicians.[13]

The Greeks created letters for their vowels from certain consonantal signs for which they had no use, since those signs referred to sounds that did not exist in their language: thus *alpha,* used to write the vowel *a,* came from *aleph,* a glottal stop; *iota,* for the vowel *i,* came from *yod,* a palatal fricative; *epsilon,* noting the vowel *e,* came from *he,* a soft aspirate. It perhaps seemed indispensable to them to mark the vowels, because their language contrasted simple vowels with diphthongs (*elipon,* "I left," contrasts with *eleipon,* "I was leaving") and included groups of consonants in an initial position (e.g., *stratos,* "army"). But the Greek privative *alpha,* which caused a word to go from a positive meaning to a negative one, must have been determinative for the writing of all the vowels, because it caused a word to go from a positive meaning to a negative one: for example, *nomos,* "the law," as opposed to *anomos,* "without law." The privative *alpha* was thus the carrier of a logical opposition that did not tolerate ambiguity, for if it had not been written, the positive and the negative would have been graphically confused (in Semitic languages negation was expressed by a syllable with a consonant).

In the earliest centuries Greek writing was oriented sometimes from left to right, sometimes right to left, like Semitic scripts, or sometimes back and forth, a practice called *boustrophedon,* "turning like an ox in the field"—the nicest looking of all. In ancient Greek inscriptions, words were not separated, and this lasted for quite some time; then dots or a hyphen were used to separate units, most often according to syntax and not always individual words, but groups of syntactically linked words. It is unbelievable how much this resembled speech itself.

The principle is well known: one sign represents one sound. The graphic unit is an isolated sign that, recognized as a signifier in the language, also constitutes the unit of analysis of language, the phoneme (Greek writing is a scholarly invention, even if the linguists who invented it did not write their memoirs). In the complete alphabet of the Greeks, vowels, liquids, consonants, and semivowels (sounds with and without formants) are graphically on the same equal footing. There is nothing to guess at, as in consonant alphabets; there are no choices to be made and nothing to add to the script, as in Old Persian cuneiform; there is no longer any concrete pictures, as in pictograms, nor any sound pictures, as in the case of the name of letters recalling the name of the depicted thing by its initial consonant; there is no sign completely independent of the language that finds its justification only in writing, such as the Mesopotamian or Egyptian determinatives. Greek writing seems to be perfectly adapted to the language of human beings.

The Greek alphabet presents a few difficulties, however. If we explain the shape and the value of two-thirds of the signs by their having been borrowed from the Phoenicians and the creation of *omicron* (little *o*) and *omega* (big *o*) by the desire to differentiate the short vowel *o* from the long *ō*, then the signs *psi* and *xi* present specific problems, because these are pure Greek creations, without earlier models, and they are not pure alphabetical signs.

The use of a single sign (*psi* and *xi*) for the groups *p* + *s* and *k* + *s* was in fact generalized rather late. Throughout the seventh, sixth, and even the fifth centuries, depending on the region, we find the groups *p* + *s* and *k* + *s* written with two letters, that is, *pi* or *kappa* followed by *sigma* or, more often, *phi* or *khi* followed by *sigma*. "Then the usage of a single sign for each of these groups is generalized. . . . Starting in the sixth century we find *ks* noted by *X* in 'western' alphabets; starting in the seventh century, we find *ps* noted by ↓ and *ks* by Ɛ in 'eastern' alphabets and it is this system that was to prevail throughout Greece starting in the fourth century."[14] From the point of view of articulation, using two letters is understandable, since two articulations are needed for the groups *p* + *s* (bilabial occlusive + sibilant) and *k* + *s* (velar occlusive + sibilant), even if the occlusive is transformed and softened by the sibilant. The speaker said and heard two sounds, and two letters were written up to the time when writing with a single letter became the rule.

This problem can be brought together with that of aspirate consonants. From the inception of the Greek alphabet, the aspirate *t* was written θ, *theta*, with the sign of the Semitic emphatic unvoiced dental occlusive (*ṭet*), while the *taw*, the simple unvoiced dental of Phoenician, was the model for its phonetic equivalent, the Greek *tau*. The aspirate occlusives *ph* and *kh*—which were simply pronounced with an occlusion followed by an aspiration and not with a spirantization, in which *p* + *h* gives *f*—did not have, in the early days of Greek writing, any special signs, as in the Mycenaean and Cypriot syllabaries. For a long time they wrote the sign for the oc-

CLARISSE HERRENSCHMIDT

clusive followed by the sign for aspiration, *H;* thus they wrote *pi* followed by *H* for the aspirate *p*, which later was written *phi, kappa,* or *qoppa* followed by *H* for the aspirate *k*, which was later written *khi.* The evolution of the Greek alphabet thus showed a tendency to write with a single sign sounds that had previously been analyzed as two distinct sounds.

This should be compared with the problem of the aspirate *h* before a vowel at the beginning of a word. In most regions of the Greek world, except in Asia Minor, archaic inscriptions attest to the writing of the aspirate *h* with the autonomous sign *H*, originally the Phoenician letter *het,* which had the same phonetic value. In the Ionic and Aeolic dialects of Asia Minor, where the aspiration had disappeared, the sign *H*, no longer tied to any sound, was used to note the open *e*, that is, the *ē*, called *eta.* In other Greek dialects aspiration was quite simply pronounced and written. We see its existence in the case of elision (*kata hemeran* being written *kaθemeran,* the initial aspiration of *hemera* being placed on the final consonant *t* of *kata,* once the final *a* had been elided), and of composition (**eishodos* becomes *eishodos,* written *eshodos* in fifth-century Athens).

Aspiration ceased to be written, even where it was still pronounced, when the Ionic alphabet of Asia became the writing system used throughout Greece. In 403 the Athenians adopted Ionic writing, even though their dialect quite clearly preserved the aspirate *h.* Athens, the capital of the ancient *Aufklärung,* created a graphic deficiency by allowing aspiration to disappear from the writing system. They did not, however, forget that the sign *H*, henceforth read as the vowel *ē* (*eta*), referred to the aspirate *h:* in the acrophonic writing of numbers, which had the first letter of the name of the number designate that number, the sign *H* was used to write the numeral one hundred, because the aspirate written *H* was the first sound and the first letter of the word *hekaton,* "hundred." This acrophonic writing of numerals was itself Athenian, however, as it typified both the living pronunciation of the aspirate and the fact it was written *H*.

The lack of a written aspirate was sorely felt, and so it was timidly reintroduced at the end of the fourth century in the form of ⊢, that is, the first half of *H;* this is the sign that became the *spiritus asper,* "rough breathing"—in Greek, *pneuma dasu,* the name the Alexandrine grammarians gave it in the third century.

Let us sum up the specific characteristics of the Greek writing system. The Greeks took the rule of consonant alphabets: one sign = one consonantal matrix of sounds—and through the writing of vowels extended it to the following new rule: one sign = one sound. This rule did not, however, become reversible: one sound = one sign. In fact, the letters *xi* and *psi* followed the rule: one sign = a group of two consonantal sounds.

In addition, the official disappearance of the aspirate in the script adopted in Athens in 403 implies the rule: one sound = zero sign. This left it to the reader to add a nonwritten sound and was at the origin of the reintroduction of aspiration with the rough breathing. Much later they began writing the *spiritus lenis,* "smooth breathing," indicating that the initial vowel was not preceded by aspiration. This too followed the rule: one sign = zero sound, which is a paradox in an alphabet.

The complete alphabet, this remarkable tool, seems to have presented some difficulties, especially to the Athenians of 403.

What are the characteristics of this writing system, beyond what we have just seen? Certain alphabetical signs—whether they are in our own alphabet or in that of the Greeks—are not used to write a sound but a nonsound. The sign used to designate the sound *a* represents a possible pronunciation of the *a*, but the character *t*, for example, designates not a sound but a nonsound, which the Greeks called *aphonos,* "lacking sound." This sign in fact designates a position of the organs of articulation that serves to pronounce a *t*, but only after a vowel has been added; for *p, t, k, b, d, g, m,* and *n* are occlusive consonants produced by a closing of the organs of articulation followed by an opening for the passage of air for the vowel. Thus certain signs of the complete alphabet note not sounds but the positions of the sound-making organs. These signs refer to the body of the reader and evoke the mute, interior, and private speech.

The act of reading the complete alphabet is linear; however, since one does not go back, one does not proceed to a grasping of the words in their totality, and one does not need to see the sign that follows to determine the value of the sign one is reading. This is why alphabetic writing is so similar to speech: it follows, without need or desire to go back, the flow of time that passes. Unlike what happens with consonant alphabets, reading the complete alphabet does not require the language, only understanding it does. We have all had the experience of reading a difficult sentence without understanding it; we read the words, the phrase, the page, and suddenly we feel that we must start over in order to understand. The complete alphabet requires a body—eyes and sound-making organs— and a mind that understands, but does not require them to work

CLARISSE HERRENSCHMIDT

together; with the complete alphabet, reading is not identical to understanding.

By the dissociation of reading from comprehension, the complete alphabet introduced a body-mind dualism. Nothing like this existed in other writing systems, nor in the picto-logographic systems, in which the whole formed by the thing in the world, the graphic sign, and the word turned writing into a tangible double of the tangible world, nor in consonant alphabets or in Old Persian cuneiform (see below), in which reading implied reading what one already knew—the lexicon and the morphological structure of the language. With the Greek alphabet, one could read everything without understanding anything.

The complete alphabet reveals both the inner workings of the speaking body and the universal nature of human language. In fact, to place consonants and vowels on the same graphic footing, sounds produced by the closing or the opening of the articulatory organs, meant writing all sounds that came out of the human body. The Greeks were aware that their writing system enabled the transcription of words of languages other than their own; this is proved by the extraordinary exactness of the phonetic rendering of the Scythian and Iranian words reported by Herodotus, for example. Transcribing the language of others into one's own phonemes amounts to showing that language comes from the human body and that all people are a part of language.

Old Persian cuneiform writing was perhaps created for Cyrus the Great (550?–530), the founder of the Achaemenid Persian Empire, when he decided to leave his name and his titles on the buildings of Pasargadae in southwestern Iran, but Darius the Great (521–486) was the only Achaemenid king who had true texts composed and took pleasure in doing so. His texts even give evidence of genius: logic, expressiveness, silence about what should be kept hidden, some obscurity in the account of a lost battle, all the rigor and rhetorical mastery needed to evoke myths and suggest rituals without naming them, but all the while referring to them implicitly so well that they fill the texts with sacredness. Darius's successors imitated him with scarcely any innovation. The use of Old Persian cuneiform died out with the Achaemenid dynasty and the conquest by Alexander the Great.

The writing system created by the great kings for inscriptions on their monuments was intended to be a synthesis of all the writing accessible to the Persians in the time of Cyrus, that is, cuneiform script—Elamite and Mesopotamian—ideograms, syllabaries, alphabetical script, and probably even other things. Old Persian writing was the reflection of the Achaemenid Empire, which was identified with the inhabited world; this in no way, however, contradicts its characteristic of being an almost private writing system of the Achaemenid kings, for it almost served exclusively to eternalize the royal speech. Fifty or so repetitive inscriptions, sometimes accessible only to divine readers because of their location on a dizzying cliff, sometimes buried in the foundations of Persepolis, sometimes decorating the walls of the great halls of Susa—this corpus is insignificant for its quantity and remarkable for its desire to mean something.

This writing system has raised impassioned discussions: is it a syllabary or an alphabet? Is its model a Semitic alphabet, or is it derived from Mesopotamian writing systems? When exactly was it made? Are the inscriptions of Ariaramnes and Arsames, ancestors of Darius I, fake antiquities? Did a Median writing system of similar form exist, since the Median and Persian languages were quite similar?

Many of these questions cannot be answered, at least for the present, but that does not prevent us from proceeding.

The signs used to write Old Persian are cuneiform, their basic constituents being the wedge-shape vertical, horizontal, or slanted, and pressed into clay, incised in stone, or molded in metal, like all cuneiform signs. The writing goes from left to right, and there is no punctuation. The writing technique is thus cuneiform, but the shape of the characters, as in the case of Ugaritic, are a cuneiform reinterpretation of Phoenician linear signs. For example: the Persian sign for m/m^a, 𐏁, derives from the tenth-century Phoenician sign m, ℳ; the inventors of Old Persian cuneiform used vertical wedges to represent the zigzags in the Phoenician m and added a small horizontal wedge to the left. This is not true for all the signs, however, for some come from Mesopotamian or Elamite cuneiform, whereas others, particularly logograms, are purely formal inventions.

As regards their value, Old Persian signs belong to three categories. First, there are five indecomposable logograms, which cannot be correlated with the sound or the true shape of the thing represented and have only a single value. These logograms refer to key concepts in Persian culture in the Achaemenid period: Ahura Mazdā (the proper name of the great god of the ancient Iranians), the king's title, the land, the earth, and the word for "god."

The second category consists of a word separator, which is always written.

All other signs represent a sound. There are three signs for vowels, long *a*, and *i* and *u* (without indication of their length), and twenty-two signs for consonants. These consonant signs can be used to write indiscriminately an isolated consonant or a consonant followed by a short *a*. This means that the same sign can be read as a single consonant or as a syllable, that is, the consonant followed by the short vowel *a* (we say these signs have "inherent *a*" and transcribe them with a superscript vowel, for example, m^a). Since at least every other vowel in the Old Persian language was a short *a*, the inventors of this writing system created an economical way of writing. With their *m* or m^a, for example, they reproduced in Old Persian—𐎶—the ambiguity of consonant alphabets, in which writing favors consonants and the sign represents a virtual syllable.

But the principle of graphic economy is thwarted by the existence of eleven signs with "inherent" *i* or *u*—four with *i*: j^i, d^i, m^i, v^i; seven with *u*: k^u, g^u, t^u, d^u, n^u, m^u, r^u. They might appear to be excellent syllabic signs, consonant + vowel, but they were not used as such, for the inherent vowel was—except in a few cases—repeated after them with its own sign: for example, to write the syllable *ku*, which appears in the name of King Cyrus (*Kuruš*), one used the symbol k^u, which has the inherent *u*, followed by the independent sign *u*, so that one actually wrote k^u-*u*.

In order to understand this system, it is necessary to describe the reading process. Faced with a sign with inherent *a*, the reader decided whether he was to read the isolated consonant or the syllable with *a*; for example, the personal subject pronoun in the first person, "I," was written *a*-d^a-m^a and could be read *adam* or *ādam* (at the beginning of a word, the sign *a* could be read short or long), *adama* or *ādama*, *adma* or *ādma*, *adm* or *ādm*. The reader of Old Persian in antiquity—just like the modern philologist—knew that it was read *adam*. In reading one had constantly to choose between the presence or absence of a short *a* that was only virtually foreseen in the graphics; this choice required reference to the language.

When the reader was confronted with the sequence consonantal sign with inherent *a* followed by the independent sign *i* or *u*, two readings were possible: one with the simple vowel, p^a + *i* = *pi*, the other with the diphthong, the *a* of the sign with inherent *a* followed by the autonomous vowel: p^a + *i* = *pai*.

This ambiguity in reading explains the existence of signs with inherent *i* and *u* followed by the same vowel. According to M. Mayrhofer, these signs were invented to prevent reading with a diphthong.[15] Indeed, insofar as, for example, the sign n^u exists alongside the sign n^a, the writing n^a-u imposes the reading *nau* and excludes the reading *nu*; for if one had wanted to write the syllable *nu*, one would have written n^u-u. By contrast, the graphic sequence p^a-i can be read *pi* and *pai*, since p^i doesn't exist. In the word written a-n^u-u-$š^a$-i-y^a-a, which at the time must have been pronounced *anušyā*, the group of signs n^u-u avoided the false reading **anaušyā*. It is highly probable that this redundant spelling practice, in this example, had as its goal to confusion between *anušyā*, "partisans of a rebel," and **anaušā*, "(the guard of the) Immortals of the Great King." We are dealing with signs that were conceived to amend the economy of using signs with inherent short *a* and to avoid erroneous readings. These are phonetic signs whose function was to prevent seeing and saying, and not to enable seeing and saying, phonetic signs conceived contrary to the principle of phoneticization.

Despite its small number of signs, Old Persian cuneiform is striking in its strange complexity—and we cannot examine here all the conventions of its writing. The cuneiform technique and the use of logograms were inherited from Mesopotamia, the interpretation of the sounds of the language in large part follows consonantal systems in which the consonant dominates and the syllable is virtual, which means that this writing system contains elements from three systems: logographic writing, syllabaries, and alphabets.

What did a reader do when he read Old Persian cuneiform? For the logograms, he read them as total signs and interpreted them as such. For the rest, he constantly discriminated between all the readings that were graphically possible in principle; he chose or declined to read the vowel *a*. To do this he called on his knowledge of the lexicon and the morphology at the same time he kept an eye on the signs that followed. In Old Persian, as well, it was necessary to understand in order to read, since reading and understanding were integral to the writing system. Old Persian cuneiform is partly syllabic in origin, but it is a really paradoxical syllabary, which does not write the syllable as the basic sound of perceived speech coming from the exterior, but as the sound chosen by the reader.

The three graphic systems we have just seen all express the sound in writing, but place its point of application in the speaking, reading, and writing subject. Cuneiform syllabaries wrote the heard syllable, the sound that strikes the eardrum and that the ear and the brain process by dividing it up. In such a system the syllable appears as a thing in the external world, comparable to the things represented by pictograms or to things in speech, the words, which stand in for the things in the world themselves. Writing syllables seems an excellent solution, with its moderate number of signs and its reproduction of heard speech, which symbolizes the first impression that the subject has of language in its ontogeny: just like life, it is something that is received. But humans were not at all content with this.

Writing had transformed their relation to language, to themselves, and to the world. Through writing, humans slowly but surely took hold of language, and systems using logograms and heard syllables were no longer sufficient. Humans wanted to write their language from within, from the point of view of the speaker. This was a radical, absolute, irremediable revolution, which condemned to oblivion the old writing worlds, Egypt, Mesopotamia, and Elam, with their logograms and their various phonetic writing systems. It was a revolution that was achieved, already in the first half of the second millennium, through alphabets with consonantal sound matrixes on which we still depend today.

In these alphabets the unit of analysis of the language remained the syllable, but this syllable changed in nature. In Mesopotamia it was thought as a heard syllable, but from then on it was thought as virtual—not written but produced in the act of reading. An invisible boundary was crossed: the syllable reduced to a consonantal sound matrix was a paradoxical syllable, spoken, but with a unique articulation. Although it was virtual, the syllable remained the indispensable stage between signs and language, between reading and understanding, but in contrast, the consonant, which alone was written, was maintained as it was in the network of its semantic function, of its lexical and grammatical adherence. In this network the consonant was not a true consonant, contrasting with the vowel and forming a pair with it; rather, it represented an articulatory matrix, but without breath, which came from elsewhere.

The syllable, sharing the reading with the consonant, was anticipated in Old Persian cuneiform; the reader chose the correct reading with or without the vowel *a*. This choice, as we shall see, was a religious one.

There are no syllables in the Greek script, which expresses in writing the positions of the sound-making organs and shows the speaking body. Writing proceeds linearly in time, as does speech. Logically, as we have seen, the Greeks had problems with consonants, for their signs for the occlusive consonants *p, t, k, b, d, g* no longer referred to sounds at all. Yet occlusives are particular phonemes; on one hand, the most recent acoustic studies still do not enable us to give a mathematical definition of these sounds; on the other, typological linguistics shows us that no known human language, past or present, is without occlusive consonants, those nonsounds that block the flow of breath, freeze the muscles, and necessitate a mastery of oneself. By contrast, *in abstracto* vowels would be perfectly sufficient to form a language.

In their universality, occlusives state that language, the human sound and speech, is intention and construction based upon intention: wanting to say is a leap into the unknown, a break with the instant when one wanted nothing at all, a risk placing the speaker in a perilous situation, between the silence he no longer wants and the impossible control of time going by.

Picto-logographic writing systems and systems of heard syllables continued to show humans that language and speech were not a field for them to experiment and create in. They protected them from the awareness of their own intentions and of their freedom in the language. Consonantal writing revealed the word and the articulatory matrix, leaving a void between the two, the void of the real syllable and real speech. Here, again, signs did not say that humans owned the language. In the Greek alphabet the consonant was in opposition to the vowel. From that time, the sign for the consonant was no longer a phonetic sign. The rationality of the complete alphabet is striking, because here each isolated sound of the language must be written in an autonomous way; it nevertheless hides the deeper irrationality that we have seen: one sound = zero sign (aspirate *h*) and one consonantal sign = one nonsound. What characterizes the complete alphabet, from the Greek alphabet to our own, remains a tension between the rational and the irrational, the impossible graphic trapping of the intention of speech and the endless current behind the passing of time.

Perhaps we have here an opportunity to ask ourselves questions about the relations between the Orient and the West. What were their respective positions with regard to writing?

The first approximation is that there were two Orients: the one whose writing systems left a remainder and the one whose writing systems left hardly any remainder, while in the Greek West, writing did not leave any at all. What is this remainder? It is what was included in the value of the signs and was not needed for reading at the time of the actual reading. In the Elamite syllabary, the sign ⟶⊤ could be read as the determinative meaning "divine" before the names of gods, or as *nap,* the Elamite name for "god," or even as the syllable *an;* all three values were possible, and all three readings were correct. When the reader chose one of them, those he rejected, although legitimate, were a remainder.

In the Old Persian cuneiform, if the reader did not read the inherent *a,* he was not making a mistake but a choice foreseen by the spelling. The vowel he left out constituted a remainder.

The remainders were not consubstantial with consonant alphabets, nevertheless, they attested to it; indeed, the weak consonants, serving as *matres lectionis* and indicating a vocalic timber, lost their consonantal character on reading and thus produced a remainder. In Greek, the complete alphabet left no remainders, for everything that was written—and nothing but that—had to be read. Thus the matter of the aspirate *h,* which disappeared from writing in Athens in 403, was related to the problem of remainders, but in the reverse sense: the Athenians preferred that writing be in deficit and that it give less rather than more.

Alphabets existed in the Orient and the West, but the graphic remainder separated them. The Orientals—some more than others—liked rich writing, which overflowed with meaning and signs; Westerners preferred theirs poor. The Orientals liked to be caught up in and enveloped by signs; Westerners liked to limit the signs.

CHAPTER SEVEN

Old Persian Cuneiform: Writing
as Cosmological Ritual and Text

In the preceding two chapters we examined three graphic systems
that brought about the blossoming, the development, and the sur-
vival of great literary civilizations to the present time.

The success of these systems is a problem in itself. Does it come
from the way the languages were written? This was assuredly so in
the beginning, because writing enabled the preservation of texts of
laws, economic dealings, accounts of victories, the content of treaties, religions and myths, mathematical research, and so on. These
writing systems participated in the growth of those civilizations.
But none of all that is enough to explain their incredible longevity,
for languages do change.

Success and longevity come from the fact that those civilizations
each developed an explanation of what language is, as they have
done for all unchanging aspects of the human condition: birth,
death, sexual difference, and family ties, among other things. Unlike us, those civilizations did not consider language to be the ex-
clusive domain of humans but rather as something invisible that
had something to do with the world of the invisible gods. The various theories of language that people have invented are actually a
sociological and historical fact.

It indeed seems that writing has played a role in the development
of those ideas. In Elam, Mesopotamia, and Egypt, writing had become the eternal meeting place between humans and their gods;
it insinuated itself alongside prayers to reproduce them, alongside
rituals in order to perpetuate them. Perhaps writing had made it
seem that language was the threshold to the invisible. By evoking
the dead, by expressing the past or the future, something potential
and virtual, that is, the unknown that is the future of mankind on
earth and, especially, after death, by the even more refined expres-

sion of the unreal, which is not possible in all languages, language had the ability to place human beings in the presence of what was not visible, of what was not or no longer present, or of what perhaps did not even exist. But this so obvious fact was not always perceived as such, for humans had long preferred to meet their gods face-to-face, through dreams, hallucination, shamanic journeys, and so on.

Writing thus became the means of acquiring access to what was invisible: just think of the many written requests for healing and compensation for an injustice sent by the faithful to the Egyptian gods in the second millennium, entrusted to the priests or thrown anywhere; of the Elamite (and other) curses in inscriptions; or of certain divinatory procedures. To reach divine justice or pity, writing turned into magic. It also represented the prestigious tool to get to know the gods in the two great scientific civilizations of antiquity. Pascal Vernus, writing on Egypt, and Jean Bottéro, writing on Mesopotamia, have shown how—by combining signs, as well as their various logographic and phonetic values, and by further combining those values to those of related signs—the intellectuals of the ancient Orient used the writing of proper names of gods to know and to describe Amon Re in Egypt and Marduk in Babylonia. These two writing systems, characterized by a potentially infinite combination among the various values of their signs—images, words, and sounds—provided the necessary terrain for experimentation in order to make progress in their knowledge of the invisible.

Considering that speech in prayer already served as a link between the gods and humans well before writing, what would symbolically become of it when writing with consonant alphabets, Old Persian cuneiform and the Greek alphabet wrote the sounds from the point of view of the speaking subject? Speech assumed a central position and now typified man as sacrificer, as well as humans in general. Since speech is a universal human phenomenon, it was not thought, lived, or made real in the same way in all cultures, civilizations, and their histories. It is fascinating to attempt to understand, thanks to the work of ethnologists, what speech must have been like in "barbaric" societies. Pierre Clastres has become well known for doing this.[16] In the societies he describes, the chief was fundamentally without power, but endowed with powerful prestige. As a good speaker, he assumed the role of moderator of the group, not that of judge; that is, he settled internal conflicts through speech. In many societies he was forced to give a speech every day, to which no one listened and whose content never varied. In essence, what he said was: We must live according to tradition, as the ancestors have set forth, in peace, honesty, and harmony. The chief therefore owed the speech; it constituted his duty, and an absolute obligation weighed upon it. Thus, speech did not belong to the chief, and it did not signify an authorization to say what he desired; rather, it necessitated the effacing of himself and typified a pure recall of tradition. The chief's speech perpetually reaffirmed that language is outside human beings and that in language the person is dependent on his ancestors and on invisible powers.

The speech of warriors—the masculine members of the group—and that of women had the very same status. Whenever they welcomed strangers, the women gathered together and sang a sad song evoking the human condition, made of birth and death; it was the song of mothers who give birth to mortals and who efface their power of giving birth in that undifferentiated, impersonal, and always identical plaint. The scene Clastres describes in which the Guayaki warriors sing around the fire by night, huddled together to stay warm, is unforgettable. Each warrior sings a recitative producing such a cacophony that no one could hear or understand anything. It is one and the same harsh speech of glorification of himself as a great conquering warrior, a speech of pride with a single and common refrain: "I, I, I." Sung in the presence of others, this speech was, however, solitary, uttered to the void. Here, too, language was not of the men and the speech was not of the subject.

We have seen that in Elam, writing was connected to the political systems, to the state, and to the sacral hierarchy among people, that it was born of the obligation of the subjects to the king or the priest—an obligation of goods and of work. To this was very frequently added the expression "I am yours," which the subject said to his king and the king to his god, in which was expressed both an ontological dependency and the obligation of speech in dependency.

Writing trickled into the theories of language and brought about a new theory of speech. By expressing in writing the language of the subject's interior, writing became the mover of a new concept of speech, language, man, the world, and the gods: the form in which human beings were to think the world.

To understand how writing became that form represents a huge undertaking, for which we can only lay the foundations here. But this undertaking has become indispensable, for photography, radio, film, television, video, and microcomputers have caused us to leave behind the practices of writing and speech that our ancestors left to us.

Compared to the longevity of other writing civilizations, Iran is the perfect counterexample. Mazdean Iran demonstrates a particularly tortuous history of writing. An Iranist who studies antiquity must consider the languages of ancient Iran (Avestan, Old Persian, Middle Persian, and, finally, Modern Persian) and their scripts (the Avestan alphabet, Old Persian cuneiform, the Pahlavi system, and the Arabo-Persian alphabet). In addition, in order to read the texts emanating from the centers of Iranian power during the Achaemenid period, one must know Greek and its alphabet, Elamite and Akkadian, written in cuneiform, and Aramaic and Hebrew, written in consonant alphabets. The same dazzling graphic and linguistic multiplicity confronts those who study Parthian and Sassanian Iran.

How is it that a civilization, in the course of two millennia, used so many writing systems and languages? Mesopotamia had at least Sumerian and Akkadian (in two principal dialects, Babylonian and Assyrian) and wrote them using cuneiform script, realized in various ways, but homogeneous in its principle and its history. Egypt developed its language throughout its long historical adventure and wrote it with three graphic systems—hieroglyphic, hieratic, and demotic—but the various states of the language and the three writing systems were all derived from each other. In Iran the writing systems did not derive from each other, and the languages are completely unrelated to each other, for example, Aramaic, Elamite, and Old Persian in Achaemenid antiquity; Greek, Arabic, Armenian, and Middle Persian for the Sassanian period.

When a civilization recognizes itself in such varied writing systems and languages, can there nevertheless be some permanence in the history of its writing systems? In order to find this permanence, which one senses vaguely, but everything denies, we must go to a level beyond linguistic analysis and show that there is a crystallization between the linguistic aspect of writing and the theory that the Iranians of Mazdean antiquity applied to symbolize and socialize language.

Iran in the strict sense, that of the Indo-Iranians and not that of the Elamites, began with the linguistic documentation of Avestan texts. The language of the Avesta, the sacred book of the Mazdeans, is in two linguistic stages. Old Avestan is the language found in the most ancient parts of the corpus: the *Gāthās*, "Hymns" (metrical), and the *Yasna Haptanghāti,* "the Sacrifice in seven chapters" (non-metrical), which, at the time of the composition of the sacred corpus, were included in the book called *Yasna,* "Sacrifice." Young(er) Avestan is the language of the later parts of the Avesta: the non-Gāthic *Yasna,* the *Yasht,* "Hymns," and the *Vidēvdāt,* "Law about how to discard the Demons," to cite only the most important ones.

The Avesta as we know it seems to have been written down only around the sixth century A.D., but the *Gāthās* and the *Yasna Haptanghāti* must have been composed orally well before that, perhaps around the tenth century B.C. This date is not meant to be a true chronological reference but to provide a relative marker without any historical substance, since we do not at all know the date of these texts, nor do we know where the community that composed them lived or how it lived, and we know nothing of Zarathustra, their alleged author. It remains that the Old Avestan texts were probably conceived without the use of writing and that it is possible to grasp the theory of language of the ancient Iranians who composed them.

The *Gāthās* and the *Yasna Haptanghāti,* the heart of the sacred Mazdean texts, are addressed to the principal god, Ahura Mazdā, "the Wise Lord." These texts were recited in front of the fire during ritual sacrifice, and in them the speakers, that is, the Gāthic community, the chanter, the sacrificer (that is, the one who ordered the sacrifice), and, finally, Zarathustra, said why they worshiped Ahura Mazdā and proclaimed their principal theologoumenon: Ahura Mazdā was responsible for the cosmogony. While they carried out the sacrifice, they recited these texts, which were specifications for the ritual, in the sense that when they acted and spoke, what they said gave the religious reason for what they were doing.

One part of the Mazdean discourse on ritual revolved around the concept of *manyu,* commonly translated as "state of mind," but which J. Kellens believes to mean "opinion," which was understood as "opinion concerning Ahura Mazdā"; it was first and foremost an "agent of thought," for *manyu* comes from the root *man,* "to think,"[17] but the *manyu* of Ahura Mazdā was also the manifestation of his power of mind, which decided and ordained, visible in the fire. The *manyu* of human beings, qualified as "primary" since it constituted a decisive act of thought, manifested itself in the judgment that stated that Ahura Mazdā alone was responsible for the cosmogony. If Ahura Mazdā was responsible for the cosmogony, then it was clear which ritual was to be chosen, which gods to be rejected, and which behavior to follow in the ritual, as in life. The

CLARISSE HERRENSCHMIDT

one who made the decision to utter this "opinion" aligned his life on the side of good words, thoughts, and deeds, on the side of the creation of Ahura Mazdā, and of the good life on earth and in the hereafter.

A Mazdean's first opinion consisted approximately in the following pronouncement, which is not found in the texts but implied therein: Ahura Mazdā, he who is characterized by being, fashioned us the Mazdeans with our corporeal being, our religious conscience, our senses, and our intelligence; he has given a body of bones for movement in life; he is the father of cosmic order; he has established the path of the sun and the stars; he has held the earth below and the clouds from falling; he has established the waters and the plants, the divisions of the day; he has instituted ritual law; he is the sole active and powerful guarantor against the evil gods, the lie, death.

This first opinion leaves the nature of death and evil only hinted at, with hints that must have been clear for the ancient Mazdeans, but which remain quite obscure for us. Death and evil are represented by lying Disorder and associated with the *daiva*—"bad gods, demons," which some people worshiped; along with death, evil, and demons, there were powers at work against the creation of Ahura Mazdā; and there was even a leader of the followers of lying Disorder, but to speak of them clearly would, to the minds of the ancient Mazdeans, have amounted to strengthening them. The allusive style of the Old Avestan text with regard to evil powers indeed makes a description of ancient Mazdean dualism quite difficult.

The *"Yasna* in seven chapters," an Old Avestan nonmetrical text, deals in a somewhat obscure way with Mazdean cosmology. From the beginning, this text is devoted to the conceptual triad that forms the basis of Mazdean anthropology. The Mazdeans knew that Ahura Mazdā put the world in order thanks to his good thoughts, words, and deeds. In turn, humans had to direct their behavior along those principles. Those who recited the *"Yasna* in seven chapters" proclaimed from the outset that they applied that triad as a framework for the sacrifice they were offering to Ahura Mazdā:

> We are the praisers of the well-thought [thoughts], of the well-spoken [words,] and of the well-performed [actions]—both [those that are now] being performed and [those] that have been performed here and elsewhere—as we are not blamers of the good [things]. (*Y* 35.2)[18]

The rest of the text explains that good thoughts, good words, and good deeds in the ritual gave power over the god. This power is the magic charm exercised by people over the gods, which enabled them to obtain what they asked of the gods: peace for their herds, health, and immortality, that is, life in the hereafter. Humans were not passive but acted within the ritual, and if they only acted according to good thoughts, words, and deeds, following the gods' desires, and with knowledge of their actions, then they expected the gods to reciprocate. The path taken by humans was the performance of the cult according to the rules, and the gods in return took the path of ensuring that the wishes addressed to them were fulfilled.

In the middle of the triad, words and speech had a specific status. Thus, the chanters say in verse 9 of the same hymn:

> With a better opinion, O Wise Ahura, we wish to proclaim these statements [and] words [as identical to] Cosmic Order. We adopt Thee [to be for us] their returner and launcher. (Y 35.9)

This brings us to the heart of the issue: Ahura Mazdā was the launcher of words and speech; human beings caught them and returned them to him. Indeed, the text specifies further on:

> Quoting the names which the Wise Ahura, giver of [what is] good, gave You [goddesses of the waters] O Good ones, when he created You, we worship You with them, we appease [You] with them, we revere [You] with them, we invigorate [You] with them. (Y 38.4)

The names of divine beings—here, the goddesses of the waters—which were invented by Ahura Mazdā and which were repeated by humans, reinforced the strength of their owners. It is a characteristic of the Iranian cult that people reinforced the gods and increased their immortality through the cult—as incomprehensible as this may be for us. The ritual uttering of divine names gave strength to the invisible ones who bore them and assured the optimal success of the ritual and access to the requests that men made to the gods. But that uttering had to be extremely precise and perfect. In serving fire, here is what had to be said to it:

> Thou art indeed the Fire of the Wise Ahura. Thou art indeed His most beneficent agent of thought. With these names or with the name "most conveyor" among your names, O Fire of the Wise Ahura, we attend thee. (Y 36.3)

The ritual fire attracted a mass of speculation, in which it is not simple to see clearly; it was the son of Ahura Mazdā and was identified with the principal entity of ancient Mazdaism, the cosmic order *(arta),* which bore the title of *ahura,* "lord," indicating a divine personification. Ahura Mazdā could use the sky as body and the fire as mouth, because the fire conveyed his linguistic creations; it made them crackle in the ears of humans. Ahura Mazdā's fire did not deceive humans but told them the truth in the form of the names of things. Humans captured and repeated those names. Here are those that had to be uttered for Ahura Mazdā:

> Him we worship [pronouncing His] Ahurian names "dear," "wise," "most beneficent." We worship him with our bones and vitalities. (*Y* 37.3)

The good Mazdeans captured the words created by Ahura Mazdā by listening to the fire, because the fire conveyed both the words of the god and the speech of humans. The flipside of the coin were the non-Mazdeans or the bad Mazdeans, who allowed themselves to be used by the followers of demons, the *daivas,* and by the followers of lying Disorder, the antithesis of the cosmic and ritual Order:

> Whether it is the supporter of the cosmic Order or the follower of lying Disorder who has the greater [power?]. Let the knowing one tell the knowing one. Let the ignorant one no longer delude [people]. Be the launcher of good thought for us, O Wise Ahura. Let no one listen to the formulas and teachings of the lying Disorder. For he will put house, village, district, and country in a bad [state of] dwelling and in ruin. (*Y* 31.17–18)

The rest of the text shows that Zarathustra served on behalf of humans as an intermediary between them and the fire, as fire, on behalf of the divine, served as an intermediary between the gods and humans. Thus:

> You listen to the formulas and teachings [of Zarathustra], he who understood Cosmic Order, the healer of existence, who is in control of his tongue with a view to a straight utterance of words, [who listens and knows the formulas of the Wise One] by means of thy Red Fire. (*Y* 31.19)

Zarathustra was therefore a prophet in the etymological sense, but in Mazdean prophecy, the status of language was different than it was in the case of the prophets of the Old Testament or of Muhammad. These prophets, standing in front of the people to whom they were speaking and having God behind them, spoke in the name of God, whereas Zarathustra, in front of Ahura Mazdā, to whom he was speaking, and standing before the fire in the very act of sacrifice, spoke in the name of the human community that surrounded him and whom he represented.

Zarathustra captured the divine acts in language, that is, names, as the fire crackled them out, an excellent conveyor of the linguistic creations of Ahura Mazdā. Zarathustra captured them through his superior intelligence, arranged these data, arranged them according to the sovereign order of his poetic language and his intelligence, and sent them back. Zarathustra—an interpreter of signs, poet, prophet, first and principal actor of the Mazdean ritual of the word—invented the formulas and the sacred corpus. It all was as if the divine Ahura Mazdā formed the names, the words, the lexicon, everything the Mazdeans thought to be the fundamental plan of language, and the mortal Zarathustra its hymnic, poetic, musical, ritual, and learned realization, in linguistic terms, syntax, rhetoric, and prosody.

Language was not the property of the divine; it was divided between gods and human beings, the former being responsible absolutely for what it was and how it was born, the latter for its realization, speech in the course of time—for human beings were in time and Ahura Mazdā outside of time.

Let us now look at how this theory of language inspired the creation of Old Persian cuneiform. But first we must envision the transformations of history, for a few centuries went by between the period of the composition of Old Avestan texts (perhaps the tenth century B.C.) and the Achaemenid period (from the sixth to the fourth century), centuries during which the Iranians moved around and perhaps created new social relationships, without our being able to say more, for we know nothing about this obscure time.

During the Achaemenid period, the king fulfilled the function of intermediary between humans and the gods; he was the supreme sacrificer and the one who ordered the sacrifices. It also appears that the king knew the sacred texts and through his speech returned to Ahura Mazdā the names that Ahura Mazdā had created and Zarathustra had expressed (captured and put into form). Several artistic representations show him alone before the fire, without one of the Magi, who were the priests of the Mazdean religion. According to their religious knowledge, the *Gāthās* placed the fire and Zarathustra in ritual and linguistic relation, whereas the Achaemenid reliefs show the Persian king and the fire. In the Achaemenid period, at

CLARISSE HERRENSCHMIDT

least under Darius I and Xerxes, Zarathustra's role was reenacted by the king.

In their Old Persian texts, Darius and his successors began by giving their "first opinion," which, as we have seen, was the basis of the Mazdean belief and consisted of the affirmation that it was Ahura Mazdā who was responsible for the cosmogony. Most of the texts began in this way:

> Ahura Mazdā is the Great God, who established that sky, who established this earth, who established man, who has given happiness in the hereafter to man who sacrifices to him, who made Darius king.

Then, in reciting the next sentence, the king turned toward the people and explained to them who he was and how far his empire extended:

> I am Darius [for example] the great king, the king of kings, the king of peoples of many tribes, the king on this great earth that extends very far, the son of Vishtaspa, the Achaemenid, Persian son of Persia, Aryan of Aryan stock.

After the "first opinion," establishing the absolute character of Mazdaism and the Mazdean legitimacy of the ruler, followed by the titles of the king, all the texts are broken into, as it were, rhythmic sections, marked by the king's statement: "King X announces." He announced that he has conquered all the lands and that he ruled over an empire identical to the inhabited earth, that those subject to him brought him tributes, that he had this text composed, that he had this palace constructed, that his actions were in the sphere of good thought, good speech, and good deeds. His speech, connecting the visible and the invisible, first offered to Ahura Mazdā the first opinion he demanded, then it turned toward the people and installed order among them and uttered the laws of the king, that is, orders to worship Ahura Mazdā and not the bad gods, to pay tribute, to construct, to keep herds, to pay workers, to offer a gift to women who have given birth. Everything followed, even if little of this is told in royal inscriptions.

The Achaemenid formulary, established under Darius in the final years of the sixth century, was resumed by the first Sassanian kings in the third century A.D. and was written in the language of that time, Middle Persian in Pahlavi script. The language changed and the writing system was entirely altered, but the symbolic status of the royal speech did not vary. In fact, it was not to vary until the end of the political and religious autonomy of Mazdean Iran. In the *Dēnkart* (III, 58), a Mazdean encyclopedia of the ninth century A.D.— written while Iran was adopting Islam—"the fundamental opinion" of the Gāthic and Achaemenid texts was expressed as follows:

> The basis of the Mazdean religion is the fundamental declaration, the founding speech bearing on the submission to Ahura Mazdā, declaring the primordial creation of Ahura Mazdā.

As in the Old Avestan text, the linguistic prototype of names and formulas was created by Ahura Mazdā. A passage from the first chapter of the *Bundahishn,* another text from the ninth century A.D., shows both the global permanence of these representations (the *ahuvar* was the most holy prayer of Mazdaism, the one that served as a prelude to the initial creation as well as to the struggle against the powers of evil) and the presence of Greek philosophy:

> Ahura Mazdā drew from the form without beginning the light without beginning.
> Out of the form without beginning he created the *ahuvar.*

In these same Mazdean texts we find the idea that the king is at the center of the exchange of speech, at the point of contact between the invisible and the visible, before the sacrificial fire (*Dēnkart,* chaps. 195–202). These are chapters that condense the advice given to humans by various sacred figures of Mazdaism: Zarathustra, the wise Āturpāt-e Māraspandān, and finally the king of kings, Khosrō Ānushīrvān, the historical king of the seventh century who became a philosophical figure. The king advises the Mazdeans to "unite one's thought, beyond the channel of one's own nature, to the highest nature of the visible and tangible world which is the supreme king, conform to Mazdean religion."

After this rapid presentation of the theory of language in archaic and in historical Mazdaism, it is appropriate to return to the scripts to observe the conceptual ties that unite the Mazdeans' theory of language with their writing system.

Old Persian cuneiform, the first writing system known in ancient Iran, was invented at the beginning of the Persian Empire, between 550 and 520. We have seen that it includes three vocalic signs; twenty-two consonantal signs with inherent *a* that can be read either as the consonant alone or as the syllable formed by that consonant with *a;* eleven signs whose inherent vowel is either *i* or *u;* a sign for separating words; and five logograms, namely, Ahura Mazdā, the title of god, the title of king, the earth, and the land. This system was used primarily to write down the royal texts, great monumental inscriptions located at central points in Achaemenid Iran.

The reader of Old Persian, and in antiquity there were undoubtedly very few, recognized the logograms and so with a single glance identified the signs that embodied the great concepts of the Achaemenid world: first the divine beings, Ahura Mazdā and the title of god; then the inanimate things created by Ahura Mazdā and ruled over by the king: the earth and the land; and finally, the king himself, not represented by his proper name but by his title, since the function was more important than the person. The logograms show us a parcel of the cosmology and the royal ideology: in the sky there are Ahura Mazdā and the other gods; below, the earth, identical to the empire with its various elements, namely, the lands and their populations. Between the two, there is the king, the unique one, creating a link and reproducing on earth through his domination over the lands that of Ahura Mazdā, identified with the sky. This simple and powerful representation of the world, which inspired all Achaemenid texts, was thus manifest in the signs: for the Achaemenids the order of the world and the order of the signs were one and the same.

But these logograms also represented the names created by Ahura Mazdā. In the first place, we have the proper name of the great god. Whereas the other logograms referred to common names, the divine logogram represented a proper name, and, as the origin of language by its principle of naming, Ahura Mazdā named himself. In Old Persian writing, divine utterances enlist the title of god—we may recall that in the "*Yasna* in seven chapters" Ahura Mazdā named the goddesses of the waters—and political concepts: earth, land, king. As the logogram is typically an indecomposable and unanalyzable graphic block, the utterances of Ahura Mazdā—which were also the pillars of the Achaemenid cosmology, legitimacy, and politics—thus escaped from the phonetic decomposition of Old Persian writing. These utterances were located outside of all division and outside all mixture and outside time. This was essential for the Mazdeans, because for them the real world resulted from the mixture of the good and the bad creations.

At the same time, those features of spelling reveal that writing restored the ritual situation in which the sacrificer, the fire, and the god met face-to-face. In fact, just as Zarathustra heard the divine words through the fire and, thanks to his superior intelligence, included them in his religious and poetic formulas, basically so did

Darius. He trapped those same supernatural signs of language and fixed them in logographic immobility, beyond anybody's grasp. We have here one of the most striking practical realizations of what we saw in Elam: the gods were present in the writing, for writing rendered language visible, just as language rendered the inaccessible accessible.

Getting back to the reader, he then had judiciously to insert in its proper place the short *a* of the signs with inherent *a*, leaning on his knowledge of the language, thus reading *adam*, "I," and not *adama* or *adm*; *daiva*, "bad god," and not *diva*; *barantiy*, "they carry," and not *brantiy*, *barntiy*, *brantiya*, or *brantaiy* (other wrong readings were also possible). While reading he employed the mental force called *manyu*, that "agent of thought," that decision at the origin of the "opinion" he uttered, which enabled him to rally to the good side of life. Writing therefore required a choice between the consonant and the syllable, similar to the choice the Mazdeans made between the gods and the demons. Reading amounted to choosing. To choose well, to utter the right reading, was to state the right opinion about the cosmology; it was being Mazdean. Clearly, the text embodied the situation of the ritual choice.

In Mazdaism, the world and history were made up of the mixture of Ahura Mazdā's good creation with the bad creation. The bad gods, the *daivas*, from the start chose the wrong camp, chose badly, opting for lying Disorder, but not knowing that they did. From then on they demanded bad rituals from humans and gave them bad advice. During his lifetime each person had to distinguish Ahura Mazdā's creation from that of the demons, true from false, good from evil, the ally from the enemy. In the confusion of the world he had to choose the good path in order to go to paradise, and he could do so without anguish if he followed the teachings of Zarathustra.

The same is true with Old Persian writing. Putting the short *a* in a vocalic environment could be perilous, since the sequence *da + i* could be read either *dai* or *di*. But the signs with inherent *i* and *u*— m^i, d^i, j^i, v^i, k^u, r^u, g^u, m^u, n^u, d^u, and t^u—prevented wrong, erroneous, even demonic readings, since they forced the sequences $C^a = i$ or u (sign with inherent *a* followed by the autonomous sign *i* or *u*) to be read as diphthongs.

Insofar as the reading of the inherent short *a* reproduced the situation of a ritual choice and the utterance of the good cosmological statement, signs with inherent *i* and *u* showed that there might have existed a bad opinion about the cosmology, but they were there to prevent it from becoming reality. The function of these signs was to prevent the reader from ruining the royal names or certain titles and, by that act alone, from uttering the teachings of the followers of lying Disorder, as we saw earlier in the *Yasna*. In the case of these spellings, reading was the same as repeating the previous elimination of the bad opinion about the cosmology, as Zarathustra had eliminated it in front of the fire and later the king by writing.

The text of the royal inscriptions was always marked by the same dividing phrase, "King X announces," in which the proper name of the signatory king appears and that introduces a new phase of the narrative or the speech. The reader therefore read *exactly* what the king announced, and all the while the text kept repeating the cosmogonic power of Ahura Mazdā and its preservation by the king.

By employing his *manyu*, his "agent of thought," in his reading of the signs, the Mazdean Persian reader uttered the good opinion about the cosmology, showed his choice in favor of Ahura Mazdā. While reading the logograms, he grasped the divine signs, and while reading the diphthongs or the vowels judiciously, he did not name the demons but chose the side of good creation and drew closer to paradise. In reading the text he carried out the ritual choice, repeating the teaching of the prophet, and the announcements and the orders of the king. He joined with the royal speech embodied in the text and so came closer to the gods. In the world as in the reading, the action of the Mazdean consisted of placing himself behind his king, for it was the king who guarded him against all evil. The situation of the ritual under royal authority was projected just as it was into the writing system, where the text was the world, confused and difficult, but writing the key that ordered it and enabled the Mazdean to find himself in it, to make sense of it.

The framework of reasoning that presided over the invention of Old Persian cuneiform was formed by the Mazdean religion, its cosmologic dualism, its speculation on the ritual, and its theory of the language, in brief, by the place of the Achaemenid king in ritual, religion, and politics.

Ritual and writing were therefore connected; in fact, recognizing, grasping, repeating, eliminating, and being careful of error were the technical and mental prerequisites of the ritual before they became those of reading Old Persian. Writing and reading in Old Persian were considered, when the writing was invented, to be ritual acts, for the sacrifice rendered to Ahura Mazdā represented the supreme human act.

The technical and mental prerequisites of ritual were very similar to those of writing. To carry out ritual, the subject had to be part of an encompassing and profoundly significant structure that dominated him, which he understood more or less, yet in which he found the fundamental answers to his condition as a human being. Reading Old Persian cuneiform required the same participation on the part of the reader.

Are we dealing here with something that is specific to Persia, or should the connections between writing and ritual be seen more generally?

From the time of Cyrus and even more so under Darius I and his successors, royal inscriptions were written in three languages—Old Persian, Elamite, and Akkadian—to which was sometimes added Aramaic. The content of these texts hardly varied in the different languages, unlike those of Kutik-Inšušnak in Susa. The Persepolitan administration under Darius I and Xerxes was in Elamite. Thousands of tablets—including receipts for payment, stock lists, travel allowances for royal envoys, permits for withdrawing from state granaries and herds—show how the royal economy functioned around Persepolis and the provinces. There is some small possibility that these tablets, written in the Elamite language and in cuneiform, may have referred to exchanges in the Persian language, that is, that one spoke Persian during administrative transactions but wrote in Elamite and that, when one read the Elamite text, it was translated into Persian.

For the most part, however, texts destined to go abroad—diplomatic documents (to which the Book of Esther in the Bible bears witness) but also internal documents, royal archives (which have, alas, disappeared)—were for the most part written in Aramaic. Most of the texts emanating from the central Achaemenid power, though thought, conceived, indeed dictated in the Persian language, were written in Elamite or in Aramaic, sometimes in Greek, but read in Persian.

Why? Because the Achaemenids were delayed in the movement of the history of writing by choosing to write their language in cuneiform. Cuneiform, requiring heavy and cumbersome materials such as stone and metal or fragile materials such as clay, was already being replaced by Aramaic in the Neo-Assyrian Empire (from the fourteenth to the seventh century), which preceded the Median and Persian Empire, for Aramaic was written in cursive on light and transportable materials (papyrus, leather, pottery shards). But there is perhaps another reason.

In the monumental texts in which the king declared the foundations of his legitimacy, he wrote in three or four languages, including his own, whereas the administrative and judicial texts were written in various languages, but never in Persian. In other words, regardless of the language the king wrote, it was not the language that counted, but the royal speech, acting as a replica of the law of Ahura Mazdā and as an ordering of the world of humans by means of that law; for the law of Ahura Mazdā was not only a ritual law, but concerned the totality of the affairs of the world caught up in the Mazdeans' struggle against the bad creation.

The Persians distrusted the principle of the division of sound. Although the principle enabled them to develop Old Persian cuneiform, a useful graphic tool comprised of a small number of signs, they did not pursue it to its end, although they knew the Greek alphabet well. The presence of the five highly symbolic logograms shows that they preferred to conserve immanence in their graphic expression. The history of writing in Iran after the Achaemenids shows the continuity of that distrust, and without going into detail one can say that the writing system used under the dynasty of the Sassanians (A.D. 224–650), Pahlavi, presented some extraordinary peculiarities.

This script served to write the living language Middle Persian, that of the king, among others, with the help of the Aramaic alphabet, thereby perpetuating the practice of the Achaemenid chancellery. In Pahlavi writing, the vowels are badly noted, as is normal when a consonantal writing system is borrowed, and there were more logograms. These logograms are not pure symbols, unanalyzable and indecomposable like the logograms of Old Persian, but are Aramaic words translating Persian words, which prolonged the strange Achaemenid practice of not differentiating the language to the benefit of the royal speech. The word šāh, "king," for example, was not written š-ā-h—which would not have presented any difficulty since the signs š, ā, and h existed—but MLKA, malek, malkā, "king," in Aramaic; the preposition abar, "on," was not written alphabetically, which would have been possible, but was represented by its Aramaic equivalent, QDM. What was most strange was that many verbs, which formed the framework of the phrase, were not written phonetically but in Aramaic heterography; for example, for "to drink, to eat," one wrote the Aramaic OŠTEN and not the

Middle Persian *xwardan,* which is how it was read. How is it that such a diabolical writing system was used for more than a thousand years, that is, from the second century B.C. to the ninth century A.D.? Is it enough to argue the importance of the Magi and the learned scribes, who alone knew how to write and wanted to preserve their power?

But there is more. At an unknown date, perhaps in the sixth century A.D., Avestan writing—which combined the signs of the Aramaic alphabet already utilized in Pahlavi with features of the Greek alphabet—was invented. This writing system contained no logograms and no syllabic sign; rather, it included sixteen vocalic signs—including six types of *a*—and thirty-seven consonantal signs, including several unvoiced dental *t*s. Avestan writing was a superalphabet: a phonetic rather than phonological script. In fact, all these signs represented not the phonemes of a living language; they noted the sounds of a dead language, ancient phonemes transformed by liturgical elocution preserved by oral tradition. It was a manic-compulsive alphabet in the way it sought to capture in writing the minute details of the pronunciation of a dead language.

Such was the situation of writing in Iran around the sixth century A.D. There was the Pahlavi script, full of mysteries to decipher, used to write the living language, and there was the precise Avestan alphabet used for the dead language of the liturgy. In short, one might say that the Sassanian kings did not want a true alphabetical writing system for the uses of everyday life, in spite of the fact that there were among the Persians educated people who knew Greek. The characteristics unique to the complete alphabet—namely, the externalizing through writing of the sound inside the body of the subject, the capturing of the inner speech, and the desymbolization of writing—were not appropriate to the Mazdean mental universe, in which the great god was the origin of language, as well as the master of time and the author of the world, and the king his representative, his interlocutor in the ritual, and his spokesman among other humans.

The fact that the Mazdeans reserved the complete alphabet for the dead language teaches us something about the alphabet. So close to fixing speech and the passage of time, does it not show what cannot be remedied? In fact, we will have the opportunity to see that the history of the complete alphabet is not linear, not that of a technical progress that was imposed without failure or regression, for Iranians and Jews did not give in to reducing their speech to such an alphabet, and the Athenians of 403 distrusted it. Things

CLARISSE HERRENSCHMIDT

are no better today; just think of the extraordinary French orthographic practices (for example, *tend, tan, taon, temps, tant,* all signifying *tã*), which almost require the reader to treat words as logograms.

The theory of language expressed in the Old Avestan texts, which, as far as we know, dates from the time when the Iranians did not have writing, is articulated in the central content of Mazdaism, the ordering of the world by Ahura Mazdā, and in the anthropology and in the foundations of the politics of the ancient Iranian world. For the scholars in the service of the first Achaemenids, it provided the mold in which they formed Old Persian cuneiform.

Revealing cosmology and showing the king positioned between men and the gods, writing represented the ritual that enabled people to be assured of their choices and of the meaning of their deeds. The text had become the world.

CHAPTER EIGHT

Writing—and Some Thoughts
on Hebrew and Greek

... When I ask a question, the response comes to me from passages in the text, which come back to life through my question, whereas the reader without questions glides right through the text. But those answers are real only when I can justify what I understand to be the "intentional meaning" of the text. When the texts of the dead do not answer with meaning, they remain mute.

—Karl Jaspers

The Old Persian script offered us a particularly fruitful field for experimentation, that of a writing system invented ad hoc for a language that did not pose any major philological problems within a fairly well-known political context and based on an oral civilization that wished to set up a language used between humans and the gods following the dualistic order of thought, much simpler than a pantheism or a monism. The hypothesis according to which writing systems endure because they contain a theory of language as a medium between the visible and the invisible enabled us to perceive the relations among writing, ritual, and cosmology.

It would therefore seem logical to investigate the Greek and Hebrew systems from this perspective, too, but the complexity of such an undertaking leads us to study only certain aspects of the history of writing among the Greeks and the Jews, without penetrating into the heart of their respective systems. We will thus not see here how writing became the mold into which humans could pour their thinking of the world and of themselves; writing—which rendered human mental activity visible and objectifiable since it represented the first steps toward the knowledge of knowledge—established a sort of equivalency between the exchange of words and that of things and between goods and words, and shattered the preeminence of group thought and forced humans to redefine themselves.

The theory of language held by the first inventors of consonant alphabets is forever concealed from us. Thus, we cannot know how the Hebrews formulated their theory in the second millennium B.C., but we can nevertheless reconstruct—here in very broad strokes—what the Judeans, having returned from exile, employed during the various stages of the fixation of their sacred corpus and of their history. This theory of language certainly constituted the conceptual framework that enabled the most fascinating feature of the Jewish writing history: the fact that Hebrew, a language of antiquity and a dead language in antiquity, once again became a living language in the twentieth century. To a great degree this concerns the history of the script, for if ancient Hebrew had not been written, no renaissance would have been possible. But this trivial interpretation forces a question that is not so trivial and that we are going to attempt to broach: did consonant writing, with its peculiarities, play a role in the revival of the Hebrew language?

That revival is generally explained by reference to history and politics, namely, that the establishment of the state of Israel in 1948 from a population that had come from a variety of horizons necessitated an oral and written linguistic link, as well as an emotional link with the common tradition. Hebrew was therefore reimplanted by the state of Israel, at the same time as the laws, the schools, and obligatory military service. Here, and for the same reasons as in the case of Kutik Inšušnak, I am a bit reluctant to retain only the political explanation, for a political will in language cannot be justified only with the immediate usefulness or the tradition that it suggests; it goes beyond politics even.

The question should be asked differently: How can a language lose its death?

Jewish civilization, more than any other, is a civilization of writing. It has symbolically exploited the characters of the consonant Hebrew alphabet. Thus, the virtual syllable enabled a particular symbolization of word and speech, whereas the logographical tendency in turn rendered the transcendence of God visible and the alphabetical sign produced a field for experimentation in knowledge. Such were perhaps the conditions that opened the path for a renaissance of Hebrew.

Archaic Hebrew is not well known: it is found in the Gezer Calendar (tenth century B.C.), which lists the months of the year and agricultural work; the most ancient parts of the Bible, the Song of Deborah, for example; and poetic texts that have been connected to certain writings of Ugarit. Classical Hebrew represents the living language between the eighth and the sixth centuries, that of the prophets Hosea, Amos, Isaiah, and Jeremiah, before the Babylonian exile. From the exile there remain the texts of Ezekiel, as well as the magnificent poem of Lamentations. The historical literature was formed during this period: Joshua, Judges, Samuel, Kings, and texts related to Deuteronomy, and the last book of the Pentateuch, but the definitive writing of the Pentateuch must have occurred later. Along with the biblical corpus, there are also a small number of archeological documents written in Hebrew, which are even more revealing, namely, tomb inscriptions, letters, and ostraca (pottery shards used as a medium for writing).

From the period of the exile, Hebrew lost some ground. Indeed, the population that remained around Jerusalem came increasingly into contact with populations from the north and the northeast, who spoke Aramaic. The exiled Judeans in Babylonia spoke several other languages, especially Aramaic, the diplomatic tongue of the Neo-Assyrian and Persian Empires. Back in Jerusalem after 539, when Cyrus the Great allowed them to return, Hebrew was no longer their vernacular language, as Nehemiah says (13:24): "And their children [those of the Jews in exile], spake half in the speech of Ashdod, and could not speak in the Jews' language, but according to the language of each people."

A great number of books composed and written in Hebrew and included in the biblical canon were written after the exile, for example, the books of the prophets of the restoration, Haggai, Zechariah, Malachi, especially Ezra and Nehemiah, Esther, Chronicles, and probably also Jonah, Psalms, and Proverbs.

As a consequence of the conquests of Alexander and of Greco-Macedonian domination, Greek became the language of culture and Aramaic the popular language, a situation that the Roman Empire did nothing to change. Hebrew was the language of the sacred corpus, a literary and religious language, unknown to most of the Jews, but it was a Hebrew exposed to an evolution that, due to the Aramean influence, was as much internal as external. The documents of Qumran, from the second century B.C. until the first century A.D., show a complex linguistic situation. One-quarter of the books of the community are canonical books; another quarter, non-

Figure 8. The Gezer Calendar: seven horizontal lines of Hebrew inscription, one vertical line at left. Wood and gypsum (from Period II), from Gezer, Israel. The first known agricultural calendar. Archaeological Mussue, Istanbul, Turkey. Photo: Erich Lessing/Art Resource, NY.

canonical books, "pseudepigrapha"; and the rest books of rules belonging to the community. A large part of these texts are in Classical Hebrew, but a few are in Aramaic and some in Greek.

The Mishnah, written in a special form of Hebrew beginning in the second century A.D., is a compilation of oral commentaries on the rules and customs contained in the Torah, which, according to the mythical Jewish representation of the word, went back to Moses himself and whose essential preoccupation was the application of the written law, for example, the arrangement necessary to Leviticus. Was Hebrew still a living language or only a language of learned men and scholars? Those living at the time knew very well that the written language of the literate was not the language of the Torah. Hebrew was still spoken at the time of the revolt of Bar Kikhba against the Roman emperor Hadrian, between 132 and 135 A.D., yet later documents, from the fourth and fifth centuries, reveal that it was henceforth a language of the literate and the learned, and so, like Latin in medieval Christianity, Hebrew became the language of exchanges between the Jews of the diaspora.

What is a dead language? It is not a language that ceases to evolve: Latin and Hebrew never stopped evolving as languages of scholars, theologians, jurists, poets, and schoolmasters. A language is dead when it is no longer heard by any baby from when it is born. This is what was understood by Eliezer ben Yehuda, the father of Modern Hebrew, whose mother tongue was Yiddish and who had studied in a Talmudic school to become a rabbi. Having arrived in Palestine in 1881, he decided no longer to speak or write any language other than Hebrew and so his eldest son, born in 1883, heard only Hebrew spoken. It is worth citing a few lines from Ben Yehuda's memoirs here:

> The child's mother was of a fragile nature. . . . Despite all that, she agreed quite willingly not to hire a servant so that the child's ears would hear no sound, no word in any other language than the Hebrew tongue. . . . In the first stages of the experiment . . . we wanted to surround the child's language with successive barriers, with a wall, then another wall, to avoid any contamination to his ear by a foreign sound. This saintly soul . . . lovingly accepted the trials of the education of a child without the least help, in spite of her weak condition, indeed, exhaustion . . . until we had the privilege of hearing the first syllables of Hebrew words uttered by the mouth of the child.[19]

The archaic, or pre-exile, texts—ostraca, scarab seals, inscriptions on stone, tombs, stelae—reveal a refined script, very close to Phoenician, with a supple ductus. This script is still recognizable on coins until around 100 B.C. But from the end of the first millennium B.C., the Torah was written with the square script derived from Aramaic and named thus because all the signs had to be inscribed within a square.

Neither of the ancient scripts, Early Hebrew or Square Hebrew, wrote the vowels. The reader grasped the words, added vowels, and made syllables in his mind. This was one of the aspects used by the later Jewish tradition, but whose origin is ancient, this act of reading in which the reader gave a voice to the text. Thanks to writing it seemed to revive the status of the most ancient speech in Jewish history, namely, when Moses, after seeing the burning bush, re-

CLARISSE HERRENSCHMIDT

ceived the order of Yahweh, he whose name means "I am," to take the people out of Egypt and to speak to them in the following terms: "Thus shalt thou say unto the children of Israel, the Lord God of your fathers, the God of Abraham, the God of Isaac, and the God of Jacob, hath sent me unto you: this (is) my name for ever, and this (is) my memorial unto all generations" (Exod. 3:15).

Then, later in history, whether it concerned Nathan facing David, Elijah facing Ahab, Amos, Hosea, the second Isaiah, Micah, or Jeremiah and Ezekiel—all the prophets were presented as the voice of Yahweh, his messenger and spokesman, the one through whom Yahweh was speaking. Here is Nathan before David: "Thus saith the Lord God of Israel, I anointed thee king over Israel, and I delivered thee out of the hand of Saul. . . . I will raise up evil against thee out of thine own house" (2 Sam. 12:7–14). And in the name of Yahweh, Nathan admonishes David for his dealings with women. Then David recognizes his sin and Nathan stops speaking as a prophet and then speaks as a judge: "The Lord also hath put away thy sin; thou shalt not die. Howbeit, because by this deed thou hast given great occasion to the enemies of the Lord to blaspheme, the child also that is born unto thee shall surely die."

Jewish tradition exploited the virtual syllabism of its script by establishing an analogy between the words of the prophet and the activity of the reader reading the ultimate text, the sacred text. Adding vowels and breath to the text, he appeared to become the one who gave God his sound-making organs and in whom the divine presence was renewed. The vocalic sound of the words, identical to the breath of life, was of divine origin, as is shown in Genesis: "And the Lord God formed man of the dust of the ground, and breathed into his nostrils the breath of life; and man became a living soul" (2:7).

The breath of vowels was therefore not written. On the contrary, the matrix of sounds, that is, the consonantal sign, in its vocalic indifferentiation enabled the reader to show the mythical affiliation that went back from the present to the beginning, from the reader to Moses, from Moses to Adam and to Yahweh. Thus the theory both of the origin of language and of the transmission of the word from the origin of time was metaphorically replayed through writing.

At the end of the first millennium the *matres lectionis,* "mothers of reading," were invented, of which we have already spoken. This process of writing vowel marks that is called *scriptio plena,* "full writing," despite its insufficiencies represented a step toward the writing of vowels. It was practiced by the Essenes of Qumran, who were therefore distinguished by their use of three languages and by the lure of the alphabet. In fact, in the Hellenistic period, the Septuaginta and the documents originating in Qumran showed that the Hebraic texts of the Torah posed problems of comprehension due to the consonant alphabet, to the growing strangeness of the language, and to the evolution of mentalities, and scribes therefore undertook additions and graphic corrections, which were only so many interpretations, however.

There were several attempts other than the *scriptio plena* to indicate vowels; only the Western system called Tiberian was in any way successful, for, invented around the fourth century A.D. and generalized in the Jewish world, it formed a basis for the Masoretic Bible or, more exactly, the Masoretic version of the Bible. The Masoretes, rabbis and scholars of the sixth to the eighth centuries, fixed the essence of their canon, including or excluding certain passages; through the notation of vowels they caused ambiguity to disappear and henceforth made possible only a single, true reading of the Bible. Although there were no autonomous signs for vowels, rather, diacritical signs above and below the consonants (small dots and check marks), the script nevertheless resembled a complete alphabet.

Thus fixed, the Masoretic text was vocalized, except for one word, the divine tetragram, the name of God written YHWH. Today it is phoneticized into "Yahweh" on the basis of its ancient spellings in Greek, but it was not read thus in post-exile Jewish antiquity; where it was not pronounced as it was written but in the forms "Adonai" or *ha šem,* "the name," for example. This sign was read as a logogram in the same way that the Mesopotamians could read the sign for "head," 𒊕, as either as *sag* in Sumerian or *rešu* in Akkadian; the meaning remained the same while the linguistic and phonetic realizations differed. One did not read the separate letters, which referred to sounds, but once they were combined one recognized a sign.

The name of God was thus written in a consonantal fashion in a quasi-alphabetical environment and was read as a logogram; in addition, this logogram resembled nothing recognizable, as Egyptian hieroglyphics or ancient Mesopotamian signs did, which made the situation rather extraordinary.

After what we have seen concerning the origin of the transmission of speech, the comparison between the tetragram and the symbol for God appearing to Moses at Sinai cannot be ignored (Exod. 3:1–6). Moses sees a "fiery" bush that "is not consumed"; he turns aside to see better, but God calls him from the center of the bush, and Moses covers his face. The burning bush as the sign of God resembles a commentary whose model would be the tetragram: a bush that burns yet does not burn; an alphabetical sign that represents a sound yet does not represent any sound; a logogram that indicates its own name, yet that one does not repeat. Moses shades his eyes, that is, he is forbidden to look. In fact, like Moses, the reader of the tetragram was not supposed to read the name of God, neither according to the vowels nor according to the consonants nor according to its aspect. And we see that "do not read" translated in the poor substance of writing, the strangeness of divine transcendence.

The Masoretic version of the Torah begs two remarks. Since almost everything is written down, the reader does not lend his voice, his articulatory organs, to the text; he does not play the role of relay for divine speech. Moreover, it is used to write a dead language, like Avestan in Sassanian Iran. The fate of the complete alphabet and the dead language seem to be linked.

But the essential nature of the consonantal system was not forgotten for all that. It was maintained in the two Talmuds, that of Palestine and that of Babylonia. The Talmuds, commentaries on the written law, came after the Mishnah and, written in two different Aramaic dialects (western and eastern), they constituted compilations of different teachings, sometimes contradictory ones, always aiming to explain the law, to multiply examples to give the Mosaic code, which was vague, a general application. They often deal with tales taken directly from daily life that are extraordinarily pedagogical and sometimes poetical and metaphysical. It was not at all by chance that for the Mishnaic and Talmudic rabbis, the speech of living human beings brought to life the letter of the Torah, for, in reading the written forms of the oral law—the Mishnah and the Talmud—the reader acted following the logic appropriate to the consonant alphabet, that is, he read while lending his breath to the text, as a prophet, as it were, for the vowels were not written down. Thus, the reader of the Talmud doubly reactivated the status of the language of the Jewish civilization; on one hand, by reading only secondary laws, applications, and interpretations, and by practicing a sort of indirect exegesis of the written Torah, he referred to the origin of the language that the latter expressed; on the other, reading the oral law, he placed himself back inside the mythical transmission of the original word.

The alphabetical nature of the signs has provided a vast field for experimentation in knowledge. Around 300 B.C. the letters of the alphabet had a numerical value: *aleph* equaled 1; *beit*, 2; *gimel*, 3; and so on, up to *taw*, which equaled 400; these values led to the blossoming of various ancient speculations. But the most accomplished science of letters, *gematria*, flourished in the Middle Ages. It consisted of calculating the value of a proper name by attributing a numerical value to each letter and then adding or subtracting. One then connected the value obtained either to the letter that represented it or to another word with the same value; the goal of all operations was to find the hidden and fundamental meaning of the word, its semantic heart.

Let us look at one of the examples given by M.-A. Ouaknin and D. Rotnemer in a book on biblical first names, a recent publication but one that introduces nothing new despite its ideological orientation.[20] In order to understand the fundamental hidden meaning, the semantic heart, of the Hebrew word *šem*—written *šm*, "name"—the authors attribute a numerical value to each letter—300 to *š*, 40 to *m*, do the subtraction, obtain 260, look for another word whose value is 260, and find the Hebrew word *sar*, which, according to the authors, means "turning away (from), revolt," but in fact is the Hebrew root SWR, "to leave the road, turn away." They then apply the traditional rule of first occurrence, which consists of looking at the first biblical occurrence of a word for its fundamental semantic orientation, and analyze the first appearance of that root, in Exodus 3:3, in the vision of the burning bush: "And Moses said, I will now turn aside, and see this great sight, why the bush is not burnt."

The authors deduce from this that the semantic heart of the word *sar* is "an ability for encounters, and that encounter is Revelation" and that thanks to numerical equivalences the word reveals the semantic heart of the word *šem*, which appears as "the ability for openness to the event." To demonstrate that it is of the greatest importance to choose the right name for a child, they have turned to the primeval myth of the transmission of the word among the Jews of antiquity, the one related in the Book of Exodus.

The alphabetical nature of Hebrew writing was thus used as a field for knowledge and was so used on the basis of alphabetical principles implying the autonomy and the combination of signs, yet the perspective remained that of an attachment to the divine origin of language. The movement here parallels that of the reading of the Talmud written in virtual syllables: in the former case the reader gives breath back to the language; in the latter the Torah is made into an absolute lexicon.

The Jewish civilization developed in its writing system from antiquity, during the Middle Ages, and up to the eighteenth and nineteenth centuries. In everyday life the Jews of the diaspora spoke various vernacular languages—Yiddish, Judeo-Spanish, Judeo-Arabic, Judeo-Persian in Iran—and gradually, as the modern world was formed, other Western languages. At the same time they continued to receive a scholarly religious education—their education in the sacred text sometimes began at the age of three—and read the Talmud; some of them even had access to the Torah. But they all, the literate and the illiterate, knew the same thing: that Yahweh belonged to the Jews just as the Jews belonged to Yahweh.

Considering that the Modern Hebrew of Israel, that of the schools, the laws, and the newspapers, is written in a consonant alphabet without vowels or diacritical signs, it seems to me that its renaissance can therefore be understood in strictly graphical terms, like the disappearance of the quasi-alphabetical way of writing the Hebrew of the Masoretes.

The resurrection of Hebrew as a language to be taught at birth has rendered obsolete, indeed, has expelled from history, both the alphabetical stage of the Masoretes, which exemplified the death of the language, and the Talmudic stage, which reflected all the exiles of the Jews and gave only an oblique breath to the mother language, the Hebrew of the Torah. This resurrection was made possible through the characters of consonantal writing and through the Hebraic theory of language, which is largely based on writing, and so its horizon is the reactivation of the absolute language, of the myth that the divine origin of language was visible in the transmission of the word. From Yahweh's revelation to Moses, the dictate of the law and the Covenant are immanently there. In writing as in language there is no history.

In 403 B.C., under the archonship of Eucleides, Athens was recovering from horror. Already conquered by Sparta, threatened with extinction by the Peloponnesian League, the humiliated city no longer had an empire that financed democracy. Civil war was tearing it apart. Then peace returned, and amnesty between the enemy parties settled in. It was then that the Athenians changed their alphabet. But let us go back a bit in time.

In 404 Athens had experienced the horrible oligarchical tyranny of the Thirty, who, installed with the complicity of Sparta, placed their own people in public offices, including the Ten in the Peiraeus, who were particularly violent. They massacred the male population of Eleusis, eliminated from Athens all those who could have organized a democratic resistance, and reduced the civil body to three thousand citizens. The majority of citizens thus found themselves deprived of any legal protection and were placed outside the law. People fled from Athens, finding refuge where they could, the poorest in Phyle, then nearby Peiraeus, where the people knew they had nothing to gain from the oligarchs.

From the autumn of that year, war broke out between the Thirty and the democrats, who were led by Thrasybulus. The democrats won battles in spite of their smaller numbers, up to the final battle in the summer of 403 in Munichia. Let us listen to Edouard Will: "An amnesty was proclaimed, from which the survivors of the Thirty and the Ten of the Peiraeus were excluded. . . . The people of Peiraeus went back to Athens after the Peloponnesians left. After a solemn sacrifice on the Acropolis, Thrasybulus exhorted the city to accept a reconciliation and the democratic institutions were put back in place. A page whose final lines had been bloody had been turned."[21]

Civil reconciliation first consisted of a prohibition against returning to the near past of the civil war:[22] "There was to be a total amnesty covering everyone except the Thirty, the Eleven and the ten governors of the Peiraeus; even they were to be immune from prosecution."[23]

A platform was agreed on, according to which a provisional government was elected comprised of twenty men to watch over the city until a code of laws could be established. This new civil order was resolutely in conformity with the ancestral constitution, implying that the Athenians used the laws, weights, and measures of Solon, as well as the ordinances of Draco. A commission of legislators (*nomothetēs*) were elected, who assembled the texts. From that date the laws formed a codified corpus of precise terms, quite different from the incoherent collection they had been up until then. Henceforth the written text was to be a guardian of society. A law of 402 established that the magistrates should in no case use a nonwritten law, that no (oral) decree, whether it was from the council or from the Assembly of the People, could have more authority than a written law. As Martin Ostwald writes: "A new social and political order was worked out that retained the characteristic institutions of the Athenian democracy while subordinating the principle of popular sovereignty to the principle of the sovereignty of law."[24]

We cannot but wonder that in such a legalistic atmosphere, one that valued the writing of the laws and in particular ancestral laws, the alphabet used and made official by the city excluded the aspirated *h* from the writing system, although aspiration remained quite alive in the language. I do not think this fact reveals "inevitable residual ambiguities," as Eric Havelock has called the imperfections of the Greek alphabet.[25] After all, if one hopes to establish a new social order based on written laws, it is necessary that writing avoid any ambiguity; if one, in addition, refers a great deal to the ancestors, one ought to pay great attention to the language, for the language is as much a part of what the ancestors have left to their descendants as are the laws. The Athenians had inherited the aspirated *h* from Draco, Solon, Cleisthenes, Ephialtes, and Pericles, and this raises the new but inevitable question: What is the connection between the way the Athenian laws were written at the time of the democratic restoration and the disappearance from the writing of the aspirated *h*, which was well attested in the spoken language of Athens?

Before answering the question in detail, let us look at two facts: on one hand, why did they choose to write the *eta*, but not the *h*, and, on the other, what did the aspirated *h* mean for the Greeks, who called it *pneuma*, "breath"?

In 403 the aspirate was no longer written in Athens, but open $\bar{e}$ (*eta*) and open $\bar{o}$ (*omega*) were. Up until then these two vowels were not differentiated in writing from the closed *e* (*epsilon*) and the closed *o* (*omicron*). In deciding between the aspirate and the $\bar{e}$, the Athenians chose to write the vowel. There was no inevitability in that; in fact, when the Ionic alphabet of Asia was adopted in Tarentum, following Athens and the entire Greek world, the open $\bar{e}$ was written with *eta* without losing the aspirate: the sign *H* lost its right half, and from then on there were two signs deriving from *H*: one for the open $\bar{e}$ (*H*) and another for the aspirate *h* (⊢). Why did the Athenians not think of this simple, though hardly mind-boggling, solution to the graphic problem? Well, they had their reasons.

Their decision to write the vowels is like starting the invention of Greek writing, which differed from its consonantal Phoenician model by the writing of vowels, all over. Thus the year 403 was a crucial one in Athens, when writing was reinvented in order to set down the laws of the city, where they seemed to be reliving the origin.

Before looking at what the aspirated *h*, which the Greeks called *pneuma*, meant to them, we must understand what aspiration is from an articulatory point of view. The sound "aspirated *h*" (an inadequate term; one should say "exhaled *h*") is produced by the free flow of air through the glottis; the acoustical organs are therefore open, not blocked as for an occlusive, nor slightly closed as for a fricative. In prescientific phonetics this openness was supposed to classify the *h* among the vowels, but unlike vowels, which necessitate facial contortions to pronounce them (*i* with the mouth tightly stretched, *o* with the lips rounded), to produce aspiration the mouth doesn't move; the sound coming from the glottis does not reverberate in the resonators (mouth and larynx) and remains without a timber—as with a consonant. In short, the *h* resembles a pure exhaled sound, going from the pulmonary breathing of the speaker outward to the vast world; it represents the matrix of speech.

Thus it is not surprising that the Alexandrian Greek philologists of the third century B.C. gave *h* the name *pneuma*, "breath, spirit," and, subsequently "rough breathing." A pseudo-Aristotelian text (*De audibilibus* 804 b 10)[26] thus distinguishes between the simple unvoiced occlusive consonants, *aphona psila* (*p, t, k*), and the aspirated unvoiced occlusive consonants, *aphona dasea* (*ph, th, kh*): the latter differing from the former by the emission of breath. This means that the aspirated unvoiced bilabial occlusive, written with the letter *phi*, was analyzed as being equal to *p* + *h* and the simple unvoiced bilabial occlusive as equal to *p*. The Alexandrian grammarians and the Aristotle of *De audibilibus* had observed the articulation of aspiration and occlusion. Thus when the Greeks had to give a name to a sound or a letter, to represent its character with a symbol, they did not do so on the basis of the shape of the sign or on any name, the first sound of which would be the sound of that sign, but by analyzing the production of the sound in the body of the subject.

The fact that it was Alexandrian grammarians and not Athenian ones of the fifth century who baptized the sound and the sign *h* in no way changes the interpretation of that *pneuma*, for the Greeks had no other choice: aspiration, from an articulatory point of view, comes from the breath, and in Greek "breath" was called *pneuma*.

This word, before becoming a linguistic concept, had an interesting variety of meanings: for Empedocles and the Hippocratic corpus and in common usage it was "air of respiration, breath," and in Aeschylus (*Persians* 507) it was "breath of life": "Happy is he who first loses the breath of life." On the other hand, for Sophocles (fragment 13) *pneuma* was only a current of air: "Man is but breath and shadow."

Two texts, one by Democritus, the other by Sophocles, have a different semantic orientation. In Democritus (B 18) the *pneuma* is sacred and seems to circulate vertically, from the divine to the humans whom god inspires: "What a poet writes under the blow of divine transport and of sacred breath is altogether beautiful." For Sophocles (in *Oedipus at Colonus*), on the other hand, *pneuma* goes between humans horizontally. One cannot resist the beauty of this passage—Oedipus speaking to Theseus:

> Most gentle son of Aegeus! The immortal
> Gods alone have neither age nor death!
> All other things almighty Time disquiets.
> Earth wastes away; the body wastes away,
> Faith dies; distrust is born.
> And imperceptibly the spirit [*pneuma*] changes
> Between a man and his friend, or between two cities.[27]

We are dealing here with something other than pulmonary air: humans bound by friendship are the citizens, and *pneuma* refers to the breath, to the spirit, that reigns in their relationships, as in those between cities. Sophocles wrote *Oedipus at Colonus* shortly before his death in 405, and this tragedy, which was performed in 401, is as much a hymn to Athens as a curse addressed to the enemies of the city. Suspicion and the breath of discord do not feature in it as poetic metaphors, for we are dealing with the war that was close at hand. Between 405 and 401, in Athens *pneuma* was understood to mean "the spirit in relationships between citizens and between cities."

These various meanings of *pneuma*—the condition of life in the form of vital breath, the breath of inspiration from on high, spirit in the relationships between citizens and cities—this wealth of denotations nevertheless does not explain the reason for the graphical disappearance of the aspirated *h*.

It is difficult to go any further on the basis of these elements alone.[28] To nourish our thought we must turn to Aristotle. The *Constitution of Athens* (paras. 39–40) relates the events of 403 and somewhat brings back the Athenian atmosphere of that time. Although written later, this text, combined, if need be, with other sources, through its precision reveals the facts of civilization we seek, namely, what speech and writing meant for the actors in history.

After summing up the agreement between the democratic and the oligarchic parties—which allowed citizens who favored the oligarchs to emigrate to Eleusis, asserted that the sanctuary of Eleusis was to be shared by both parties, established the amnesty between citizens, and called for the reimbursement of the money that the Thirty had borrowed from the Spartans for the war—the Stagirite continues: "After the conclusion of a settlement along these lines, those who had fought with the Thirty were afraid, and many intended to move out of the city, but put off registration until the last moment, as men always do. Archinus saw the number involved, and canceled the remaining days for registration [*tēs apographēs*] because he wished to keep them in the city; many were compelled to remain, much against their will, until they recovered their confidence" (40, 1).

Archinus, an influential politician in Athens, retained those who were worried through the manipulation of writing, by removing the remaining days for registration. He cheated on the date established in the text in order to retain the citizens in Athens, regardless of political tendencies. He used writing fraudulently to preserve the integrity of the civil body.

Let us continue with Aristotle: "This was a sound move by Archinus, as was his later indictment of Thrasybulus for illegal proposals [*grapsamenos paranomōn*] when the latter tried to give citizenship to all who had had a part in the return from the Peiraeus although some were manifestly slaves" (40, 2). At the beginning of the democratic restoration, Thrasybulus had attempted to have a decree passed conferring citizenship on anyone who had returned from Peiraeus with the Athenian populace, including slaves and foreigners, among them the orator Lysias. Archinus, a more moderate democrat, attacked this decree as being illegal, not only because of its content, but also (as we learn from sources other than Aristotle) because it had not been previously examined by the council. Archinus won, and the rejection of the very democratic decree of Thrasybulus did not put people in the street, which means Archinus's intervention had received the support of a notable percentage of democrats. Another proposal concerning citizenship was later rejected, that of Theozotides, who suggested that citizenship be limited to the wealthy. In short, Athens was returning to the statutes of Pericles: to be a citizen of Athens, one had to be born of a father and mother who were citizens of Athens.

CLARISSE HERRENSCHMIDT

Let us stay with the matter at hand between Thrasybulus and Archinus. Writing played a primary role in it, for the action brought by Archinus bears the name of *graphē paranomōn*, literally, "(written) indictment for illegal proposals" (Aristotle uses *grapsamenos*, "being indicted [in writing]"). In the Athenian constitution, any citizen could bring an accusation of illegality against a proposal or a decree that he thought to be contrary to the laws of the city. Although the Greek word *graphē* certainly means "indictment (in public law)," its primary meaning is nothing other than "writing." By taking this basic meaning, we must understand *graphē paranomōn* as "writing (accusing a decree) from a legal point of view."

Using writing a second time to save the city, Archinus prevented Thrasybulus's decree and helped maintain the former right of access to citizenship, that of the constitution of the ancestors. Writing was already a guarantor of the integrity of the social body, but here it is also the guarantor of respect for political practices and for civil continuity. Aristotle continues:

> [Archinus seems to have acted as a good citizen a third time] when he seized one of the returned exiles who was attempting to disregard the amnesty, brought him before the Boule [council], and persuaded them to execute him without trial. He argued that their actions would show whether they intended to preserve the democracy and stand by their oaths; if they let the man go, they would encourage others, while, if they executed him, they would establish an example for all. This is just what happened, for after his execution nobody ever again tried to flout the amnesty. (40, 2)

Amnesty and the oath that accompanied it required a citizen who recalled the civil war, in which he had quite certainly suffered, to lose his life, the vital breath, even if the word *pneuma* does not appear in the text. His death served to foster forgetfulness and to preserve in silence the cohesion of the Athenian social body. There was no allusion to writing here, and the dead person did not even leave his name, for what was condemned concerned individual speech in contradiction with the public oath. Aristotle continues:

> The Athenians appear to have handled their affairs, both private and public, as well and with as much statesmanship as any people ever have shown in a similar situation. They not only refused to entertain any charges based on previous events, but they also repaid as a state the money which the Thirty had borrowed from the Spartans for the war, although the agreement had specified that the men of the city and those of Peiraeus should repay their debts separately; they felt that this ought to be the first step in

restoring unity and concord in the state. In other states the democrats, far from making contributions themselves in similar circumstances, redistribute the land. Athens was reunited with Eleusis in
the third year after the oligarchs moved there, in the Archonship
of Xenainetus. (40, 3–4)

By paying their debts to the Spartans collectively and not according to their political divisions, as had been anticipated, the
Athenians disobeyed their own convention, but that did not lead
to anyone's death. The collective disregard for what was written was
not important, as long as the individual disregard for the oral oath
was punishable by death.

We cannot spend much time on the connection between alphabetical writing and coinage in ancient Greece, on which the works
of F. Lenormant and B. Jurdan have cast a fascinating light.[29] Let us
nevertheless mention that until the passage against the decree of
Thrasybulus (40, 2), writing was the guarantor of the integrity and
of the composition of the Athenian civil body and yet personal
speech and remembrance then constituted a threat for the restored
democracy (40, 2); but it was suddenly coinage (40, 3) that took
over from writing and assembled the Athenians in the liberating
payment of a debt that they had assumed collectively. Writing and
money went hand in hand not only in fact but in spirit: Archinus
cheated on the deadline for inscription to retain certain citizens in
the city; the debt was paid by everyone, contrary to the agreement,
and therefore no one was in danger of being put to death.

The democrats of 403 decidedly did not start all over again the
errors of the democracy in the time of the empire, which imposed
its ideas, its tributes, and a new division of lands. Paying the debts
of their conquered enemies, the Thirty, they renounced the practices of the empire, on the basis of competition with Sparta. They
even renounced a straightforward domination over Eleusis, finding
an agreement with the small city—but here we have gone far beyond the archonship of Eucleides.

Writing is very much at issue in Aristotle's text. Let us see how
we can connect the facts of Athenian political history with the facts
of the Greek alphabet and of the history of the language. The laws
protected the city in its fragile renewal, and their written form
maintained the civil body: integrity, continuity, and definition. Let
us recall (1) that the invention of Greek writing meant the writing
of vowels, (2) that quite early on the Greeks wrote their laws, and
(3) that in Athens in particular democracy began with the written
laws of Solon, displayed in the Agora. Keeping all this in mind, one

might think that there is an analogy between the fixing of the laws of the democracy that was restored in 403 and the writing of the *eta* and the *omega*. One might say that the citizen population of Athens, once democracy was restored, remained pretty much the same, without a lot of emigration and without a massive influx of foreigners or slaves, just as the transformation of the alphabet used in Athens affected neither the alphabetical principle nor the essence of the signs, as the majority of the letters were common to the two writing systems.

But an individual's expression of resentment for the suffering endured during the civil war was punishable by death. Similarly, when the moderate Athenian democrats renounced the empire, they renounced in their writing that which constituted one of the peculiarities of the Athenian dialect, the aspirated *h*. It is appropriate here to mention what P. Vidal-Naquet brought to my attention, namely, that the alphabet adopted by the Athenians in 403 was the Ionic alphabet. Now, Ionia had constituted the largest part of the Athenian Empire, perhaps the richest and the most populated, the one that the Persian kings coveted. Athens therefore adopted the writing of its former subjects. The Athenians' desire for external peace in 403 was related to the summary execution of a citizen who did not respect the law of silence and to the elimination of the aspirated *h*.

The Athenians' writing down of the laws following the civil war represented an enormous effort, an infinite will for peace and for a common life, a courageous ordering process after a horrible period in their lives. It was an atmosphere of collectivity that we have difficulty imagining. It required the writing system used for the laws to be stamped with the same civil seal, to contain in its substance and the essence of its letters that which was allowed and that which was forbidden and to show in its signs that no one would speak of the ill that the city had done him and that Athens promised never again to dominate all Greeks with its language.

The prohibition of individual speech and the renunciation of the empire in the language are symbolized in the exclusion of the aspirated *h* from the writing system: the writing down of the laws in 403 pushed both the individual and the empire out of the field of action of the new democracy.

But this restoration affected neither the sanctuary of Eleusis, where citizens with full rights and slaves were initiated in the same capacity, nor the coinage, which divided the civil body itself into rich and poor.

Here we touch on a profound fact of civilization, namely, that a political will couched in writing went beyond politics, for it concerned the placement in concrete signs of the entire communal life, of all the connections that are made through language and outside it.

The exclusion of the aspirated *h* from the writing system of the new order was a minimal correction to alphabetical power, but a correction all the same. It shows that in 403 the moderate democrats of Athens did not want the full extent of logic and alphabetical power. On the contrary, they limited their effects. This splendid earlier writing system had enabled them to found an order of which the sovereignty of the law was the cornerstone, yet through the same movement that system had placed the order in danger, for the complete alphabet noted nonsounds, simple positions of the sound-making organs, and intention to speak, and so, through its strict rules of writing, it states that the language has been appropriated by the individual.

This correction was not made in isolation or like a bolt from the blue, because even before 403 the Athenians were wondering what was happening not only in their city and within the political situation of this city—the empire—but among themselves, in their friendly relations as citizens, and in their relationships of internal and external exchange. The passage from *Oedipus at Colonus* translated above shows this well. Something was disturbing Athenian consciences, something that was said in the theater, a place of edification, the school of the citizen population, to be "no longer the same breath (of confidence, of political life) that always went between the citizens"; in other words, the Athenians said to themselves through the mouths of Sophocles and Oedipus that they no longer spoke to each other in the same way.

This correction, this limitation placed on the complete alphabet, was necessary because for the Greeks uninterrupted exchange was the face of reality. In nature, the exchange was the state of becoming, which unfolded as if within a cycle and in which the elements—water, fire, air, earth—were transformed without becoming something else. Humans and the gods were face-to-face in the exchange of nouns and adjectives in Heraclitus: *aθanatoi θnētoi, θnētoi aθanatoi,* "mortal immortals, immortal mortals."[30] Gods and heroes talk to each other a lot in Homer, especially in the *Iliad;* from the beginning of Greek civilization they had a common language, which in turn brought about the theater, nothing but an immense religious ceremony.

CLARISSE HERRENSCHMIDT

There were other exchanges between human beings: of goods, of blows, and of words. Based on the experiences of the Mermnads of Sardis, the Greeks invented minted currency, which liberated them from the obligation of speech, placed stores of goods, stolen wealth, and unfair tributes back into the flow of economic movement, and carried the emblem of the cities that struck the coins, the symbols by which cities recognized each other, far abroad. Men spoke, and spoke to each other in the assembly, managing the archaic city of the eighth and seventh centuries and passing to each other the scepter that authorized speakers to take the podium, the symbol of political speech. The one who very briefly held the scepter, who had received it from a neighbor and was preparing to pass it on to someone else, spoke, and no one was the owner of it.

It was also in this uninterrupted series of exchanges that self-knowledge and the knowledge of the other were established, for the "Know thyself" of Socrates and Plato did not typify a direct introspection but, as Jean Pepin writes, "a complex operation that included a detour through the knowledge of others" and an anchoring in the divine.[31] Just as the eye could not see itself except when it is reflected in another eye, as in a mirror, so, too, the soul, to know itself, had to look at another soul; this is the essential message of Plato's *Alcibiades I*.

Thus the Greeks could hardly establish a religion of the book but could only establish dialogues: the dialogues of the epic and of poetry, the dialogue that formed the basis of their enigma literature— Oedipus solved the Sphinx's enigma through a dialogue, the dialogues of the theater, and above all those of philosophy. In this manner they invented the writing of vowels, which are shapes of the voice (in Greek, "vowels" were called *ta phōnēenta*, "that which produces sound"), variations so close to speech, identifiable with the breath of breathing, and so are from breath, which is itself only air, one of the elements in infinite transformation, always at work in nature's becoming.

They therefore found themselves face-to-face with a flagrant contradiction; on the one hand, their writing, which trapped speech like the flow of time, appeared as flexible and simple as the exchange of conversation between friends, but put the point of application of the signs in the body of each person; on the other hand, their theory of language as uninterrupted exchange, in no way excluding the gods.

Let us express this contradiction in another way. Signs referred to simple sonorous experiences, to positions of inner muscles that everyone has; alone, even isolated, the subject could read anything and make language his own. With the complete alphabet, the meaning was no longer in common signs, but resided in the appropriation of the text by the reader. For the ancients, however, meaning resided only in their common life, made up of exchanges carried out under a traditional law. In a certain sense the appropriation of language through the complete alphabet was outside of the law.

Therefore Archinus, Thrasybulus, the oligarchs, and the moderate democrats were in agreement about eliminating the aspirated *h* from writing, without saying so, without even doing it deliberately, for it went hand in hand with the reinstituted political life. They thus prohibited the privatization of breath through writing, because speech was for everyone, and that included the gods.

As a society they limited the ideas that meaning rested on convention, that man was free in language, that philosophical dialectics and maieutics constituted the eminent art of language, that on the distant horizon the sign was arbitrary—and too bad for the philosophers who were going to insist on thinking so—and that meaning resided elsewhere than in the uninterrupted exchange in the cosmos and with the gods.

But to forbid the privatization of breath through writing and of the principle of exchange was also to put the exchange back *en meson,* in the middle, as at a superior logical level. Although the moderate democrats of 403 were also the assassins of Socrates, they were nevertheless not strangers to the eternity of Athens, for its written language, having lost its dialectical specificity, became the Greek thought for all Greeks, while awaiting the others.

And so the moderate Athenians of 403 wanted to have nothing to do with our situation in language, caught between the inconceivable universal and the subject who soliloquizes.

By the way, it was going to require twenty more centuries of history to get that far, to Christianity and its double theory of language—God, master of the words that create, Christ made man in the word, the birth of nations or that which is within linguistic borders, implying grammar and spelling as being median locations between the subject and the universal, and the printing press or the duplicating of time that it implies.

But that is another story.

THREE

Writing and Civil Religion in Greece

CHAPTER NINE

Myths and Reasonings

When we consider the origins of our civilization, of our forms of thought and perhaps of some aspects of our social life, we must first set aside certain assertions that flourished in the nineteenth century that are still made today and that have absolutely nothing to do with scientific knowledge. Suppose a former government minister, reflecting on the true sources common to all of Europe, thinks he can locate them in the primitive culture of the Indo-Europeans. He writes: "Those men who directly preceded us are, through us, at the origin of the most advanced civilizations and knowledge, of the most refined art and culture. The spirit of invention, of creation, in four thousand five hundred years led them through a long progressive walk from the banks of the Baltic Sea to the surface of the moon." We would therefore be the descendants of the Indo-Europeans who left the banks of the Baltic four thousand five hundred years ago.

Who were these Indo-Europeans? Why the Baltic? How did they arrive in Greece? None of the minister's theory is derived in any way from what we know or from reasoned conjecture, but comes out of pure ideology. People want to find Indo-Germanic origins in Greece. That being the case, one of the salutary aspects of Jean Bottéro's work is to have shown that history began in Sumer, as indicated by the title of the book by S. N. Kramer that he translated. Bottéro has indeed clarified the constituent traits of Mesopotamian civilization: first, the presence of large urban environments and the constitution of complex societies; second, the existence of an organized pantheon, with a multitude of great gods, each having his or her own name, unique personality, ways of acting, and realms of intervention; third, the invention of writing, which makes that region the point of departure for our history; fourth, the great myths, responding to essential questions; fifth, the important place held on the level of intellectual activities by divination, for the rules of divination show that the Mesopotamians already possessed the mastery of a thought process that enabled them to establish a certain order in the universe. Consequently, Bottéro is right to have concluded that our history originated in Mesopotamia. With this in mind, it is quite true that the small corner of the world and of history that I am going to discuss—Greece—can only be understood against that Mesopotamian background, which is older than Greece. My feeling is that certain continuities, perhaps even influences, do exist, but that it is essential at the same time to note differences. So how, then, do we begin to approach the question of the origins of the Greek world?

There is some disagreement as to whether it was around 2100 or 1900 B.C. that Greece would have seen the arrival of populations whose Indo-European origins—they spoke an archaic Greek dialect—can be verified only later, in the Mycenaean era. Archeologists disagree about the date, but they are generally in agreement that it was after that period that new things, revealed by archeological data, appeared in continental Greece: essentially, a type of ceramic called Minyan, which is very different from what came before it, was discovered there. What is certain is that between the sixteenth and the fourteenth centuries B.C. in continental Greece—in a very extensive area that included Peloponnesus, Argolis, but also Attica, Thessaly, and Boeotia—a civilization that we call the Mycaenean world was established. It reached its height in the fourteenth century; certain monumental fortresses were erected in the thirteenth century; the decline, the destruction of palaces occurred at the end of the twelfth century. There is an extraordinary wealth of funerary objects in the different types of tombs (*tholoi* and two different grave circles, one from between 1650 and 1550, the other from between 1570 and 1500), such as those that Schliemann revealed in what he called the "tomb of Agamemnon." At the same time a number of characteristics indicate that we are dealing with a population in which bellicose aspects were important. We find figured stelae on which there are chariots, scenes of the hunt or of war. We are therefore faced with a population that was rather different from that of Crete at the same time. In Crete the civilization was palatial, and we distinguish the era of the first palaces from that of the second. What is of interest to us is that following the first destruction of the palaces, we see how the Mycenaeans, who were then in continental Greece, settled in Crete in the second half of the fifteenth century and played a dominant role there. Around 1700, the destruction of the Cretan palaces was complete. Was it due to those Mycenaeans? This is doubtful. Perhaps it was due to earthquakes, or perhaps there were other reasons. In any event, we note that only the palace of Cnossos remained intact and that, at that time, in Crete and in Mycenae, there was the same type of civilization. Moreover, after 1400, the moment when the Mycenaean civilization was at its most powerful, we have tablets. Crete had known a syllabic writing system, Linear A, which no one has ever deciphered, and then another type of writing appeared in continental Greece among the Mycenaeans, and even in Crete, a system derived from the first, called Linear B. This writing has been deciphered. It is Greek—which means that we can be sure that around 1400 there occurred a relative unification of those two systems, Linear A and Linear B. Linear B is difficult, which implies that there had already been some form of education. Of course, it was Cretan scribes who taught those proto-Greeks how to write, but here we have a type of culture that, through a second version of Cretan writing, transmitted an Indo-European language that was already Greek.

Those Greeks surely did not come from the Baltic, but then where did they come from? Were they from the Anatolian plateau? They were perhaps from the same period as other Indo-European advances such as that of the Hittites in Asia. Perhaps they came from the steppes located between the Caspian Sea and the Black Sea. In any event, they certainly joined very quickly with a local non–Indo-European population that the Greek authors from time to time also called the "Barbarians." Herodotus would be able to say, for example, that earlier, in Greece, there were Barbarians, Minyans, or Pelasgians.

By joining up with these populations, the Greeks became in a certain sense a mixed breed. Their culture took on the essential elements of what the Cretans, who were not Indo-Europeans, had built. At the same time the Cretans' mobility had already established them on the entire coast of Asia, and even beyond. The Myceneans took their place in 1400. We know that Mycenaean establishments existed, not only on many of the Cyclades islands and in the Mediterranean as far as southern Italy, but also in Asia. The principal Mycenaean palaces were very different from the Cretan palaces. They were fortresses that, starting in 1300, were surrounded with walls, like those that one sees in Tiryns or in many other places in Greece. Whereas the Cretan palaces were very complicated constructions but opened directly on to the countryside and were without defenses, the Mycenaean palaces were true military fortresses.

Between the twelfth and the eleventh centuries those vast urban constructions, with their fortified palaces, disappeared. There was then a true regression, in every respect. By excavating tombs and studying the occupation of the territory, archeologists have been able to show that there was an enormous demographic decline. The countryside lost its population. At the same time their writing, which had played a role comparable to the one it played in the empires or the city-states of the Middle East, had been used to keep accounts of all the economic and religious activities that took place in the palaces. Writing had disappeared completely, except on Cyprus, but that was a particular case: it was a syllabic system derived from Linear B, and it created a type of Cypriot script that was still in use during the classical period. Everywhere else, writing disappeared completely, and it did not reappear, roughly speaking, until around the eighth century, perhaps at the end of the ninth. This was a true civilization, one that was already Greek in its language, that was extraordinarily rich and powerful, that demonstrated a refinement in the manufacturing of certain objects, such as those that have been found in tombs. The Mycenaeans, then, had created all of that, and then suddenly everything was interrupted. This is the period that is called the "dark centuries": there was a loss of population and perhaps, according to one theory, even abandonment. Two explanations prevail: the first claims that this decline of Mycenaean hegemony was due to the invasion of the Dorians, a group of Greek people who spoke a specific dialect, Doric, as used in the Peloponnesus. This hypothesis, which was held for a long time, is rarely advanced anymore, because when archeologists look closely, they see nothing to suggest that a different population appeared between the twelfth and the ninth centuries. The second theory asserts that internal battles or other phenomena caused that civilization gradually to be weakened and diffused. In other words, for us Greece started up again in the eighth century. In this eighth-century Greece, whose origins are very difficult to define clearly, as we have just seen, we know that there had been contacts and, consequently, possible borrowings between continental Greece, Crete, and all of the regions of the Mediterranean periphery.

There Greece had been a part of a world where, until the twelfth century, travel and exchanges were incessant. Between the twelfth and the ninth centuries communication between the Greeks and Asia was essentially interrupted. At that time there was a decline in commerce, a very great slowdown in shipping. In the ninth century, and even at the end of the tenth, things started up again, thanks to a vast movement of colonization: the population grew, and urban sites were developed. The Greeks of continental Greece settled colonies not only on the opposite coast of Asia (the coast of Asia Minor was colonized in 950) but also on the Black Sea, in Sicily, and farther west, in Marseille and even in Spain. We are now entering the period that is truly that of the Greece on which we are focusing.

How was that Greece both similar to and very different from Mesopotamia? Let us first look at the similarities. In archaic Greece, details of which appear in a certain number of texts such as the Homeric epic or Hesiod's poetry in the genre of wisdom literature—the *Theogony,* the *Works and Days*—it seems to me that the myths, the legends, the very organization of the pantheon evoke what we have seen in Sumer, in Akkad, and in the Assyro-Babylonian world. We are indeed dealing with polytheist systems. A large portion of the myths consist of tales that in their own way, through the narration itself and without raising any questions, provide not a solution but a way of seeing how the world is organized. There have been many attempts to see connections between particular Greek myths and Hittite or Babylonian myths. Although my knowledge of the myths of the ancient Middle East is very superficial—I have simply read the texts—I think that if there are resemblances, they are not that much greater than those found in the myths of other great, very different civilizations—those of pre-Columbian America or Africa, for example. It happens that there are cases where correlations are completely clear, as in the case of the struggle of Zeus and Typhon. It can be shown that there are particular Hittite myths that are very similar to that tale. Yet these analogous Greek tales concerning Typhon are only cited by Apollodorus, Plutarch, and Nonnus of Panopolis; that is, they span from the first century B.C. to the fourth century A.D. Consequently, we find ourselves in a world that was both Greek and Oriental, and it is completely natural that we find relationships between them.

But if we look at Hesiod's *Theogony,* a poem that has been dated around the seventh century, just after Homer, it seems to me that there are already certain differences in tone. In Hesiod's tale there is a concern with order, both on the cosmic level and on the level of Zeus's power, a concern with showing that such power was based on what the Greeks called *dike,* "justice." This cosmological and ethical tendency appears to me to be more evident in Hesiod's

Theogony than in the corresponding myths with which it has often been compared. In the *Enūma Eliš*, for example, the battle of Marduk and Tiamat indeed corresponds to Zeus's battle with Typhon in the *Theogony*. We know that Marduk kills Tiamat with the help of winds that rush into the stomach of that monster, that he throws a part of her body above, which makes the sky, and a part below, which makes the earth. In the *Theogony* there is a similar situation: at a certain point the sky and the earth are on top of each other and it is necessary to separate them. A blow from Kronos's sickle accomplishes this. Obviously, a connection has been drawn between these two texts. If the earth and the sky are separated, however, it is because Kronos, having castrated his father Ouranos, forces him to go far away, which is after all quite different from what happens to Tiamat. The connection comes out of the fact that Typhon's cadaver, once Zeus has triumphed over him—not without some difficulty—emits winds: not regular winds, which are quite common, but on the contrary, tempestuous winds, winds of disorder, chaotic winds. Here is a good example of the approach of certain mythologists: they take some small points in the thread of the tale, show that they overlap, and attempt to say that there had been an influence. I believe that that approach is not only futile but leads to a distortion of the meaning of a myth in general. We are dealing with different things. But where is the problem?

What is different in the Greek world seems to be this: in the eighth century, the historical moment on which we are focusing, Greece was not a civilization of the written word. It was an oral civilization. All the great spiritual forms—the epic, lyric poetry, poems of wisdom—had not yet been written down. People lived in a culture in which the spoken word played a fundamental role; it continued to do so for a very long time, until almost the fifth century, and perhaps even later, as the use of writing became customary only very slowly. We are in the world of the sung, mimed, danced word, the poetic word. Communication occurred within the framework of a life that was both civil and religious. It was a religious life that differed from what we know of elsewhere. In the eighth century the divinities evoked in the *Theogony* already existed in the Mycenaean world. The names of the gods that we find on the Mycenaean tablets were already the names of the great Greek gods, who were for the most part Indo-European. Zeus is obviously the counterpart of the Roman Jupiter or of the Indian Vedic Dyaus. But, as Dumézil has shown well, what made up the skeletal structure of the religious system of the great Indo-European religions (whether that of India or Rome, of the Germans or the Scandinavians) was the trifunctional concept of the gods, society, and human beings. This concept did not exist in Greece, or, if it did exist, it was in the form of completely scattered scraps that were found hither and yon. Thus there were in fact gods, most of whom were Indo-European, but who constituted a pantheon that was not organized according to the model corresponding to what we find in other Indo-European religions. Dumézil himself was well aware of this: after attempting to apply his schema to the Greek case, he ultimately gave up.

Greek religion was characterized by two facts that seem contradictory but actually are not. As we will see, communities of the kind called *poleis,* "city-states," began to appear: communities where people considered themselves fellow citizens, that in general had an urban center and a countryside. Each city had its own special god, its tutelary god, who was called the divinity of the polis, for example, Hera in Argos or Athena in Athens. The tale was told of how Hera and Athena at a given moment had a conflict with another god in order to ascertain who would be the patron of a certain civil community. There was a religious particularism. The gods were profoundly integrated into the system of the city. They were gods who had the same status as the group of human beings who recognized them—they were city gods. At the same time they anchored heaven in a specific territory, with some sanctuaries in the center, others on the urban periphery, and still others on the borders of the state. And processions went through the entire territory on a regular basis, starting out from the center, crossing the city limits, and going as far as the borders before returning. This was in a certain sense a way of marking the gods' territory. At the same time, it was the eighth century, the time of Homer, when the great Panhellenic sanctuaries were established, when the sanctuary of Delphi was beginning to be important, as were the Olympiads. When it came to invoking the gods, engaging in cultic exchange with them, it was this particularism of the cities that was at play. At the same time, on an intellectual level, as Herodotus said in the fifth century B.C., men, poets such as Homer or Hesiod, began to formulate a sort of Panhellenic religion. They named the gods and put them in order. Thus a pantheon was created that was largely the canonical pantheon of Greece, even if each city had its own; and that creation occurred within the context of an oral culture. This land, which had a type of syllabic writing system based on the knowledge of specialized scribes—writing professionals—forgot it completely and

chose a very rich oral culture, one that would produce lyrical poetry, the epic, and even, initially, a certain number of philosophical
works. Indeed, philosophers such as Parmenides, Empedocles, Heraclitus, and Xenophanes wrote in verse. But their poems were created to be read aloud. And this is essential.

Out of that oral tradition, in which what everyone knew was
transmitted in the form of sung poetry, a form of writing appeared
that—compared to that of the Mycenaean era, to Cretan writing,
and even to other types of writing—was completely new. This was
alphabetical writing. It was borrowed from the Phoenicians, which
is not surprising. It is clear that as of the ninth century the Greeks
were in contact with the Phoenicians in the trading stations where
they each had a small colony. The Phoenicians were familiar with
alphabetical writing since the Canaanites as well as the Hebrews
used it. The Greeks transformed that alphabetical writing system in
such a way that it became the exact translation of speech. That is,
they used a certain number of signs to note vowels. At that moment, writing ceased to be what it had been in palaces of the Mycenaean era and what it had been in many places: the scholarly
specialty of a class of learned men, professionals, and scribes. Its
function took a different turn: it was no longer used to portray objects or even, through different techniques, to follow the flow of
language. Writing became nothing other than the translation of the
spoken word. Speech became everything. Moreover, that writing
system was much easier to learn because the number of signs was
quite limited. It was no longer a specialty, even if, in the course of
social development, it took a long time for it to penetrate all areas
of society. For example, although Greek law was until a very late
date—the Hellenistic era—an oral law and was not written down,
and although we are dealing with a civilization that was deeply
rooted in the oral, the written word nevertheless played a role that
it had not played elsewhere. Here is an example: the Greeks went
to Pithekousai on the island of Ischia. In a Mycenaean and Greek
trading station of Pithekousai, we have found decorated vases dating from the eighth century on which the potter not only put his
name but also cited a verse from Homer relating to the scene that
is described. We know of cases of mercenaries in Egypt who signed
their names to graffiti. Consequently, we have proof that from early
on this alphabetical writing was quite different from what up until
then had been a scholarly specialization. At the same time, the fundamental role of this writing system was to make a certain number
of texts public for the benefit of all citizens. Thus there was a move-

ment from oral performance to the written word: when a bard sang part of the *Iliad* or the *Odyssey,* he was remembering at the same time he was improvising, as he himself admitted and as anthropologists have demonstrated. He composed out of a tradition with which his audience was already familiar. Thus what he was telling had a circumstantial character: it depended on his audience as well as on the juncture in time.

This point is very important. In the sixth century in the Greek colonies of Asia Minor, specifically in Miletus, a new type of writing appeared: this is seen first in Thales, then in one of his pupils, Anaximenes, then in Anaximander. Thales played a political role in his city and quite probably made use of writing. For Anaximander, this is an established fact. Thales's thoughts and the explanations he sets forth are written in prose. Thus there was a movement from oral poetry to written prose, and it had considerable consequences. From the time that the speaker abandoned the former manner of delivering "philosophical" discourses in verse before an assembled crowd, as figures such as Empedocles still did in the middle of the fifth century, to the time that the text was written down in prose, when it was "placed in the center," as the Greek expression goes, that is, made public, placed in the middle of the community, it was henceforth by that very fact subject to controversies and criticism.

In my opinion, we are now delving into a completely new system compared to what we know of those of the ancient Middle East, one that was also new compared to the myths of Hesiod, which in a certain way recall Mesopotamian or Hittite myths, even if they demonstrate certain changes. In myth we have tales that do not immediately raise any questions and that explain how, in the beginning, there was a chaotic, disorganized world, and how gradually order was established. But in the legendary poetry, such as that of Hesiod, everything occurs through divine genealogies, as in the Middle East. First of all, a group of gods occupies the primary position; they battle each other, or give birth to each other, and succeed each other. Better, or in any case, differently than the texts of the ancient Middle East, Hesiod's poetry perhaps sheds light on the fact that, to have order in the world, it was necessary to have a ruler among the gods, and the ruler had to establish the order. Another important point was made: it was necessary that that order never again be questioned. One might say that the entire *Theogony* is a huge narration that begins with primal powers, with chaos—a gap, a dark gulf, without direction, where nothing can be seen, that is foggy, nocturnal—which in a certain way might also evoke the myth of the flood, where all the borders between objects are obliterated. This is what Hesiod places at the beginning of the emergence of the cosmos: there was Chaos, then Gaia, the opposite of chaos, was born, which was solid, visible, stable; and then, through a sort of movement whose vicissitudes the poet follows, we come to Ouranos, to Kronos, to the struggle of the gods, and finally to Zeus. The issue then was to see how Zeus might act so that the order he had instilled when he was conqueror would endure; all the gods then decided to grant him *basileia,* "royalty," and asked him to distribute to each of them portions of honor, *timai.* Each god would have his own, and that was never to change . . . even though Zeus also had children. Consequently, the myth raises the question of temporality. Since he had children, they would be younger than he. Since they were younger, they would one day be stronger. Rivalry would ensue, and Zeus risked enduring what he had inflicted on Kronos and Kronos on Ouranos, as in the myths of the Middle East. The myth brought the answer, showing how Zeus found the means to have a daughter, Athena, and at the same time not to have a son stronger than he. I will not go into the details of the procedures he used to achieve this. Briefly, he swallowed his first wife, Metis, who was wisdom, skill, cunning. Once he had swallowed her he could rest easy, for if he hadn't done it, he would have had a son stronger than he and there would have been battles for sovereignty enduring from generation to generation. This is what was told in the myth: genealogy, childbirth, marriage, battles, ploys, struggles against monsters, and finally the fundamental idea that the order of the world assumed a ruler, a superior power, and that it was that power and the stability of that power that could establish the constancy of the cosmic order.

If we look at the first philosophical texts—a few fragments from Thales and Anaximenes, a few more from Anaximander (but we know of them through the commentaries that have been written on them)—we see that in what has been called the "first philosophy," that of the physicists, the gods had disappeared from the authors' explanations of things. In Pherecydes there was still a god whom he called Zas—he loved plays on words—but in Thales and those who followed, the gods were finished. The gods of the pantheon, the gods of the cult, had disappeared completely. In other words, a new form of reflection was developed that from its inception was located outside the traditional religious sphere. It was no longer a poetic narration but an explanation of the world, of phenomena. And to accomplish that, to explain the phenomena such

JEAN-PIERRE VERNANT

as we see them, the authors used explanatory schemas that were the same sort as those that were seen every day. For example, consider material sifted with a sieve. The light material disappears, and the heavy matter remains. This is a good way to explain certain phenomena. To explain vision one might also use a lamp. In other words, these were simple procedures—technical or natural—that would enable people to understand how the cosmos was organized.

Through a fundamental change in perspective, this philosophy completely modified the relations of order and power. In the myths there was an order of the world since at a given moment there was a power. For there to have been order there had to have been a power that founded it, established it, instilled it, and preserved it. That perspective was completely altered. Henceforth, for there to have been order, it was necessary for no power to possess complete supremacy, because if one power possessed more strength than any others, then it would overwhelm them. For example, if warmth were more powerful than cold, dampness, and so on, everything would ultimately be hot.

Thus it became necessary to present not a tale but a text, an exposé—which was not yet a demonstration—in which the author would show that there was order in the cosmos insofar as there was a balance of powers. One might say that in this type of thinking, order was more important than power. The idea of a ruler over the world had disappeared—the opposite notion now prevailed. Anaximander was the most characteristic of this point of view. He explained that Thales thought that the *archē*, "the principle," that which was primary and dominated everything, was water. Why didn't the earth fall? Because it floated on water. Consequently, water was the primary element; it could assume all forms, and it dominated the earth. This was an old theme that recalled the myth of the flood, because all these philosophies were also rooted in old mythical concepts. But at the same time the vocabulary changed: instead of the names of gods they used words, qualities—warm, cold, dry, moist—and they added *to*, the neuter article. They believed it was those abstract substantified qualities that formed the fabric from which the world was cut. Thus it was truly a revolution in the conception of reality. Anaximander said that what was principle, *archē*, could be neither warm, cold, dry, nor moist, because if there were such a principle, then the sovereignty of that principle would destroy the others. The principle was what he called *apeiron*, "the nonlimited." And it could be shown that the only function of this *apeiron* was to make sure that none of the principles of which the world was comprised could overpower any of the others. As Anaximander said: If warmth or any other power in the world went beyond its share of power and invaded the rest, it would then be necessary for it to make amends, for it to pay for the mistake that it had made, and for it to return as much. In other words, there was a balance; the powers came and went, and the *apeiron* served as follows: as it was not a power like the others, it did not risk assuming supremacy.

Anaximander went further still. The consequences of this state of affairs are important: we see a system of thought in which it was no longer power that was sovereign but order, law, *nomos,* as the Greeks would say a bit later, and it was only *dike* that was *basileus,* "king." There was no king beyond that. In this conception, the world itself was seen as something that obeyed a primary order. The word *archē,* which I am translating as "principle," has this meaning only in the philosophy of Anaximander. In Hesiod the term means both what is primary, the primordial—chaos, what existed before Gaia—and what, at the end of his narration, was deposited and concentrated in the hands of Zeus, the power, the commander, supremacy, whereas in the new system *archē* implied the principle, order, the law of equitable distribution that formed the foundation of being. In the mythical system, the *archē* as point of departure and the *archē* as sovereignty were temporally separated from each other. Aristotle said that Zeus and the Olympian gods were "latecomers." They arrived at the end of history, at the end of the tale. The entire myth consists of showing how we went from the *archē* that was primordial to the *archē* that was sovereignty. In Anaximander's conception *archē* was indeed that which ruled—but it was not a ruler who appeared late in the day—it was that order which at the original establishment of the world never ceased and would never cease to regulate the world's course. Anaximander asked the question that the others had asked: Why doesn't the earth fall? He answered: The earth doesn't fall because it has no reason to fall. Being at the center of the celestial circumference, it has no reason to go either higher or lower, more to the right or to the left. This is how such transformations, what we might call a geometrization of thought, occurred; Anaximander's text even presents the order of the world in the form of what the Greeks called a *theoria,* vision and theory at the same time. The earth is there, in the middle, consequently, why would it fall? Or as Anaximander further says: It doesn't fall because, being at an equal distance from all the points of the celestial circumference, it is dominated by nothing. The earth was in the center, and we will see later the political values that came out of that notion. What was already becoming predominant, through the abandonment of all those stories, all those dramatic narrations, and poetry, was the use of prose, of the written text—a form of writing that was also placed in the center, and that, in this sense, escaped its creator and became the object of a public and contradictory debate.

It was also the moment when maps were being invented: Anaximander invented the first map of the inhabited universe. Henceforth reality was presented spatially. And this sort of spatialization of thought, which was manifest also on the social and political levels in the great urban plans, ended in what, to me, highlights perfectly the originality of Greece. The Babylonians, Egyptians, Chinese, and Indians all had very well-developed, in general algebraic, mathematics. They certainly knew the Pythagorean theorem, among others. But the Greeks did something completely different. They produced what was to result in Euclid's geometry. In a certain sense, the physicists of Ionia instigated this revolution in thought. They were interested in phenomena, in what could be seen. They sought explicative schemas to account for appearances. But precisely because Greece was a civilization of the spoken word, poetry, religious poetry, and hymns also continued to be produced.

A completely different philosophical current, which also dates from the end of the sixth and the beginning of the fifth century, brought together inspired poets who, in order to explain phenomena, did not do what the physicists did—seek out positive schemas; positivism was rampant in the physicists' texts—but attempted to see what was hidden behind appearances. Then, beginning in the sixth century and developing in the fifth, there was that great philosophical idea of the contrast between appearances and Being, the one and absolute. A whole series of philosophers set out on this path. And in that current, truth, the true, was no longer the truth of mythical tales, nor was it the truth of the philosophers of Ionia who tried to explain appearances. The truth of a given discourse came solely out of its internal coherence: what caused discourse to be true was not the fact that what one saw seemed to confirm it, but that the discourse, as it was articulated within itself, was irrefutable. This was the definition of the principle of identity among adherents of the Eleatic School. Combined with other factors, it led to the definition of a mathematical science that entirely marked Western civilization, because it was a science that linked together a series of demonstrations based on principles and definitions that it posited, in such a way that the truth of the final proposition was completely independent of any external confirmation in the world.

The truth of the final proposition hung entirely from the internal rationality of the discourse, from its coherence, from its systematic nature, or one could even say, using the words of historians of mathematics, that the Greeks ultimately came to define—and this was not by chance—the ideal nature of mathematical objects. Mathematics could not be done without drawing figures: a triangle, a circle, or a square. But what the Greeks became perfectly aware of was that the drawn triangle was not the triangle on which one was reflecting, because, naturally, it was a triangle whose lines had a thickness and a certain irregularity. In other words, they defined a knowledge whose rationality was based on objects that were not of the phenomenal order but were mental objects of an ideal type that naturally, for the Greeks, and not only the Greeks, corresponded to true essences. Thinking made a true leap here, in that mathematics represented something entirely different. It represented a type of rationality that was not easily found elsewhere. But we must take care: I do not at all mean to say that on Greek soil, through a sort of miracle, there emerged on one hand a philosophy of nature striving to find positive explanations for the order of the world and on the other a philosophy of Being, of the logos, of rationality, that initiated the whole philosophical movement. It is completely clear that Anaximander's *apeiron,* which in his system served to eliminate the sovereignty of a unique divine power, found its origin in the old chaos of Hesiod's *Theogony.* He never would have thought of the *apeiron* if the myth had not spoken of chaos, which indeed was defined by the fact that it could be anything, it was no more one thing than another. Similarly, the Greek mathematicians never would have been able to envision the type of studies they pursued if one of their schools, the Pythagoreans, had not at the same time been a sect that believed there were perfect numbers. For, while they were engaged in mathematics, they were also involved in spiritual ascetic exercises; they attempted to join the beginning to the end, that is, to rediscover the entire cycle of the reincarnations that we might have lived. There was not, on one hand, reason, reflective intelligence, and demonstration, and on the other, religion, myth, and superstition. These things coexisted. The discovery of the ideality of mathematical objects occurred in a certain sense against the background of an initiatory and sectarian group such as the Pythagoreans. Things are never simple. There was no struggle of the rational against the mystical, the lay against the religious. Nor was

　　　　　　　　　　　　　　　JEAN-PIERRE VERNANT

there a reasoning, a Western reasoning, that came out of it. The reasoning of the people of Ionia was not the same as that of Parmenides, founder of the Eleatic School. The reasoning of philosophers and mathematicians is not that of doctors; doctors have several versions, moreover, depending on the different types of medicine being practiced. Depending on the person who wrote and the realm of the real that that intellectual orientation enabled him to explore, the intellectual procedures were not the same. The historian—Herodotus, Thucydides, or one of those that might have preceded them—did not reason exactly as the philosopher did. Such a broad field of multiple rationalities nevertheless had a relative unity; it was for all that fundamentally rooted in what one might call the universe of the political, the intellectual horizon of the polis.

CHAPTER TEN

The Polis: Shared Power

After broadly describing the conditions and the forms in which a rationality different from myth developed, let us now, beginning with the emergence of the polis, look at the invention of the political and of democracy in Greece. In *Democracy Ancient and Modern*, Moses Finley writes: "It was the Greeks, after all, who discovered not only democracy but also politics, the art of reaching decisions by public discussion and then of obeying those decisions as a necessary condition of civilized social existence. . . . The Greeks, and only the Greeks, discovered democracy in that sense."[1] Although on the whole I agree with this assertion, things seem a bit less simple than Finley suggests. In the Greece that we have seen developing, what was important were the public places, the spaces where the entire community gathered together to make decisions, venues, public locations for practices involving speech. People came to those places to speak, to discuss, to argue, to set discourse against discourse. Thus there was a definite language-oriented practice and, at the same time, an institution that fixed that fundamental element. The group had common interests. And those interests were expressed in the space of the group, in locales that were privileged as compared to others, that is, which were no longer individual, domestic, familial places but common places where the entire group in a certain sense felt rooted. Briefly, one might say that the logic for this current was Athenian democracy: the idea that the entire group participated in public affairs, had the right of free speech, and could demand accountability from all magistrates; the same group made political decisions—those that bore on common business—and was represented in the courts of law. Consequently, through the forms of social life, the entire institutional system consisted of perfecting the notion of a space where the community was gathered and where it sovereignly made its decisions. Such was democracy—from *dēmos,* whose meaning included both the people in its entirety and that portion of the people who were the poorest. But in *democracy* there is not only *dēmos* but also *cratos,* "power"— the sovereignty of the people. Of course, all of this created many difficulties, because the word *democracy* for the ancients could designate a regime in which it was truly all of the citizens who decided, independent of their status, that is, independent of the fact that they were more or less large landowners or that they had a different land-based revenue. People from all the different social categories were represented, whether they were artisans, farmers, or nonproducers. As Pericles says in the speech Thucydides attributes to him: "No one, so long as he has it in him to be of service to the state, is kept in political obscurity because of poverty."[2] This is the primary meaning of *democracy.* There is a second meaning, as well: *dēmos* also designates the poorest and most destitute people, the masses, *to plethos,* the most numerous, who benefited from the power, who seized it, and who consequently made the tyranny of that power of the greatest number weigh upon an elite, on the *aristoi,* the best, the *oligoi,* those who were fewer in number.

This is an important notion on which we need to reflect. I believe it is incontestable that the political is connected to the institution of public debate, of argued discussion, of opposing speeches. This implies that speech acquired a function and a weight that were entirely different from what they once were. Speech exchanged in a public place no longer had the same decisive value as the speech of a king or a priest, nor did it have the value of a revelation of truth, as for example that of an inspired prophet or a poet. This speech, uttered by anyone in the course of a debate, was seen as argumentation and persuasion, the exposé of a reasoned opinion about what was best for the collectivity. The first point, then, is this: Such speech had a function that was no longer to utter a religious truth. Already in Homer we see the appearance of something along these lines; for example, in Ithaca, at the moment when Telemachus assembles the Elders, or at the end of the *Odyssey,* when Ulysses kills the suitors, there is once again a gathering of the people of Ithaca or of their representatives. There is almost a functioning city-state here. And there are more serious elements that indicate the beginning of the notion of the polis, in particular a Cretan inscription from Dreros that dates from the second half of the seventh century in which we find this formula: "This has been decided by the polis," or rather, "It has pleased the city of Dreros to . . ." Here we see that there was a polis, a community, and we see an indication that the city had decided that one could not serve another term as magistrate before ten years had passed. Similarly, a decree on the Constitution of Chios that can be dated from the beginning of the sixth century indicates that there existed a *boule dēmosie,* a popular council, perhaps alongside an aristocratic *boule.* Finally, if we believe the text that is called the great *rhētra* of Sparta, from around 650, information that Plutarch and Tyrtaeus reported as well, we see that this great *rhētra* gave the *dēmos* the right of *antagoria,* that is, to reply, to contradict what the aristocratic members of the Council of the Elders might have decided. Not only did they have this right to reply, but they also had *to cratos,* power. Thus we can see the power that was placed in the hands of the *dēmos.* Normally, it was the ruler who possessed the *cratos.*

In order to fully understand, it would be necessary to analyze the group of terms that are connected to *cratos* and *cratein.* There was on one hand a *cratos* that indicated "prevalence," which can also mean power, authority, mastery, in the military realm or in all realms, and there was a *cratos* that meant "hard, difficult." It appears that these two terms were connected. What is important is to see the way in which the Greeks represented another *cratos,* "sovereign power." For example, in the *Theogony,* after conquering the Titans, Zeus was assigned the task by all the other gods of taking the *basileia* in hand and distributing to each of them their due, their honors, their portions: their *timai* and their *moirai.* But Zeus was above that distribution; he imposed and presided over it. The entire poem specifies this: when the merciless struggle between the Titans and the Olympians began, a divinity who belonged to the age of the Titans and who was called Styx decided to become a turncoat by abandoning the Titans and joining forces with Zeus. She brought Cratus, strength, and Bia, force, with her. This means that in Greek language and thought, sovereign power was envisioned as a sort of brutal power of domination that bent others to its will, and it brings to mind a remark that I often repeat since I find it very astute, one attributed to the anthropologist, botanist, historian of technology, and Orientalist Andre-Georges Haudricourt. He shows that in the representation of sovereignty and the power of domination over others, two conceptions can be contrasted: that of the Chinese of classical tradition and that of the Indo-Europeans. The Chinese, he says, were gardeners and farmers. Consequently they believed that it was necessary to clear the land, to level it, to break up clods of dirt, so that each plant could grow according to its own nature, its essence. So the best king—the Chinese did not take pains to explain this—was the one who did nothing, and who had nothing to do, because everything grew by itself and because through his presence alone he incarnated the balance of universal forms, a sort of harmony. Thus the *mana* that emanated from him, so to speak, assured that each thing followed its natural inclination. This conception of gardeners and farmers was different from that of the Indo-Europeans, says Haudricourt. For the Indo-Europeans, who were herders, the king, the ruler, was the shepherd of the people, the one who led his flock. And he led it with a scepter that was also the staff used to give the people beatings if they did not go fast enough. At the same time the king imposed the yoke, the brake, on them. This meant that royal power was seen as Cratus and Bia, as a power to impose force on others.

But in *Le Vocabulaire des institutions indo-européennes,* Emile Benveniste makes some remarks that indicate that it is necessary to temper this conception. There were not, on one hand, Chinese farmers, and on the other, Indo-European shepherds. Benveniste indeed shows, along with Dumézil, that the Indian *rex* was much more religious than political. His mission was not to impose an order and to exercise a power, but, according to Benveniste, to set rules, to determine what was just, which meant that the *rex* thus defined was much more like a priest than a king. Benveniste notes that the Celts and the Italic peoples, as well as the Indians, preserved this category of royalty, which was of course connected to the existence of the great colleges of priests that watched over the strict observance of rituals. In Greece the king was not at all that quasi divinity who came to earth as in the laws of Manu. Here we find a type of royalty that contrasts with both the Indian and the Roman conceptions. The king was defined not as he who watched over the proper carrying out of rituals, without which society could not prosper, but as a *despotēs.* The king's relationship with his subjects was like a father's with his children. The same type of *cratos* was found in the king, in the father of a family, and in the free man in his relations with his slaves. Domination had a universal value, independent of the person who assumed it. At home a man was a *despotēs* in relation to his children, his wife, and his slaves, as well as the Barbarians, should it fall to him to rule over them.

Thus that type of power highlighted a fundamental inequality in the nature of people. Consequently, the *despotēs* had the right, as did the father, to make those beneath him bend to his will, and, since there were no longer any colleges of priests, we witness a sort of laicization. Sovereign power was viewed with this type of realism, this type of positivity, as an imposed power. Henceforth, in a bellicose and aristocratic society, such as the one of the ninth and eighth centuries, the great problem was to neutralize that power which, in the myths of Hesiod, established order. It was the duty of the community to find the means to neutralize it. This was not easy and did not take the same path everywhere; but fundamentally it was a matter of finding institutions, places, and practices based on an equality not of everyone but of a defined circle: citizens. Thus came the necessity of dissociating the exercise of power from the rule of violence of Cratus and Bia and of instilling a regulation, a control over power. It was even deemed necessary to find a way to depersonalize it, to laicize it, and, at the same time, to neutralize it entirely, or to act as if one could neutralize it.

This tendency appeared very quickly. Let us take a look, for example, at the beginning of the sixth century, at the figure of Solon, a philosopher, poet, and political man who was almost the contemporary of Thales. He was asked to intervene when Athens was experiencing great troubles. The city had fallen prey to *stasis,* to sedition, to rebellion. The body of citizens was divided. Solon came as a man of the state, as a wise man and poet, because his poetry was not indifferent or foreign to his action as a reformer. Solon brought with him a sort of inspired seer, Epimenides, who publicly recited his poems to calm people's minds and to appease the furor of some and the anger of others. He also established rituals; thus the entire area of Athens was to be symbolically marked. He began at the Areopagus and released white sheep and black sheep that scattered over the entire area of the city. Wherever they stopped, their stopping place was considered to have a religious value. If a black sheep stopped it was necessary to make a sacrifice to the Chthonic powers; if a white sheep stopped, that meant there was a celestial and Olympian god who was to be honored on that spot. Space was blocked out religiously so that the seething of passions that divided the community was eased. In one of his poems Solon declared that he was going to act: he eradicated the debts and the slavery of a certain number of small peasants who had not been able to pay what they owed. He said that he was "rendering the earth, the divine earth, free," and he wrote that he did not want to act *turannidos biei,* "through tyrannical violence" (30, 31), but through *cratos* of the law, *cratei nomou.*[3] This is a considerable change: the idea that true *cratos* belonged to *nomos,* "the law." Thus here we have in political thought what we had perceived in philosophical thought. What is

JEAN-PIERRE VERNANT

fundamental is that it was not the ruler who established a balanced order; it was the balanced order that dominated and controlled the *cratos.*

The same echo is heard in both cases. By rejecting tyrannical violence, Solon was acting through the *cratos* of the law, amending, *sunarmosas bien kai diken,* "seeing to it that violence and justice were combined" (30, 31). Here, at the dawn of the sixth century, we see a poet, a traveler, a man who was rejecting tyranny, who was remaining in the center of the city "so that neither those who were on one side or those who were on the other could triumph and succeed in conquering unjustly," *nikan adikos* (3). But in this he is joining *cratos* and *nomos, bie* and *dike.* Hesiod tells us that Cratus and Bia were the two acolytes of Zeus who sat on either side of him. He could not take a step without the others following him. Now *cratos* is linked to *nomos, bie* to *dike.* This association was made on both the intellectual and the institutional levels. Like Anaximander, Solon valued the idea of an egalitarian order, which meant that the world would not be composed entirely of fire, or water, or snow, or air, but depending on the seasons, the heat would be greater, then the cold, then the damp, then the dry. That is, there was an order of compensation, the *archē,* the principle, which he called *apeiron.* There was no longer Gaia, Ouranos, Zeus, or Poseidon; all those gods disappeared from the realm of philosophical thought. Note how Solon proceeded in the same way on the level of civil and political thought. He wrote: "The strength, *menos,* the violence, of snow and hail come from clouds, and thunder is produced by the brilliant lightning, but the city perishes from its overly great men" (7). If there were people who were indeed above others, that was bad. Everyone should have had approximately the same stature. Here, too, we have a completely positive conception; phenomena were at the level of what could be seen. The same thing occurred with cities. The city would be destroyed if men were too great. Solon adds: "It is ignorance that leads a people to slavery at the hands of a single power" (7). There was nothing mysterious in this process, which occurred for completely objective reasons. This is why he, the lawgiver, regulated the harmony of the city, which was divided, because the rich and "those that were too great" (7) could not halt their ambitions, their will for power, and because the poor wanted to take everything from the rich. And Solon represented *nomos kai dike,* a just distribution at the center of the city. "Like a boar," he said, "he will push back the two packs. He will therefore prevent an unjust victory: *nikan adikos*" (30, 31).

This is exactly what Anaximander recounted. I will cite one of the rare fragments we have of Anaximander's writing. He speaks of elements such as warmth and cold that were already conceived as powers, the almost divine *dunameis,* because for the Greeks the world was divine. And it was divine for philosophers and physicists, as well as for theologians. Out of those *dunameis* there was therefore birth, and at the same time, the ruin of things, which occurred following an order of necessity. For "various things must make amends to each other and compensate each other for the injustices that they committed with regard to each other." For example, in the summer, the fire, heat, and aridity go too far and begin to take over. They do injustice to the cold and humidity. But in the course of time they are obliged to pay the *poine,* "the fine," to make amends to those whom they had wronged by pulling back as much as they had advanced. This meant that the human cosmos and the physical cosmos were conceived truly as an order.

The second question is, how were these things instituted? In particular, how did the idea of a public space appear, a space for debating with defined practices and a space that instilled a community with the consciousness of being a community, while at the same time the practice of coming to a majority decision at the end of the debate was being developed? Community, publicness, the equality of citizens . . . how was the connection made? Compared to what we know about Assur, Babylon, or Egypt, the Greeks' invention is extraordinary: it is indeed astonishing, even strange, for a group to say, "We are forming a group of equals. This means we are going to regulate *ta koina,* common affairs, together, by coming to a common decision. The world will begin to be divided between common things, public affairs, and private affairs. In his own home, each person is master of his decision; no one must meddle in them." But for the Greeks—to a degree that varied from one city to another; this took hold much more strongly in Sparta than in Athens—there was an immense world of affairs that were considered common, and where no one was to make a decision in the place of another, where the group was considered as a group, a human community in its totality of individuals who were similar to each other. In Greek they were called *isoi,* "equals," or *homoioi,* "similar, interchangeable." It was this community that was to take *cratos* in hand in the assembly so that the only violence was that of the decision that was taken and became the law. This is better understood when we consider that, in Homer, in the small kingdoms and in the few small cities, warriors had an aristocratic conception of existence and of personality. Those men did not want to be dominated. Let us look at the *Iliad:* Agamemnon, who had to give up his concubine (on Apollo's order, since Apollo was intervening on behalf of his priest, the father of the young girl), then demands Briseis, Achilles' concubine, as compensation. Agamemnon was the king of kings. He was the *basileutatos,* the most royal among the kings. But we must beware—there was already a great difference: a word such as *anax,* which was already found in Mycenaean, was an absolute proper noun. One was simply *anax.* But in Greek, *basileus* included a comparative and a superlative: one was more of a king than another. Agamemnon was the *basileutatos,* the "most king" of all.

But others were also kings: in this Homeric world, the society was not a society of the Asian type where the king played the role of intermediary between the gods and human beings and where all other people formed a hierarchy that was subjected to him. There was a series of different poles of power. Each one of those poles tolerated very badly being subjected to the domination of another. Very quickly there appeared a series of indications and formulas that are quite revealing. These formulas consisted of saying that someone had decided, at a given moment, to place the power of sovereignty within the community. Herodotus tells us (around 522) what occurred with a certain Maeandrius. He says that *to cratos* had fallen to him because Polycrates had given it to him before he died. We are familiar with the speech he made to his co-citizens: "I can now be your ruler [*archein*]. But what I find fault with in others I will not do myself, if I can help it. I did not like it when Polycrates held absolute authority over men [*despozon*] as good as himself [*homoioi*] . . . so now I wish to open his power to all of you, and I proclaim equality before the law [*isonomie,* 'equality before the *nomos*'] for the commonalty entire. It is I . . . who now offer you this freedom."[4] What does he mean? "I don't want to dominate you because you are my equals. Consequently, I grant you your freedom, I recognize your *isonomia.* And for this I place the *cratos es meson,* or I see to it that it remains *en mesoi,* in the center." There are many other texts that say the same thing, some of which are even older.

Once it is placed in the center, power no longer belongs to anyone; it is depersonalized, socialized, laicized. The origin of this formula, so revealing as to the neutralization of the *cratos* through its being deposited in the center, must be sought in the practices that are revealed in archaic poetry, especially that of Homer. In particular, as is seen in Homer, there is the fact that in the assembly of warriors, the booty, the prizes of competitions, goods, the distribution of properties, all obeyed a certain number of rules that conveyed the same conception, the same public and communal value of the center. When the spoils of a military campaign were assembled, everything was put in the middle. The army stood in a circle around the spoils; the circle created the sacred *kuklos,* the *agora.* The word *agora* means both "assembly" and "game," because the people were assembled around it. When the people were no longer under arms, those who had the status of warrior made the circle in the same way as those who later would have the status of citizen. They were all at an equal distance from the point where the spoils were deposited. Then began a process that happened in two phases, as did the sacrificial ritual. The shares of honor, taken from the booty, were given to the most glorious hero. Then, what remained did not belong to anyone in particular, because it belonged to everyone. It was distributed equally among all those who had fought. Subsequently, as we see, Agamemnon stole Achilles' share of honor, Briseis, from him, and then he wanted to make amends, because he realized his actions had resulted in a catastrophe. The Greeks were beaten badly, and Achilles watched their downfall from his tent, not wanting to move. He had to be convinced to return to battle. Agamemnon offered him gifts. Achilles refused. Why? Here we must distinguish two very different things. In archaic societies everything related to a gift and to the gesture of offering a gift revolved around the placing of the gift in the hand of the receiver. Thus Agamemnon could not directly give Achilles the fifty tripods, the horses, the servants, and all the jewelry he proposed. The gesture of giving a gift, which was called "placing into the hands," implied, by the very fact that a thing had been offered, the gratitude of the one who was receiving toward the one who was giving. The object that passed from one person to another was not neutral; it wove a connection of dependency between the receiver and the giver. It was the *charis,* which assumed a counter-*charis.* For that gift, as Mauss has shown, was likely to subject the person who received it, the person who was then required to free himself of that gift. Consequently, Achilles could not receive his share of the booty from Agamemnon. What happened, then? The Myrmidons of Achilles took all the gifts from Agamemnon's tent. But they did not take them directly to Achilles' tent. They placed them *en meso agores,* in the middle of the *agora.* They brought the booty back. By returning the booty, they cut the personal ties that united such and such a tripod, such and such a servant, such and such a horse to its

JEAN-PIERRE VERNANT

original owner. So when Achilles went to get the goods, they were completely his and did not create any ties of dependency. Placing the booty *en mesoi* made it common, public, and depersonalized it.

The same thing occurred in the same way in games, for example, in the funerary games held in honor of Patroclus. The dead man was cremated according to the ritual, then people organized games, horse races, foot races, and boxing matches. Of course, the one who organized these games had prizes to award. But he would not hand them out directly. He requested that a circle be formed, and he deposited the prizes *en mesoi*. In this way, the prizes no longer belonged to him. They were under public scrutiny and became common property. He who won the race went to collect his prize himself without being in a position of dependency with regard to the one who deposited it. Moreover, the winner took something that was common property, he appropriated it, and that taking— he took it in his hand—occurred within sight of everyone. Thus a social control was exercised at each moment of the affair: the community was always present.

In the warrior's world of the *Iliad,* when an assembly was called, the veteran warriors formed a circle, and they were all at an equal distance from the center. In Homer there is a tendency to ensure that each person could and should enter the circle in turn, place himself *en mesoi.* Once there, the herald gave him the scepter, which was much less the symbol of a power than the symbol of the community. It was the ambassadors who ordinarily had the scepter and who were placed under the protection of a common law. By taking hold of the scepter, which gave the person the opportunity to speak, the warrior spoke not of his personal affairs, but obligatorily of *ta koina,* the common affairs of the group. Consequently, the center of the circle, a public and depersonalized place, was reserved for a series of debates that we call political, because they dealt with what concerned the common interest in cities: decisions of war and peace, the dispatching of ambassadors, the laws. As for the laws that were decreed in this place, they always began with the formula "It pleased the Athenians that . . ." In this context, the city, the polis, was seen less as an institution than as the collection of those who made up the community. It was that community that would sovereignly decide. It was the law, then, that had the *basileia;* the law was king. There was no longer any personal, individual sovereignty; it was the community that was, in a certain sense, completely invested with the responsibility for a sovereign decision. All the same, those decisions included a religious aspect that they preserved during the entire ancient period, first because the opening, the closing, and the purification of the place involved religious rituals, and second because that law was seen as the reflection of divine justice. Greek man and the Greek city were not cut off from the cosmos. They were all a part of it. There was a universal order. But the Greek citizen was persuaded that it was only by being a member of a community that he had the right to speak, to participate in the discussion, and the duty first to regulate divine things that concerned the city. It was communally decided, for example, that it was necessary to make a sacrifice to such and such a god, or even that a god from somewhere else could be introduced into their religion. The gods were themselves political. There was religion in politics, and religion itself had a political dimension. In the end, the gods were citizens. They defended the interests of the city and were concerned with it.

For the Greek man it was only when he was a member of a community of that type that he truly was a man, in the strict sense of the term. If he was not free, if he was a barbarian, a slave, a child, or a woman, he was only halfway so. That is, as often happens in history, that unbelievable change, that advancement that turned a human community into the master of the most important things concerning it could only take place by reducing the members of that community to a fairly small circle, depending on the institutions involved. In other words, to invent the free citizen was at the same time to invent the slave, to establish a statute under which those who were not part of the civil community were rejected not only from the city but also in a certain way from that which was human. A person was a man only if he was in some sense placed around that center from which the violences and injustice of a tyrannical power had been exorcised. Consequently, as often happens, the step forward, which occurred very differently depending on the cases, implied that those who were not part of that civil community could not have access to the center. We should also perhaps mention something else, which brings us back to the notion of "democracy." In such a system, every political decision made in the center, in that public space that belonged to no one, obligatorily implied a debate and thus at least two sides. That freedom of debate, that *isegoria,* that right of free speech implied that at a given moment the city was divided into a minority and a majority. The minority was then subject to the *nomos* in the form of *bie,* the violence that was done to it. And, in a certain sense, the entire history of cities is the history of those violences, of those struggles, in particular the struggles between the rich and the poor. Among the solutions that have been found, Athens's is a good example. The wealth of the rich of the ancient world essentially served to finance the poor by way of the liturgy. All the great functions of the state were assigned to the very rich families, who took care of all the related expenses. The public treasury then paid those who sat on the courts of law, who participated in the deliberating assembly, and who came to the theater. There was therefore a certain redistribution of wealth, just as Solon wanted: "Stand like a boar in the center," to ensure that the center did not explode owing to the violences of some toward others. This occurred, depending on the year, more or less successfully. But sometimes it was quite unsuccessful: there were extremely difficult periods. Just as one could not invent the freedom of the citizen without at the same time inventing the servitude of the slave, one could not instill the rationality of free debate, of a critical mind, without at the same time inciting passionately contrasting speeches, thus potentially unleashing the threat of a violence that would overthrow the law and the justice that were to preserve the community from the tyranny of a power out of control.

Notes

Foreword
1. Compare Jack Goody, *La Logique de l'écriture*, p. 24.
2. Jean Bottéro, *Mesopotamia: Writing, Reasoning, and the Gods*, p. 23.
3. Ibn Khaldun, *Peuples et nations du monde*, 1:109.

Part One: *Religion and Reasoning in Mesopotamia*
1. The original text, in French translation, is discussed in Miquel Civil, "Sur les 'Livres d'écolier' à l'époque Paléo-Babylonienne."
2. These citations are taken from Bottéro, *Mesopotamia: Writing, Reasoning, and the Gods*, p. 130. Trans.
3. From *The Epic of Gilgamesh*, p. 102. Trans.

Part Two: *Writing between Visible and Invisible*
Worlds in Iran, Israel, and Greece
1. P. Amiet, in André-Leicknam and Ziegler, *Naissance de l'écriture: Cunéiformes et hiéroglyphes*, p. 49.
2. V. Scheil, *Textes de comptabilité proto-élamites*, p. 2.
3. Here I am following the ideas of P. Clastres, *La Société contre l'état* and *Recherches en anthropologie politique;* and of M. Gauchet, *Le Désenchantement du monde.*
4. B. André and M. Salvini, "Réflexions sur Puzur (= Kutik) Inshushnak," pp. 54–72.
5. A.-M. d'Ans, *Le Dit des vrais hommes.*
6. M.-J. Steve, *Le Syllabaire élamite: Histoire et paléographie*, p. 9.
7. F. Grillot-Susini, *Eléments de grammaire élamite*, p. 54.
8. I. J. Gelb, *A Study of Writing;* J. Février, *Histoire de l'écriture*, "Les Sémites et l'alphabet: Ecritures concrètes et écritures abstraites," in Février, *L'Ecriture et la psychologie des peuples*, pp. 117–29.
9. Gelb, *A Study of Writing*, p. 149.
10. H. A. Gleason, *Introduction à la linguistique* (1969), p. 326, cited by M. Sznycer, "L'origine de l'alphabet sémitique."
11. These are harmonics amplified by resonators in an acoustical definition of sounds. From an acoustical point of view, there is no opposition

between consonants and vowels, but there is between sounds with formants and sounds without formants.

12. J.-M. Durand, "Diffusion et pratique des écritures cunéiformes au Proche-Orient ancien."

13. Herodotus, *The History*, 5:58.

14. M. Lejeune, *Phonétique historique du mycénien et du grec ancien*, p. 72 et seq.

15. M. Mayrhofer, "Überlegungen zur Entstehung der altpersischen Keilschrift," pp. 290–96.

16. P. Clastres, "Exchange and Power: Philosophy of the Indian Chieftainship," pp. 19–37, "The Bow and the Basket," pp. 83–107, and "The Duty to Speak," pp. 128–31, all in *Society against the State*. From my point of view, it is Clastres's ideas on language, ideas based on an exceptional sensitivity to speech, that make his work an irreplaceable monument.

17. J. Kellens, "Un avis sur vieil-avestique *mainiiu-*," pp. 97–123.

18. Cf. J. Kellens and E. Pirart, *Textes vieil-avestiques;* J. Kellens, *Zoroastre et l'Avesta ancien;* and H. Humbach, *The Gāthās of Zarathustra*. Translations given here may diverge from these.

19. E. ben Yehuda, *Le Rêve traversé*, pp. 114–15. It is worthwhile also to know that the child's mother died very soon afterward. I am grateful to M. Masson for pointing this book out to me.

20. M. A. Ouaknin and D. Rotnemer, *Le Grand Livre des prénoms bibliques et hébraïques*, p. 26 et seq.

21. E. Will, *Le Monde grec et l'Orient*, 1:399.

22. Aristotle, *The Politics* and *The Constitution of Athens*, 39, 6. All citations from the *Constitution of Athens* are to this edition. Trans.

23. The Eleven were in charge of the prisons.

24. M. Ostwald, *From Popular Sovereignty to the Sovereignty of the Law*, p. 497.

25. Eric Havelock, *Aux origines de la civilisation écrite en Occident*, pp. 67–70.

26. A. Schmitt, "Der Buchstabe H im Griechischen," pp. 3–51.

27. Sophocles, *Oedipus at Colonus*, p. 115.

28. The hypotheses expressed here are subject to caution, for I know that any research on the unconscious collective meaning of a sign is a risky undertaking.

29. F. Lenormant, *Monnaies et médailles de l'Antiquité;* B. Jurdant, "Écriture, monnaie et connaissance." My "Écriture, monnaie, réseaux. Inventions des Anciens, inventions des Modernes," *Le Debát* 106 (Septembre–Octobre 1999), pp. 37–65, approaches the issue in a new way.

30. J. Pépin, *Idées grecques sur l'homme et sur Dieu*, p. 34 et seq.

31. Ibid.

Part Three: *Writing and Civil Religion in Greece*

1. Moses Finley, *Democracy Ancient and Modern*, pp. 13–14. Trans.

2. Thucydides, *The Peloponnesian War*, p. 145. Trans.

3. The quotations from Solon's poems may be found in Freeman, *The Work and Life of Solon*, pp. 207–16. The specific fragment from which each quotation is taken is given in parentheses. Trans.

4. Herodotus, *The History*, 3:142. Trans.

Bibliography

André, B., and M. Salvini. "Réflexions sur Puzur (= Kutik) Inshushnak." *Iranica Antiqua* 24 (1989): 54–72.

André-Leicknam, B., and C. Ziegler, eds. *Naissance de l'écriture: Cunéiformes et hiéroglyphes.* Editions des Musées Nationaux, 1982.

Aristotle. *The Politics* and *The Constitution of Athens.* Edited by Stephen Everson. Cambridge University Press, 1996.

Benveniste, Emile. *Indo-European Language and Society.* Translated by Elizabeth Palmer; summaries, table, and index by Jean Lallot. Faber, 1973.

ben Yehuda, E. *Le Rêve traversé: L'autobiographie du père de l'hébreu en Israël.* Edited and with a preface by G. Haddad. Seribe, 1988.

Bottéro, Jean. *Mesopotamia: Writing, Reasoning, and the Gods.* Translated by Zainab Bahrani and Marc Van de Mieroop. University of Chicago Press, 1992. Originally published as *Mésopotamie: La raison, l'écriture et les dieux* (Gallimard, 1986).

———. *Naissance de Dieu: La Bible et l'historien.* Gallimard, 1986; Folio, 1992.

Bottéro, Jean, and Samuel Noah Kramer. *Lorsque les dieux faisaient l'homme: Mythologie mésopotamienne.* Gallimard, 1989.

Christensen, Arthur. *L'Iran sous les Sassanides.* 1944. Reprint, O. Zeller, 1971.

Civil, Miquel. "Sur les 'Livres d'écolier' à l'époque Paléo-Babylonienne." In *Miscellanea Babylonica: Mélanges offerts à Maurice Birot,* edited by Jean-Marie Durand and Jean-Robert Kupper, pp. 67–78. Recherches sur les Civilisations, 1985.

Clastres, Pierre. *Recherches en anthropologie politique.* Editions du Seuil, 1980.

———. *Society against the State: Essays in Political Anthropology.* Translated by Robert Hurley in collaboration with Abe Stein. Zone, 1987. Originally published as *La Société contre l'état* (Editions de Minuit, 1974).

d'Ans, André-Marcel. *Le Dit des vrais hommes.* UGE, 1978.

de Meyer, L., H. Gasche, and F. Vallat, eds. *Fragmenta historiae elamicae: Mélanges offerts à M.-J. Steve.* Recherches sur les Civilisations, 1986.

Dentzer, Jean-Marie, and Winfried Orthmann. *Archéologie et histoire de la Syrie II: La Syrie de l'époque achéménide à l'avènement de l'Islam.* Saarbrücker Druckerei und Verlag, 1989.

de Prémare, André-Louis, ed. *Les premières Ecritures islamiques.* Revue du monde musulman et de la Méditerranée, no. 58. Edisud, 1990.

Deshayes, J.-M. *Le Plateau iranien et l'Asie centrale des origines à la conquête islamique: Leurs relations à la lumière des documents archéologiques.* Editions du CNRS, 1978.

Détienne, Marcel, ed. *Les Savoirs de l'écriture en Grèce ancienne.* Presses universitaires de Lille, 1992.

Durand, J.-M. "Diffusion et pratique des écritures cunéiformes au Proche-Orient ancien." In *L'Espace et la lettre,* edited by A.-M. Christin, pp. 13–59. UGE, 1977.

Eph'al, Israel. *The Ancient Arabs: Nomads on the Borders of the Fertile Crescent, 9th–5th Centuries* B.C. Magnes Press/Brill, 1982.

The Epic of Gilgamesh. Trans. and with an introduction by N. K. Sandars. Penguin, 1960.

Février, James. *L'Ecriture et la psychologie des peuples.* Armand Colin, 1963.

———. *Histoire de l'écriture.* 1948. Reprint, Grande Bibliothèque Payot, 1995.

Finley, Moses. *Democracy Ancient and Modern.* Rutgers University Press, 1973.

Gauchet, Marcel. *The Disenchantment of the World: A Political History of Religion.* Translated by Oscar Burge; with a foreword by Charles Taylor. Princeton University Press, 1997. Originally published as *Le Désenchantement du monde* (Gallimard, 1985).

Gelb, I. J. *A Study of Writing.* University of Chicago Press, 1963.

Gleason, Henry Allan. *An Introduction to Descriptive Linguistics.* Holt, 1955.

Gnoli, Gherardo. *De Zoroastre à Mani: Quatre leçons au Collège de France.* Klincksieck, 1986.

Goody, Jack. *The Domestication of the Savage Mind.* Cambridge University Press, 1977.

———. *L'Homme, l'écriture et la mort: Entretiens avec Pierre-Emmanuel Dauzat.* Belles Lettres, 1996.

———. *The Logic of Writing and the Organization of Society.* Cambridge University Press, 1986.

Grillot, F. *Eléments de grammaire élamite.* Recherches sur les Civilisations, 1987.

Havelock, Eric. *Aux origines de la civilisation écrite en Occident.* La Découverte, 1981.

Herodotus. *The History.* Translated by David Grene. University of Chicago Press, 1987.

Herrenschmidt, Clarisse. "Le Tout, l'énigma et l'illusion." *Le Débat* 62 (1990): 95–118.

Humbach, Helmut. *The Gāthās of Zarathustra,* pt. 1. K. Winter, 1991.

Huot, Jean-Louis. *Iran I: Des origines aux Achéménides.* Nagel, 1970.

Jaspers, Karl. *Les Grands Philosophes.* Vol. 1, *Socrate, Bouddha, Confucius, Jesus.* Agora, 1990.

Jurdant, B. "Ecriture, monnaie et connaissance." Ph.D. diss. University of Strasbourg, 1984.

Kellens, Jean. "Un avis sur vieil-avestique *mainiiu-.*" *Münchener Studien zur Sprachwissenschaft* 51 (1990): 97–123.

———. *Zoroastre et l'Avesta ancien.* Peeters, 1991.

Kellens, Jean, and Eric Pirart. *Textes vieil-avestiques.* Reichert, 1988.

Khaldun, Ibn. *Peuples et nations du monde.* Vol. 1. Editions Sindbad/Actes Sud, 1986, 1995.

Lejeune, Michel. *Phonétique historique du mycénien et du grec ancien.* Klincksieck, 1972.

Lenormant, François. *Monnaies et médailles de l'Antiquité.* [1870?].

Lozachmeur, Hélène, ed. *Présence arabe dans le croissant fertile avant l'Hégire.* Recherches sur les Civilisations, 1995.

Lukonin, Vladimir G. *Iran II: Des Séleucides aux Sassanides.* Nagel, 1967.

Martin, Henri-Jean. *Histoire et pouvoirs de l'écrit.* Rev. ed. with the collaboration of Bruno Delmas. Albin Michel, 1996.

Mayrhofer, M. "Überlegungen zur Entstehung der altpersischen Keilschrift." *Bulletin of the School of Oriental and African Studies* 42, no. 2 (1979): 290–96.

Olender, Maurice. *The Languages of Paradise: Race, Religion, and Philology in the Nineteenth Century.* Translated by Arthur Goldhammer. Harvard University Press, 1992. Originally published as *Les Langues du paradis: Aryens et Sémites: Le couple providentiel* (Seuil/Points, 1989).

Ostwald, Martin. *From Popular Sovereignty to the Sovereignty of the Law: Society and Politics in Fifth-Century Athens.* University of California Press, 1986.

Ouaknin, Marc-Alain, and D. Rotnemer. *Le Grand Livre des prénoms bibliques et hébraïques.* Albin Michel, 1993.

Pépin, Jean. *Idées grecques sur l'homme et sur Dieu.* Belles-Lettres, 1971.

Robin, Christian, ed. *L'Arabie antique de Karab'îl à Mahomet.* Revue du monde musulman et de la Méditerranée, no. 61. Edisud, 1992.

Sader, Hélène. *Les Etats araméens de Syrie depuis leur fondation jusqu'à leur transformation en provinces assyriennes.* Orient-Institut der Deutschen Morgenländischen Gesellschaft, 1987.

Scheil, Vincent. *Textes de comptabilité proto-élamites.* Mémoires de la Mission archéologique en Perse, vol. 17. E. Leroux, 1923.

Schmitt, A. "Der Buchstabe H im Griechischen." *Orbis Antiquus* 6 (1952): 3–51.

Sophocles. *Oedipus at Colonus.* Translated by Robert Fitzgerald. Harcourt Brace, 1949.

Steve, Marie-Joseph. *Le Syllabaire élamite: Histoire et paléographie.* Recherches et Publications, 1992.

Sznycer, M. "L'origine de l'alphabet sémitique." In *L'Espace et la lettre,* edited by A.-M. Christin, pp. 79124. UGE, 1977.

Thucydides. *The Peloponnesian War.* Translated by Rex Warner, with an introduction and notes by M. I. Finley. Penguin, 1954.

Vernant, Jean-Pierre. *Myth and Thought among the Greeks.* Routledge and Keegan Paul, 1983. Originally published as *Mythe et pensée chez les Grecs* (1965; reprint, La Découverte, 1985).

———. *Mythe et religion en Grèce ancienne.* Editions du Seuil, 1990.

———. *Myth and Society in Ancient Greece.* Translated by Janet Lloyd. Harvester/Humanities, 1980. Originally published as *Mythe et société en Grèce ancienne* (1974; reprint, La Découverte, 1988).

Will, Edouard. *Le Monde grec et l'Orient.* Vol. 1. PUF, 1972.

Index

Athens (*continued*)
136–37, 142–43; political history,
135–36, 140. *See also* Greece
Atrahasīs, 40, 42
Āturpāt-e Māraspandān, 118
Avestan language: alphabet of ancient
Iran, 111; invention of writing, 124
Awan, 69, 82

Babylonia, 8, 153
bārū, 44–45
basileia, 171
basileutatos, 171
beer, 8
Benveniste, Emile, 167
ben Yehuda, Eliezer, 130, 178 n. 19
Bible, 4, 5
Bottéro, Jean, 109, 149
boule dēmosie, 166
boustrophedon, 97
bullae, 71, 72, 81
Bundahishn, 118

calculi, 71, 72, 81
Cashinahua, 86
Chinese and sovereign power, 166–67
civilizations: origin of, 4, 5; precursor
to modern, vii–viii, 66; traits of,
149–50
Classical Hebrew, 128
Clastres, Pierre, 109, 110, 178 n. 16
Cnossos palace, 151
consonant alphabet: aspirates, 98–99;
characteristics of, 91, 94; contribution to writing, 106, 131; Hebrew
language and, 131, 133–34; importance of, 105; in Old Persian, 103;
origins of, 92; point of view of written expression, 90; reading process,
94–95; sign and sound relationship, 95–96; syllables and signs,
92–93; vowel use, 93–94; word-
language-subject continuum, 96
Constitution of Athens, 139
cosmology: conception as an order in
Greece, 170; conceptual triad in
Mazdean Iran, 113–14; earth and
sky origin myths, 37, 153–54; emergence of order in Greek myths,
158; first map of universe, 161;
writing and, 125. *See also* astrology
counting devices in Elam, 71, 72, 81
cratein, 166
cratos, 166
creation myths, 39–42

Crete, 150–51
culinary arts, 62
cuneiforms
consonant alphabet and, 92
expression of sound using, 77
Old Persian: belief in divine utterances, 119–20: categories of,
102–3; connection between ritual
and writing, 121–22; disappearance of, 122–25; framework for
reasoning, 121; history, 101–2,
111; inherent vowel use, 103;
king's role as intermediary,
116–17; phonetic signs function,
104; reading process, 103–4, 105,
119, 120–21; ritual choice elements, 121; structure of, 118–19;
syllabaries, 104–5; symbolic status of royal speech, 117–18; writing technique, 102
pictograms use in Mesopotamia: artistic tradition as beginning, 20–21;
complexity of, 26; evolution as
accounting device, 7, 21–22; precursor to writing, 21, 22; sign
use, 22–23, 24; syllable use, 24;
transformation from signs to
words, 23–24; transition to abstract characters, 25
replacement by Aramaic, 122–23
syllabic sign use in Elamite, 81–82, 84
writing technique, 102
cylinder seals, 71, 72, 81
Cyprus, 152
Cyrus the Great, 101

Darius the Great, 101, 117, 122
death, Mesopotamian view of, 43, 63–
64, 65
deductive divination, 48–49, 56
democracy, invention of: bilateral implications of a *democracy*, 174–75; centralization and neutralization of
power, 171–73; community sovereignty, 173–74; function and
weight of speech, 165–66; idea of
egalitarian order, 169–70; idea
of the law in political thought,
168–69; importance of public
places, 164; instilling control over
power, 168; meaning of *democracy*,
165; notion of community gathering space, 164–65; public space for
the community, 170–71; representation of sovereign power, 166–68

Democracy Ancient and Modern (Finley), 164
Dēnkart, 118
despotēs, 167
determinatives, 87–88
divination, 43–45, 48–49, 56
divinatory treatises, 45–47
Dorians, 152
Dumézil, 154, 155
dunameis, 170
Dur Untash, 88

earth and sky origin myths, 37, 153–54
education and training in writing: in Mesopotamia, 26–28, 31–32; scholarly focus of Hebrew, 129–30
Egypt: consonant alphabet origins, 92; origin of civilization and, 5
Elamite civilization
    city-state society, 78–79
    lack of comprehension of language, 83
    language origin, 70
    location, 69
    Mesopotamian influences on, 71, 76–77, 81
    name origin, 69
    political history, 84
    prevalence of language, 122
    religion in: representation of gods, 79–80; writing's role in, 89
    writing system: connection with speech, 110; counting devices, 71–72; cuneiform sign use, 81–82; depiction of quantities, 73–74; difficulty of reading texts, 77–78; Linear similarity to proto-Elamite, 82–83; mental process for writing, 75–76; overview of history, 70–71, 81; pictogram use, 76; portrayal of objects, 86–87; proto-Elamite signs, 77, 78–79, 82; purpose of writing in social order, 80; reading process, 87–88; separation from language, 85–87; simplification of Sumerian syllabary, 87; social order maintenance and, 79–80; spread of cuneiform writing, 82, 84; style of representation, 78; syllabic phoneticization use, 81–83, 85; tablet use, 74; text subjects, 88–89; transaction recording devices, 71–72
Elba, 5, 16

Eleatic School, 163
Eleusis, 140, 143
Empedocles, 157
empiricism, 47
Enki, 41–42
Enlil, 41–42
Enūma Eliš, 154
Epic of Gilgamesh, 16, 63–64
Epimenides, 168
Essenes of Qumran, 132
Euclidean geometry, 161
Euphrates River, 8
exorcism in Mesopotamian religion, 60–61

Février, James, 93
Finley, Moses, 164
fire ritual in Mazdean Iran, 114–17
flood myth, 16; in Greek mythology, 158, 159; Supersage, 41–42, 53
fortune-telling in Mesopotamia: cause-and-effect observations, 46–48; divination, 43–45; divinatory treatises, 45–47

Gaia, 160
Gāthās, 111–12, 116
Gauchet, Marcel, 35
Gelb, Ignace, 92–93, 94
gematria, 134
Gilgamesh parable, 16, 63–64
God's name in Hebrew language, 132
gods. *See also* mythology; religion
    Ahura Mazdā: Mazdean texts and, 112–13; in Old Persian texts, 102, 117, 118–19; spoken language as reverence for, 114, 123
    in Elam: representation of, 79–80; writing and, 89
    in Greece: city-state patrons, 155; disappearance from philosophical thought, 169; establishment of order in cosmology, 157–58; political dimension of, 174
    in Mesopotamia: Akkadian influence, 11; anthropomorphism, 54–55; demons sent as punishment, 58–59; depiction in mythological poem, 41–42; exorcism, 60–61; governmental will of, 58; metaphor of earthly world, 57, 65; notion of divinity, 55; omnipotence of, 56; polytheist hierarchy, 54; relationship with humans, 42,

gods (*continued*)
53–54, 61–64; role of, 38, 39;
Sumerian influence, 11
as motivation for invention of writing, 80
role of writing and, 108–9
graphēparanomōn, 141
grapsamenos paranomōn, 140
Greece
alphabet: aspirate consonants, 98–99;
disappearance of aspirate, 100;
dissociation of reading from comprehension, 100–101; lack of consonants, 105–6; letters for vowels, 97; origins of, 96–97; sign
and sound relationship, 97–98,
99–100; two letters for one sign,
98
Athens political background, 135–37,
140
cosmology in, 158, 178
democracy, invention of: bilateral implications of a *democracy,* 174–75;
centralization and neutralization
of power, 171–73; community
sovereignty, 173–74; function
and weight of speech, 165–66;
idea of egalitarian order, 169–70;
idea of the law in political
thought, 168–69; importance of
public places, 164; instilling control over power, 168; meaning of
democracy, 165; notion of community gathering space, 164–65;
public space for the community,
170–71; representation of sovereign power, 166–68
language: aspirated *h* description,
138; changes in vowel use,
137–38; culture of spoken word,
154–55; function and weight of
speech, 165–66; impact of writing on civil decrees, 140–42; impact of written laws, 136–37,
142–43; meaning of signs,
145–46; oral culture and religion,
155–57; oral culture in politics,
164–65; *pneuma* meanings, 138–
39, 178 n. 28; relation to breathing, 138; symbolism of aspirated
h, 145; symbolism of excluded aspirant, 143–45; writing and coinage, 142
language of culture in Rome, 128
Mesopotamia and, 153, 154–55

Mycenaean era: adoption of Cretan
writing system, 151; arrival of
populations, 150; decline in civilization, 152–53; disappearance
of early writing system, 152; mixing of populations, 151; settlement of Crete, 150–51
mythology: coexistence with religion,
162–63; concern with order,
153–54; establishment of order
depicted, 157–58; order from
power, 159, 160; similarities to
other polytheist systems, 153; origin of civilization and, 4
reasoning: coexistence with religion
and myths, 162–63; concept of
power belonging to the law,
168–69; nature of mathematical
objects, 162; notion of polis, 163,
165–66; order from balance,
159–60; philosophical idea of
truth and appearances, 161–62;
theory of universal order, 160–61
religion: change in function of
speech, 165–66; city-state patron
gods, 155; coexistence with
myths, 162–63; disappearance
of gods from philosophical
thought, 169; order from balance, 159–60; order in cosmology, 157–58; order through oral
culture, 155–56; politics and,
174; replacement by philosophy,
158–59; uniqueness of religious
framework, 154–55
writing system: alphabetical writing
beginnings, 155; Athenian laws
and, 136–37, 142–43; consequences of change to written
prose, 157; depiction of order
from balance, 159–60; disappearance of, 152; impact on civil decrees, 140–42; meaning of signs,
145–46; philosophy replacing religion, 158–59; transition from
oral, 156–57
Guayaki warriors, 110

Hammurabi, 56
Haudricourt, Andre-Georges, 166
Havelock, Eric, 137
Hebrew language
alphabetical nature of writing,
134–35
documents using, 128–29

Qumran, 128, 132

reading processes: consonant alphabet, 94–95; Elamite writing, 87–88; Hebrew language, 130–31; logograms, 119; Old Persian cuneiform, 103–4, 105, 119, 120–21
reasoning
definition of principle of identity, 161
in Greece: coexistence with religion and myths, 162–63; concept of power belonging to the law, 168–69; nature of mathematical objects, 162; notion of polis, 163, 165–66; order from balance, 159–60; philosophical idea of truth and appearances, 161–62; theory of universal order, 160–61
in Mesopotamia: cause-and-effect observations, 49–50; connecting of phenomena, 47–48; deductive divination, 48–49, 56; divination, 43–45; divinatory treatises, 45–47
Old Persian cuneiform as framework for, 121
religion. *See also* gods; mythology
Akkadian contributions to, 11
categories of, 52–53
in Elam: representation of gods, 79–80; writing's role in, 89
essential elements, 51–52
in Greece: change in function of speech, 165–66; city-state patron gods, 155; coexistence with myths, 162–63; common language between men and gods, 144; disappearance of gods from philosophical thought, 169; establishment of order in cosmology, 157–58; order from balance, 159–60; order through oral culture, 155–56; politics and, 174; reliance on dialogues, 145; replacement by philosophy, 158–59; uniqueness of religious framework, 154–55
in Mazdean Iran: cosmology, 113–14; evil powers inferences, 113; king's role as intermediary, 116–17; meaning of recited texts, 112–13; ritual uttering of divine names, 114–15; status of words and speech, 114; theory of language and, 115–16

in Mesopotamia: Akkadian influence on, 11; anthropomorphism, 54–55; conclusion of mythological age, 42; creation myths variances, 39–40; demons sent as punishment, 58–59; exorcism, 60–61; governmental will of gods, 58; issue of evil, 57, 59–60; metaphor of earthly world, 57, 65; morality's place in, 62–64; mythology as form of explanation, 36–37, 38; notion of divinity, 55; omnipotence of gods, 56; polytheist hierarchy, 54; "popular" aspects, 53; prayers and rituals, 58, 60–63; relationship between gods and humans, 53–54, 62–64; religious behavior, 61–63; role in world, 35; sin and, 56–61; Sumerian influence on, 11
in Old Persian, 121
Sumerian contributions, 11
Writing's role in, 108–9
remainders in writing, 106–7
reverential religions, 52
rex, 167
rhētra, 166

Sargon I, 81
Sassanian kings, 117
Scheil, Vincent, 77
scholarly languages: dominance of Sumerian, 13; focus of Hebrew, 129–30; in Mesopotamia, 26–28
scriptio plena, 131–32
Semites: ethnic merging, 12; eventual dominance of Mesopotamia, 14–15; influence of writing on Greeks, 97; origin of civilization and, 5, 9; qualities of, 34; treatment of gods, 11. *See also* Akkadians
Serābīt el-Hādem, 92
"The Seven Wise Men" myth, 9
Shiraz region, 69
signs: first uses of, 22–23; function in Old Persian, 104; meaning in Greek, 145–46; proto-Elamite, 77, 78–79, 82; simplification of, 24; sound relationship, 95–96; syllables and, 92–93; transition to abstract characters, 25
Simashki, 69
Sinai, 92
sin in Mesopotamia: exorcism, 60–61;

writing systems (*continued*)
    prose, 157; depiction of order
    from balance, 159–60; disappear-
    ance of, 152; impact on civil de-
    crees, 140–42; meaning of signs,
    145–46; philosophy replacing re-
    ligion, 158–59; transition from
    oral, 156–57
    Hebrew language: alphabetical nature
    of writing, 134–35; documents us-
    ing, 128–29; historic background,
    128; numerical equivalences and
    meaning, 134; reading process,
    130–31; revival of, 127, 130–35;
    scholarly focus, 129–30
    impact of, 110
    as a means to gods, 109
    in Mesopotamia: alphabet introduc-
    tion, 17; artistic tradition as be-
    ginning of, 20–21; business docu-
    ments, 5, 28–29; complexity of,
    26; date of origin, 19; divination
    treatises, 45–47; economic activi-
    ties recorded, 28; education and
    training in writing, 26–28, 31–32;
    evolution as accounting device,
7, 21–22; historic chronologies,
30; impact of written speech, 20;
legal decisions recorded, 29; letter-writing, 29–30; limitation of
spoken language, 19–20; literary
works, 32–33; preservation of
tradition using, 32; quantity of
documents found, 7; sign use,
22–23, 24; syllable use, 24; transformation from signs to words,
23–24; transition to abstract characters, 25

Orient vs. West remainders, 106–7
revolution in point of view, 105
role between humans and gods,
    108–9

Xerxes, 122

Yahweh, 131, 132
Yasna Haptanghāti, 112, 113–14

Zagros, 82
Zarathustra, 112–13, 115–16, 118
Zas, 158
Zeus, 153, 154